Sociology of Law

Qiliang Wang

Sociology of Law

A Study of Cultural Contextualism

SSAP

Springer

Qiliang Wang
Yunnan University
Kunming, China

Translated by
Li Yiyang
Contract translator at Global Tone
Communication Technology Corporation
Beijing, China

Reviewed by
Wei Yuanlin
Global Tone Communication Technology
Corporation
Beijing, China

Supported by a Grant from the Yunnan University Double First-Class Initiative

ISBN 978-981-16-5508-1 ISBN 978-981-16-5509-8 (eBook)
https://doi.org/10.1007/978-981-16-5509-8

Jointly published with Social Sciences Academic Press
The print edition is not for sale in China (Mainland). Customers from China (Mainland) please order the print book from: Social Sciences Academic Press.

This Springer imprint is published by the registered company Springer Nature Singapore Pte Ltd.
The registered company address is: 152 Beach Road, #21-01/04 Gateway East, Singapore 189721, Singapore

This book is dedicated to

Li Na and Our Qiyue

Foreword

Empirical Approach in Sociology of Law

More than ten years have passed since the publication of Su Li's *The Rule of Law in the Chinese Context* in 1996. During this period, the sociology of law developed rapidly, producing methodologically and substantively rich and diverse literature that also increased in analytic rigor. The growing literature is a sign of the field's maturation and its growing influence among legal scholars. Despite recent progress, growth has been slow. Over the past decade, while a considerable number of monographs and papers have been published, including some that have offered more insightful analysis on specific questions than was found in Su Li's book, none have surpassed it in terms of overall theoretical significance and quality of discourse. Recent scholarly writings on the relationship between law and society are still largely built on Su's discussions of law in a national or local context and of how to establish the rule of law in rural areas. The paucity of new ideas on the theoretical front stands in sharp contrast to the remarkable progress in the rule of law in China in the past decade.

In *the Rule of Law in the Chinese Context*, Su Li's sternly worded question: "What contributions have you made to this field of study?" was a wake-up call, perhaps a somewhat unpleasant call, for many of Su's fellow legal scholars. Even today, young scholars such as myself must take Su's question as seriously as those from Su's generation had to do. It makes us realize that unless we can expand our research horizon beyond the one defined in Su's work, we may indeed end up making little, if any, contribution to either sociology of law or indeed sociology. Therefore, going beyond Su's Li remains a formidable challenge facing younger scholars in the sociology of law. This is not to say that anybody should try to be different from Su just for the sake of being different, but it is high time for us to posit new ideas based on empirical studies of the rule of law in China, which was precisely what Su did more than a decade ago.

Case study is the predominant method in this field. Common resources for cases suitable for researchers in the sociology of law include literature and media reports. However, the analysis of such cases in previous studies has often been superficial. Jumping to conclusions prematurely and over-generalizations were common. This is one of the reasons there has been no real breakthrough in the sociology of law in China. Many researchers' interpretations of cases were based on their life experiences and understandings of social theories rather than in-depth empirical research. For arguments not supported by empirical evidence, researchers resort to presumptions or common senses to explain them. Many studies contain extensive theoretical discussions but lack in-depth analysis of source materials of empirical data, which inevitably leads to unsubstantiated conclusions. Furthermore, compared with the older generations of scholars, our younger generations of researchers are still very inexperienced, which means our observation and theoretical analysis may lack depth. Therefore, it would be much wiser for us to base our research on solid empirical evidence.

Over one hundred years ago, the first Opium War put an end to the last golden age of Imperial China. In over 60 years since the People's Republic of China was founded, a traditional agrarian society has been transformed into a modern industrial society. Thirty years of economic reform and development have brought tremendous social changes. In the first three decades of the People's Republic of China, traditional values and customs still prevailed in society, but rapid socioeconomic development was producing momentum for modernization. After China began the nationwide economic reform, modernization accelerated, reaching a pace unseen in human history. What took European countries and the USA two hundred years to complete took us only 30 years to complete. Chinese social scientists should take upon themselves to uncover the forces behind this transition and related social phenomena and propose solutions to problems arising therefrom. The importance of social theories, public policy, and public opinion is beyond dispute.

The study of the relationship between law and the social transition must be informed by the understanding of the development of the rule of law in the country. Specifically, Chinese sociologists of law need to answer at least three questions: (i) What is the historical and social context of the development of the rule of law in China? (ii) How is the rule of law implemented in China, and what impact does it have on society? (iii) What impact does the rule of law have on people's everyday lives?

The conventional research paradigm in jurisprudence or the economic analysis of law is not particularly helpful here. The economic analysis of law has a strong explanatory power for specific problems under a given structure but is impotent in explaining the structure itself. More importantly, a structure often means abstraction of real-life phenomena. The lack of in-depth qualitative analysis may skew the conclusion. Therefore, we need to focus on political and social aspects of law. As Su Li pointed out not long ago, Chinese sociologists of law should not only focus on judicial systems but also pay attention to the interaction between law and political and social factors in China; in addition to sociology of law, they should also employ social theories and research methods in political science.

While much of life may be quite simple and straightforward, the need for theoretical explanation is also very real for many. Confucianism has given philosophical speculations about ancient Chinese society. Today, we rely on sociologists to analyze what is going on around us. *From the Soil: The Foundations of Chinese Society* by Fei

Xiaotong, which is regarded a cornerstone of modern sociology in China, uses social science methods to study the life of people in rural China founded on Confucian values. Modern Chinese society is completely different from the traditional society illustrated in the book. These differences can be explained by social sciences. In the past three decades, China has undergone great changes, including rising social mobility, changes in social structure, and the shift in residence of the population from rural to urban areas. Modern factors have penetrated every crevice of society. Consumerism, armed with tools such as advertising, fashion and mass media, is one of the strongest forces that shape our lives in the modern world. The protection of individual rights is considered an essential part of the modern legal system. These trends have driven the disintegration of inward-looking traditional communities, and Chinese people are voluntarily or involuntarily involved in the process of globalization. This is the context for the development of the rule of law in China. The research methods of anthropology may have an irreplaceable role in the studies of the relationship between law and social factors because the subject–object dichotomy of the positivist school, a mainstream school in Western sociology, is unhelpful in the analysis of daily lives, whereas quintessential research methods in anthropology, such as observation as an outside observer, participant observation, and in-depth interviews, are better ways to truly get to know the everyday life of the members of a society.

To gain insight into the historical and social context of the development of the rule of law in China as well as how the rule of law is practiced in China, we must recognize that law does not operate in a vacuum but in a very complex political and social environment. It is affected by various factors in the environment and reflects the interplay between different actors. Researchers studying political and governance issues do not set predetermined values or targets. They just observe and record the interplay between actors in real-world governance and use existing political and social theories to interpret observation. In this respect, the theories and methods of political science and sociology have an irreplaceable role in understanding the broader context of law.

In short, I believe legal sociologists should refine theoretical propositions based on empirical findings and draw inspiration from political science, sociology, and anthropology. There is no doubt that Wang Qiliang has the ability to achieve theoretical breakthroughs in this field of study. He did much fieldwork when pursuing a bachelor's degree in law. He also conducted research near the border between China and Vietnam when studying for a master's degree. I admire his passion and pioneering spirit. He began his academic career in a remote area near the border between China and Vietnam and has since then gradually shifted his focus to the core issues in sociology in China. He has acquired detailed knowledge of theories and methods of anthropology, which he skillfully employed to treat issues discussed in this book. Wang Qiliang secured a postdoctoral position at the Center for Rural Governance Studies at Huazhong University of Science and Technology and conducted research on rural governance issues. During this period, he became familiar with theories and methods of political science and sociology, which he also employed in the discussion of research questions in this book. Because of his background in law, anthropology, political science, and sociology, I believe he has the potential to surpass Su Li.

Even if he does not surpass Su Li, he will definitely have a bright future ahead of him in academia because he has embarked on a right path. Taking the right path may not necessarily lead to success, but taking the wrong path will definitely lead to failure. I am looking forward to seeing more works of Wang.

The first time I met Wang was at a conference on law and social science research in the spring of 2006. We met once or twice a year since then to discuss academic matters. We also had animated telephone and email conversations. I have benefited a lot from these discussions and conversations. I have read the entire draft of this book. This book presents the results of a series of explorations made by Wang regarding research methodologies and paths. It is the prelude of another book of his—*The Origin of Order—Law and Social Control in Contemporary Chinese Villages*. In *The Origin of Order*, Wang employs a diverse range of methods and theories to study law in the context of contemporary China. *Social and Cultural Context of Law* is a great book. It is an honor for me to write the preface for this book. I am younger than Wang. If my discussions above appear ignorant and frivolous, please forgive me. Nevertheless, by writing this preface, my one hope is to encourage Wang and other peer scholars to surpass themselves.

Summer 2010

Chen Baifeng
Zhongnan University of Economics and Law
Wuhan, China

Introduction

Observing Law and Order

Whether we like it or not, we are all subjected to the system of constraints imposed on us by laws and social customs. We study the law because it has real-life consequences for each and every one of us.

For over a millennium, we have looked to classic jurisprudence for answers to questions regarding the relationship between norms and facts. Law simplifies the world in its own way. Legal professionals such as judges and lawyers usually only need to focus on facts and factors that are of significance according to the law. In this sense, the law system is decontextualized. The parties in this closed system are nothing more than code names. Their behaviors are merely codes. Legal professionals apply law in a manner similar to that mathematicians apply formula. For example, a judge does not need to care about why a robber robbed someone. His responsibility is to determine whether the defendant's behavior constitutes robbery. Law schools prepare students for the world of practice by teaching with selected court cases. Law is like a set of formulas incomprehensible to ordinary people.

However, the problem is that law is intended to simplify the world, but the world itself is complicated. In other words, sufficient understanding of the complexity of the world around us is the premise for our ability to build a law system that can truly simplify the world. If the sole purpose of legal education and studies is to spread legal skills and knowledge, legal systems will become increasingly disconnected from the real world. The behaviors of human beings are not driven by codes. We are all messy flesh and blood, with emotions, selfish desires, and ability to know right from wrong. Behaviors lead to consequences. However, this does not mean we should just abandon existing legal research methods and approaches. There is no absolute superiority among legal research methods. What we should do is to look at law from more perspectives and experiment with more research methods. I believe, in addition to employing the traditional legal research paradigm, we should put law back in its social and cultural context and examine how it is practiced in daily life. In a word, I want to study sociology of law. This book is just the beginning of my journey in this field.

It presents the results of a series of studies I have done in recent years on how to observe law and order. [1]The book is divided into two parts: Actions, Culture, and Order and Legal Pluralism, Social Control, and Social Order. As seen from the titles of the two parts, how order is formed is a central question of my research. The two-part structure of this book is based on the following considerations: (i) Social order is the combined result of actions of all members in a society. Then, how does an action occur? What are its dimensions? What effects does law have on people's actions? (ii) Based on my observations and fieldwork, I believe there are different sets of social norms and multiple social control systems in a legally pluralist society. We must recognize not only the dimensions of action but also the context in which actions take place. Only by this way, we can have a deeper understanding of factors influencing our actions, the logic in human behavior, the nature of law, the role of law in the formation of social order, and the position of law in relation to other social systems. The book consists of eight chapters that have different themes and focuses and tries to approach the above questions from different angles. Part I focuses on social structure (including institutions) and how culture affects human behavior. Part II places emphasis on how legal pluralism and the interactions between sociocultural factors affect people's actions. Therefore, the content of the introduction is not arranged in a strictly linear manner based on the order of chapters but based on themes. In the concluding chapter, I originally decided to discuss issues presented in *The Future of Legal Studies in China* (Deng, 2005). After revision, the concluding chapter presents my views on how to construct a new paradigm for legal studies in the Chinese context and theories guiding my academic research.

Dimensions of Human Behavior and Emergence of Social Order

Mr. Liang Zhiping once said:

Law confers on a civilization the right to use violence legitimately. It is a means of social control. Different civilizations have different norms, values, mindsets, and customs, which shape their cultures and spirit of laws. (Liang, 1991, p.1)

Mr. Liang approaches the spirit of laws from a new perspective—the cultural perspective. Culture studies allow us to see the complexity of life and the subjective aspect of law. Culture shapes law and affects the operation of the legal system. Although we know culture gives rise to reasons for action and guides behavior, much of the difficulty in studying law from the culture perspective stems from the difficulty in observing culture. I believe that culture, as an abstract concept, can only be understood through observation of practices of a cultural group. Humans express culture through activities. Culture is shaped by actions of and interactions between

[1] I have included published works (revised) in my book. There are a number of cases discussed from different perspectives in different chapters. Their repetitive appearance in this book is for the structural integrity and coherence of the chapters.

people. It in turn influences the behavior of people living within the culture. Culture also changes with the environment and group interest.

To put it briefly, I focus on the actions of individuals and groups because social order is the ultimate result of collective actions of a social group. The environment where actors (individuals and groups) live in and institutions in force constitutes the objective dimension of actions. The objective dimension not only determines the possibility of an action but also provides rules and resources for actions. Culture is the subjective dimension of actions. It influences individuals' understanding of the objective world and decision-making. For social groups, culture can be defined as their tendency to form an order. Therefore, each actor is both subject to structural constraints and capable of making choices. Eventually, the interaction between actors and their interaction with the environment give rise to order. From birth, individuals live in a society shaped by existing social structures, social relations, systems, and culture created by our predecessors. In this sense, they are passive recipients of historical and environmental conditions. However, individuals also have the capacity to act of their own volition (human agency). Therefore, they are also actors. Human conflict and cooperation driven by interest or purpose shape and reshape social structure, culture, and social order. We are like spiders crawling around in the webs weaved by our predecessors. We constantly destroy existing webs and weave new ones to replace them.

The reason why we study law and informal social control such as social customs is that they are an important part of social order that makes our daily life, and we are all living in a web made up by them. Regardless of our choices and actions, we must take this web seriously. It is real and powerful. It restricts, guides, and empowers us. Therefore, its perfection is crucial because the rules and resources it provides are not necessarily equal.

In Chap. 1 ("Use of Violence in the Struggle for Survival and Its Devastating Effects"), to use violence to destroy life, I examined the structural causes of *vigilante* remedies. When talking about structure, we mean more than social and natural factors such as social structure, gender structure, and spatial structure. When a system is in full force and affects a society, the system constitutes a structural constraint on members of society and their actions. Members of society must behave within the framework of the system, which not only influences their decision-making but also provides resources for their actions. It is the imperfection of the formal social control system of a state that restricts citizens' access to judicial remedies, which forces injured persons to resort to *vigilante* remedies. The reason behind the use of *vigilante* is system failure. Chapter 4 ("Causes of Corruption") discusses why corruption occurs. Corruption, as an abuse of power, can occur in everyday situations. The soil of corruption is nourished by flaws in the systems. Failure of a system to produce moral citizens is the cause of corruption. Under a corrupted system, individuals are prone to expect undue rewards. All mishaps caused by a system can be solved by improving the system.

The complexity of human beings lies in the fact that human actions are not just conditioned reflexes, and humans possess the cognitive abilities to understand and think creatively. Chapter 3 ("Religion and Civil Disputes: How Disputes Arise and

Get Resolved") discusses the importance of the subjective dimension of society (values, beliefs, meanings, etc.) for understanding the causes of actions and the formation of social order. When mentioning disputes, we often think of interest disputes. However, it should be noted that there is another type of dispute, such as religious disputes, that involve differences in values and worldviews. Moreover, we must realize that the connection between the subjective world (values and worldviews) and disputes does not only manifest in religious disputes or disputes resolved through the involvement of religious actors. Values and worldviews affect every aspect of our life—an important fact that we tend to overlook in discussion and resolution of disputes. We often focus only on the objective aspect of disputes and ignore their subjective aspect, resulting in failure of dispute resolution. Culture (including religion) influences our judgment and actions. By this token, if people are not aware of their rights or lack perception of justice or morality, they will not resort to violence, which has detrimental effects not only on the life of others but also on their own, to redress personal grievances. Our views, values, and beliefs influence our behaviors.

However, the objective dimension (structure) of actions is not completely separate from the subjective dimension (culture) of actions. In contrast, there is a close relationship between the two. An action only occurs when both dimensions act on the actor at the same time.

When I participated in a burial memorial for a Nakhi youngster who committed suicide to escape arranged marriage, I asked myself what I would do if I was in his shoes. Would I kill myself? The answer is no. I might run away or succumb to parental pressure, but I would definitely not commit suicide. Chapter 2 ("Suicides of Nakhi Lovers and Failure of Law") discusses why there have been so many love suicides among the Nakhi people. Lijiang, where many Nakhi young people commit suicide over forced marriage, is known as the capital of lovers' suicide. During the Qing Dynasty, the Imperial Court rolled out a reform initiative to centralize its control over ethnic minorities. This reform accelerated the assimilation of the Nakhi people and other ethnic minorities and forced them to adopt the social customs of the Han people, including arranged marriage practice. More seriously, due to this reform, love suicide became a social custom or an informal institution through which young lovers express their defiance against forced marriage by taking their own lives together. It was considered by the Nakhi a plausible way to resolve the conflict between forced marriage and the pursuit of true love. However, we must see that conflicts between social systems and the oppression of Confucianism are not enough to create a large number of love suicides. There were few Romeos and Juliets in the history of China. Only when a system is in line with the values, beliefs, and worldviews of a social group, it will become meaningful and have an impact. Nakhi youngsters ended their own lives in defiance of the uncompromising Confucius marriage code gleaned courage and strength from their religious belief in afterlife. For Nakhi, lovers' suicide became a customary way to fight arranged marriages advocated by Confucianism. This informal institution arose from the clash between the external formal institutions (legal system) imposed by the Imperial Court of the Qing Dynasty and Nakhi culture (values, beliefs, etc.). The combination of a formal institution such as a state law and the culture of a social group leads to the creation of a unique informal system.

It is obvious that human behaviors are subject to the structural constraints of formal institutions, while the subjective dimension of a society—culture and religion—decides people's response to formal institutions. Actions and order are the result of the interaction between the objective and subjective dimensions.

Chapter 4 ("Causes of Corruption") in the novel *The Water of Blue Waves* (*cang lang zhi shui*) depicts the marginalization of a young official who tries to battle bureaucracy. In the end, he "comes to his senses" and realizes what a "fool" he has been. This novel vividly portrays the "relationship cluster" (structure) of the Chinese political scene and their attitude toward corruption, which is considered a necessary evil by most of them. Malignant people–people, people–institution, and people–environment interactions under the influence of such structural constraints lead to the dissociation between corruption and morality. The interaction between bureaucratic structure and the attitude of the political scene enables the production and reproduction of unethical political relations, thereby producing an order that encourages unscrupulous behaviors.

I would also like to emphasize that among factors affecting human behaviors and social order, and formal institutions established by the state are the most important. As mentioned before, this does not mean that the actions of citizens are entirely determined by formal institutions, but the only factor we have control over is formal institutions. We will also find through discussion that formal institutions are also the driving force behind culture, customs, informal social control, etc.

Dilemmas in life are related to the natural environment and, more importantly, social relationships. Social status, opportunities, perception of human dignity, and social relationships have a stronger influence on the happiness of a person than human biology, technology, and wealth. As pointed out in this book, social status, opportunities, perception of human dignity, and social relationships do not exist naturally. They are the products of formal institutions. For those who use violence as a means to redress personal grievances, the root cause of their unhappiness is not violence but the institutions that force them to resort to violence. The conflict between the formal marriage system imposed by the Qing government, which led to inequality in the family setting, and the traditional Nakhi marriage customs is to be blamed for tragic deaths of young Nakhi lovers, whereas the plight of the villagers in Ping Village arose from failure of the state to enforce formal institutions in the village during social transition, resulting in an increase in violent incidents.

We cannot change every factor that affects actions and social order or eliminate all causes of tragedies. What we can do is to improve the legal system and promote the rule of law. We cannot expect everyone to do what is right, but the state must at least establish institutions that encourage good behaviors and deter bad behaviors. Justice and morality are translated into actions by people through the implementation of institutions.

Therefore, the central question regarding the dimensions of actions and the formation of social order is what effects institutions do have on human behaviors and social order.

Understanding Actions, Law, and Order in the Context of Legal Pluralism

It is the responsibility of the state to introduce norms that apply to all social groups—that is, state laws—within its boundaries. Interactions between people of different cultural backgrounds within the state are governed by state laws. State laws apply to everyone in the state. However, it is also true that the laws of a country do not obliterate informal social norms embedded in daily life.

Therefore, legal pluralism is inevitable. Society is a complex whole consisting of norms and rules at different levels (such as national, village, group, and family levels) that govern the interactions among members of society.

The laws of a sovereign state form only one part of the legal systems of a legally pluralistic society. Therefore, if we want to observe the formation of social order and the operation of plural legal systems, we need to return to the society and culture in which the law is embedded. In other words, we need to put the law back to its social and cultural context.

By studying law and other means of social control side by side and examining their interactions and their effects on the formation of social order, we will be able to gain a glimpse into the nature of law and challenges facing the rule of law. Social norms, deviant behavior, and social control should not be taken out of their specific social context. Rules of formal social control, informal social control, and quasi-formal social control institutions are not necessarily consistent, as are deviant behaviors under different social control systems. The same behavior may invoke different sorts of social controls. Therefore, there are bound to be conflicts and collaboration between different social controls. The concordance between social controls can translate into a decline in social conflicts, whereas discordance between social controls will only lead to chaos. Therefore, discussing the interrelationship and operation of different social controls as components of social order and exploring ways to achieve concordance between different social controls are of great significance to the promotion of the rule of law.

Relationships, especially human–nature relationships, relationships with other humans, and self-relationships (Li, 1997, p. 101), are very important facets of society. Chapter 5 ("Law as a Classification System That Creates Order") discusses the roles of laws and norms in the formation of social order and their effects on the order of things, behaviors, and social values. Here, we discuss classification in cultural terms. Culture can be considered the set of solutions conceived by a social group to challenges posed by its environment. It has a tendency to give rise to social order. Culture influences social rules. Every society has its own classification system. Apart from solutions to challenges posed by the environment, different societies often have different solutions to even the same problem, which is why a society has plural legal systems that are considered local knowledge. Compared to state laws, local norms take into consideration more non-technical factors such as worldviews. As mentioned before, legal pluralism is inevitable. State laws, free from the constraints of local norms, provide a source of authority rather than beliefs.

Legal pluralism or the existence of multiple social controls is one of the reasons why human behavior is a complex issue. In addition to state law, there are also customary laws and folk laws. We have seen the conflict between social customs and formal institutions in the Nakhi community (Chap. 2), unscrupulous exploitation of legal loopholes in the Pingcun Village case (Chap. 8), the operation of informal social controls in parallel with state law in the Mancun Village case (Chap. 7), and religion acting as a means of social control (Chap. 6). The complex relationships between formal institutions and informal social controls are reflected in people's actions. People are subject to both law and social norms. The interactions between plural legal systems affect daily life and give rise to social order.

Law, society, and culture are deeply intertwined, which is why legal pluralism is inevitable.

Even relationships are considered a form of social norms. Relationships involve rights and obligations and allocation of power and thus constrain human behavior. From the perspective of legal pluralism in legal anthropology, relationships can be considered "soft law," which is embedded in every aspect of social life. Although relationships are considered social structures (objective dimension of society), they also influence our attitude toward life and therefore have the characteristics of the subjective dimension of society. Relationships change slowly but continuously and are passed down from generation to generation. Social relationships are the experience of past generations and shape the pattern of group life. They are internalized and become part of our values and worldviews that guide our actions. In social activities, we conform to the unwritten rules of social relationships, seeking to maximize resources and benefits brought by social relationships and minimize their negative effects. Therefore, in regard to the practice of law and dispute settlement, social relationships are existing structures that affect decision-making. However, at the same time, people will not completely succumb to constraints posed by existing relationships, especially when they are at a disadvantage. Human beings will try to seek external resources (state law, stronger relationships, etc.) to change the pattern of existing relationships. Therefore, social relationships such as structure and attitude are constantly being reproduced, thereby giving rise to new structures and new orders. The political circle, as a relationship cluster, thus features an alternative normative order to state law. The justice system needs to break the dynamic mechanism of corruption caused by this alternative order (Chap. 4).

In the Mancun Village case, religious beliefs strongly influence villagers' worldviews, way of life, and opinion of what is right and wrong (i.e., justice). Religion as a social control institution establishes social norms. Although religion is often considered a source of disputes, it also provides alternative dispute resolution and shapes local legal culture. Suffice to say, religion is a part of culture. As part of the subjective dimension of group life, religion has a strong influence on people's actions and the formation of normative orders (Chap. 6). The Mancun Village case (Chap. 7) provides evidence for the fundamental role played by local informal social controls in the formation of social order, the complementarity between formal institutions and folk law, the influence of the state on local customs, and the plurality of normative order created by diverse social controls, including state law and folk law.

However, suicides of Nakhi lovers (Chap. 2) show the destructive effects of state law and mainstream culture on local social order. This tells us that state coercion does not always have a destructive effect on the way of life and values of social groups. Although the above two cases seem to support contradictory conclusions, they in fact reflect the nature of the law. Law not only mirrors society but also shapes society. Whether an individual can learn to navigate pluralistic normative/legal orders does not depend entirely on the individuals. A large part of it depends on the extent to which state law mirrors and shapes society. On the one hand, if state law only acts as a "mirror," it will not contribute to social progress. On the other hand, if state law causes excessive interference in society, it will produce a variety of tragedies.

In contrast to the Mancun Village case, what occurred in Pingcun Village shows that if a village's internal or traditional social control system is broken or weakened to an extent that it is unable to maintain the existing social order or give rise to a new social order and, at the same time, state law fails to come into full effect or respond to the normative needs of the village, which will result in a lack of normative underpinning in social transition, the village is very likely to form an informal social control institution in conflict with state law. A lack of beneficial interactions between state law and informal social control will in turn exacerbate the negative effects of the absence of normative order, resulting in a malignant circle that can lead to social chaos. A takeaway from the Pingcun Village case is that when a traditional system of a village has been changed/destroyed, the lack of a new system in its stead will cause the collapse of the cultural system that supports the way of life, values, and worldviews of the villagers, leading to social chaos in the process of modernization. This is a dilemma faced by many villages in the process of modernization and the root cause of the sustained absence of social order in these villages. To solve this dilemma, we need to recognize that "modernization" and "traditions" are not mutually exclusive. It is important to transform local social control institutions in a prudent and gentle manner rather than forcefully. The law imposed must be able to promote the formation of an endogenous social control system in the village (Chap. 8). A similar case is the case of the Yi people in the Liangshan Yi Autonomous Prefecture. Due to the failure of state law, the Yi people resorted to vigilantism, including violence and suicide, to resolve disputes between clan branches (Wang, 2007). On the one hand, excessive involvement of law in society and culture can lead to social chaos and collapse of culture. On the other hand, the lack of effective intervention will also lead to social chaos. This is the biggest dilemma of law.

Law is an important variable that can change the pluralistic pattern of law, social structure, and relationships, and this variable is relatively controllable. The effectiveness of law, which is discussed in Chap. 4 ("Causes of Corruption"), largely depends on whether it aims to solve social problems. Corruption is often discussed in the context of criminal law. Therefore, the focus of anti-corruption efforts is often on how to prevent and control corruption as a criminal activity. However, corruption is not just a criminal activity. It is also a political process. It occurs in specific or daily political situations. Bureaucracy is a breeding ground for corruption. There is a set of unwritten rules governing every individual in the political circle, distorting their values and sense of morality and leading to the reproduction and spread of corruption in daily situations. The blurring of the boundary between private and public life of political figures can lead to corruption. There are both macro- and microdeterminants of corruption. Only by constructing a fair system and controlling the daily operation of power we can truly reduce the incidence of corruption.

As mentioned earlier, law, society, and culture interact in various ways. This prompts scholars to ponder a potential risk faced by the justice system: If state law departs from social reality too much, it will become foreign to members of society. State law cannot be a perfect mirror that reflects every need, value, and belief of members of society. It is normal for law to depart from society. State law is similar to a map. We cannot mark every route and terrain of a place in all particulars on the map. Otherwise, it will be a huge, unusable map. As there can only be key geographical information on a map, state law only addresses issues legislators consider to be important. However, at present, the disconnection between state law and social reality in China has reached an extent that state law cannot answer basic questions closely related to Chinese people's daily life, such as why the hand-to-mouth existence problem leads to huge inequalities between people, why corruption cannot be rooted out, why the wealth gap is widening, and why house prices are so high. The failure of state law to answer these questions has shaken people's belief in the rule of law and undermined their trust in the country's legal system. The root cause of this crisis is the failure of state law to effectively respond to social needs. As Ann Seidman and Robert B. Seidman have pointed out, state law is just a set of highly selective and biased rules and institutionalized procedures (Seidman and Seidman, 1992, p.14). The excessive departure of law from society will undermine the trust of people in the rule of law and the legitimacy of the justice system as a whole, resulting in an increase in informal social controls and the use of vigilantism. To solve all these problems and give full play to the role of law as the mirror of society as well as a means to "make society," we need to put law back to its social and cultural context.

Last but not least, I believe studying law in its social and cultural context can help us gain insight into legal questions and theories. Only by proposing and testing assumptions based on observations of the day-to-day practice of law in Chinese society, we can find answers to legal questions that are closely related to Chinese people's daily lives.

References

Deng, Z. (2005). The future of legal studies in China. *Tribune of Political Science and Law*, (1–4).

Li, Y. (1997). *Human vision*. Shanghai Literature and Art Press.

Liang, Z. (1991). *Searching for harmony in the natural order*. Shanghai People's Publishing House.

Seidman, A. W., & Seidman, R. B. (1992). *Legislative Drafting for market reform: Some lessons from China* (Y. Shi, Trans.). China University of Political Science and Law Press.

Wang, Q. (2007). Meanings, values, and use of violence in vigilante--subjective dimension of human action. *Journal of Yunnan University (Law Edition)*, (3).

Contents

Part I
Actions, Culture, and Order

Chapter 1
Use of Violence in the Struggle for Survival and Its Devastating Effects: Structural Causes of Violent Vigilantism

1.1 Introduction: Research Problem and Methodology

The famous historian Jonathan D. Spence recalled an incident of collective violence during the Ming-Qing transition period:

> One such army (of bandits), several thousand strong, moved down into T'anch'eng (Tancheng) County from I-chou (Yizhou) in April 1641. They looted the market town of Li-chia-chuang (Lijiazhuang) on the county border and marched southwest to the Ma-t'ou (Matou) market. This they looted too, and spent three days there before [...] moving east to T'an-ch'eng city, which they besieged. However, the days the bandits spent in Ma-t'ou had given the people of T'an-ch'eng time to organize their defenses. They blocked the city gates with stones and earth, placed cannons ready for firing on walls, and marshed the local defense forces under men like Wang Ying [...] This group, and other unnamed citizens, fought off the bandits through the morning of April 15 and finally repulsed them [...] (Spence, 2005, p. 6–7).

This story provides a compelling example of self-defense involving the use of violence. The people of Tancheng were forced to use violence to defend their homes in the absence of government protection.

The Tancheng incident occurred in the late Ming Dynasty, a historical period scarred by bandits and rebellions. What is certain is that collective violence is not uncommon in the history of China. In fact, it was a recurring theme at the time of dynasty changes and social instability. One of the research interests of Jonathan D. Spence is humanity behind history. Many of his works show how helpless people were when history threw them into situations they had no control over. Historical background is an external structural constraint for all human beings. Every choice is made within a specific historical setting. In the case of Tancheng County, in the historical background of dynasty change, ordinary people, including peasants, literati, and the gentry, took up weapons to protect themselves in a life-or-death situation. Rise in violent incidents seems to be inevitable in such a historical context.

Research on collective violence in the Ming and Qing Dynasties can help us gain a glimpse into why and how vigilantism had occurred. Collective violence, as a way for ordinary people to resolve disputes and seek redress, was rampant in rural areas

Q. Wang, *Sociology of Law*,
https://doi.org/10.1007/978-981-16-5509-8_1

of Fujian and Guangdong in the old days. According to Mr. Wang Rigen, "rampant collective violence was largely fueled by corrupt local government which obstructed the bottom-up reporting of such incidents. Under the rule of a corrupt government […], collective violence and political corruption were mutually causal […]" (Wang, 2003, p. 49–52).

When interpreting the Tancheng County case and rampant collective violence in Fujian and Guangdong during the Ming and Qing Dynasties, we should not stop at historical inevitability. Otherwise, it would only show our incapability to uncover the truth. The studies of two historians have prompted me to ask the following question: What are the key factors behind the occurrence of vigilantism?

Many researchers have tried to find the causes of vigilantism from different angles. For example, some researchers believe that vigilantism occurs in contemporary China because "in the past 100 years, legal modernization programs in China simply focused on the transplantation of Western laws, and failed to recognize the importance of customs, social structure, religion, etc." (Liu & Zhao, 2003). In other words, China's existing legislation is not compatible with its current social and cultural background. Some researchers have studied vigilantism from the economic perspective and come to the conclusion which explains why some people choose vigilantism over judicial recourse: (1) vigilantism is less time-consuming than litigation; (2) litigation is expensive; (3) litigation is complicated […] (4) impulses of self-defense and desires for revenge […] "Benefits are one of the primary motivations. Real or expected gains drive people to choose vigilantism remedies. Vigilantism has certain advantages over other remedies in predictability of outcomes, costs, efficiency, and convenience" (Xu, 2003). These explanations of the causation of vigilantism, especially the economic cost-based explanation by Mr. Xu Xin, are fascinating and instructive. However, the causation of vigilantism is complicated. Different research approaches and points of departures lead to different views. By combining all of these different views, we may have a holistic understanding of the causal mechanism of vigilantism.

The point of departure in this chapter is in sociological terms. This chapter aims to determine the structural causes of vigilantism. Famous sociologist Anthony Giddens wrote, "Individuals produce society, but they do so as historically located actors, and not under conditions of their own choosing" (Giddens 2003, p. 278). He also posits that "structures must be conceptualized not only as constraints upon human agency, but as enablers as well" (Giddens, 2003, p. 278). That is, structures can both constrain and enable human actions. If, based on Giddens' theory, vigilantism is a product of human agency, then vigilantism is both constrained and enabled by certain structures. This chapter focuses on these structurally constraining factors that restrict the possibility of people redressing wrongs through recourse to legal proceedings, forcing people to take matters into their own hands. The research materials used in this chapter primarily come from two sources: (i) legal anthropological studies conducted by me in recent years and (ii) existing ethnographic literature and relevant investigative reports and historical studies. These materials have one thing in common. All of them focus on life at the bottom. This chapter tries to interpret daily life events and questions from a legal sociological perspective. After all, the fundamental purpose of law should be to improve people's lives. Therefore, it is necessary for legal researchers to study problems associated with daily life.

1.2 Vigilantism and the Use of Violence

Vigilantism refers to actions taken by a party to a dispute to redress the alleged injury on their own. In this situation, no impartial third party intervenes, and the allegedly injured party resorts to their own resources, rather than the help of government authority or legal proceedings, to solve the dispute and to claim their due rights (Xu, 2004b). Forms of vigilantism include the use of any means—violent, manipulative, persuasive, and authoritative (involving coercion or controlling behavior)—that may affect the rights and remedies concerned (Xu, 2005). Similar terms that might be used in this context include self-redress, private remedy, self-defense, self-preservation, extrajudicial enforcement, and lynch (Xu, 2005).

Incidents involving invocation of vigilantism, as a form of informal social control and a means for an injured party to implement their legitimate rights,[1] are very common in human history, whether in ancient or modern society. For example, in primitive societies, vigilantism is the most important redress (Hoebel 1992); the *Law of Twelve Tables* of ancient Rome did not recognize retaliation as a legitimate right but allowed vigilantism to some extent. For example, the *Law of Twelve Tables* stipulated that if anyone was caught stealing at night and was killed unfortunately, this killing was with impunity and that if a person committed a theft during the day and attempted to defend himself with weapons, it was legal for the defender to kill the thief in the defense of his person and property (Nicholas 2000, p. 219). For another example, the law of the Tang Dynasty prohibited revenge but recognized the legality and rationality of vigilantism. The *Law and Litigation of Tang Dynasty* stipulated that if one's grandparent or parent was attacked by others, he was legally allowed to use reasonable forces to defend his grandparent or parent without hurting the perpetrator. Even if the perpetrator was hurt during the process, the penalty would be three times less than that under normal circumstances (Zhang 1995, p. 229). In modern societies, reasonable self-defense and vigilantism are also permitted by laws but with stricter restrictions. Under modern justice systems, vigilantism is permitted only in limited circumstances. They serve as supplements to judicial relief but definitely are not considered to be the primary recourse.[2] Therefore, some scholars believe that the justice systems in human history went through three stages: (i) Stage-1, where vigilantism was the primary means to seek redress; (ii) Stage-2, where juridical

[1] Wang Qiliang. *Informal Social Control in Daily Life.* Unpublished manuscript.

[2] However, in real life, vigilantism is a fundamental means of social control. As a widely used alternative to the formal legal process, vigilantism is of great significance for the maintenance of social order. Its importance is not necessarily less than that of judicial remedies (Xin, 2004a).

remedies were introduced as supplements to vigilantism; and (iii) Stage-3, where vigilantism is a supplement to judicial remedies (He, 2004).

Violent vigilantism is but one form of vigilantism whose basic features include the absence of any formal legal process or the consultation of any neutral third party (Xu, 2005). The only difference between violent vigilantism and other vigilantism is that violence is used instead of other nonviolent means (such as negotiations). The word "violence" has different definitions (Lin, 2001; Guo, 2005). In this chapter, it refers to the use of physical forces, threatened or actual, against oneself, another person, or an object. Violent behaviors range from battering to simple assault to aggravated assault to homicide. Violent forms of vigilantism can be directed against the person, such as body search, restrictions on freedom of movement, acts of intimidation and coercion, or against property, such as trespassing on property or theft, destruction and violent dealing of property. Some violent vigilantism (use of defensive force, etc.) are permitted by law, and others are illegal or may even be considered criminal offences.

Although vigilantism is an important way to redress grievances, the use of violent vigilantism must be subject to legal restrictions. Reasonable legal measures should be adopted to reduce the incidence of *vigilante incidents. Vigilante*, as a powerful remedy, may cause damage to the existing pattern of law and disrupt social order. Furthermore, the use of violent vigilantism often leads to devastating consequences even if the perpetrators have some legitimate objectives. Even if the law of a society allows people to use physical force to protect their lives and property in the face of burglary, when burglary becomes an every-day situation, such violent vigilantism is not very helpful in restoring social order or creating conditions for peace. In the case of Tancheng, in the two decades following the incident, local defense forces ultimately failed to repulse bandits and the Manchu army. The lives of the people of Tancheng began to disintegrate before their eyes in their uncountable encounters with violence. Tancheng became a city of destitution (Spence, 2005: p. 7–9). The impact of unlawful vigilantism on social security and the authority of law is more detrimental. The lives of people who resort to or are victims of violence are inevitably destroyed by violence. It is imperative to control and reduce the incidence of unlawful violent gigilantism.

If the use of violence by civilians is a result of structural constraints, it is even more tragic when people use physical force in defense of their lives, and their lives will still be destroyed in the process.

1.3 Structural Causes of Violent Vigilantism

1.3.1 Failure of Government Protection Mechanisms

There are many reasons to support the establishment of norms and the monopoly of the legitimate use of violence by the state. However, what is more important is that the state must use the power conferred by citizens to make laws and legitimately use violence to protect citizens, support the orderly operation of society, and raise the wellbeing of citizens.[3] The government should take effective measures to protect citizens' civil rights and individual rights, the environment, and national security. Failure of the government to perform this protective function effectively and faithfully may lead to social turmoil and the abuse of violent self-remedies.

Through my fieldwork in Guoshan Village in Jinping County, Yunnan Province in 1999, I came to believe that the failure of government to protect citizens' property rights will ultimately lead to the rise in violent vigilantism incidents[4]:

Case 1: Death of Villager Deng

A villager named Deng Xiaosan escaped after being caught in the act of stealing. Deng had been caught red-handed several times. This time, the villagers were really angry over his lack of repentance. On the night when Deng was caught again, dozens of villagers dragged Deng with his hand tied behind him to a local school and beat Deng to death. Local police investigated the death of Deng but failed to pin down the mastermind behind this incident of collective violence.

I do not believe the root cause of this incident is an outburst of anger of the villagers because vigilante killing of thieves had happened more than once in Guoshan Village. It is impossible to treat collective violence in the same pattern every time as an impulse. On one occasion where Deng and his accomplices were caught red-handed, the villagers did not punish Deng's accomplices. They only punished Deng, a known habitual thief. When I interviewed the villagers, few villagers expressed strong opposition to the vigilante killing of thieves.

Tragedies such as the Guoshan Village case give pause for reflection. Should the occurrence of tragedies be attributed to the cruelty of villagers? If this is the case, why had the villagers not killed Deng's accomplices? Why not kill all the thieves regardless of the value of the stolen items or whether it was the first offense of the thieves? Was vigilante killing a tradition in the village? The answer is no. Theft is punishable by monetary penalties according to local regulations. Physical punishment was never a popular form of punishment for theft before the 1990s. What prompted the villagers to resort to collective violence?

Through investigation, I learned that the local government had done a very bad job in maintaining social order. Local police were responsible for six administrative villages, and 42 natural villages dispersed over wide areas, making local policing a challenging task. Due to limited police resources, it was impossible for local law enforcement to respond to every crime promptly. They had to prioritize those high-harm crimes. In such a context, local police were unable to effectively crack down on

[3] The so-called protective function of government includes "design, implementation, and supervision of various external institutions to support the operation of internal institutions of civil society and to adjust behaviors related to public policy".

[4] As a rule of thumb in social and cultural anthropology, "Ping County", "Guoshan Village" and "Pingcun Village" in this book are all pseudonyms given to the places and communities I studied.

petty offenses (such as theft and violations of the *public order regulations*). Administration problems and inefficiencies further hindered the local police from providing protection for local communities.

State law does not encourage citizens to use physical force. In the Guoshan Village case, the villagers already knew that the local police could not effectively control theft. Therefore, they took matters into their own hand and resorted to vigilantism, which they believed would be a means of social control more effective than law. The inability of state law has spurred villagers to resort to the use of physical force to defend their property. Similar cases were also reported in a nearby village, Pingcun Village, where trafficking in women was rampant. In the face of local law enforcement's inability, villagers often resort to vigilantism, including the use of violence, to rescue human trafficking victims (Wang, 2007c).

In 2005, a high-profile violent incident occurred in Zhejiang Province. This was a typical case of the failure of the government to provide protection to local communities. In this case, the government failed to protect the local environment, putting citizens' rights to health and development at risk and therefore triggering a violent response.

Case 2: The Huashui Town Case

On April 10, 2005, in Huashui Town, Dongyang City, Zhejiang Province, a team of over 3000 law enforcement officers, including policemen and urban administration officers, was encircled by more than 20,000 villagers. In the confrontation, dozens of villagers, including more than ten senior citizens, were injured. More law enforcement officers were injured, including the deputy mayor and the head of a local police station. No death was reported. According to *Phoenix Weekly* (*feng huang zhou kang*), the temporary bamboo sheds built along the road had not been removed after the incident. There was a long string of items left by the police when they retreated: police helmets, tear-proof shells, batons, rubber sticks, watermelon knives, scissors, police uniforms, and so on. From April 10 to 15, forty-eight damaged vehicles were parked in a local middle school in Haixi Town (Song, 2005).

The cause of this incident of mass violence was the government's failure to respond to public concern about environmental pollution. After their petition for industrial pollution control fell on deaf ears, the people of Huashui Town built roadblocks to prevent chemical companies from transporting raw materials into the town. Law enforcement officers sent to demolish these roadblocks were surrounded by local residents. Serious pollution has put local residents' health at risk. Local residents believed that large chemical companies had persuaded the local government to meet their interests and ignored the calls of local residents for pollution control (Song, 2005). The post-incident investigation conducted by the State Environmental Protection Administration proved that dereliction of duty by the local government was to be blame for this incident.[5]

[5] Dai Yuda. (2015). *The Root Cause of the Huashuihe Pollution Incident in Zhejiang Province: Improper Planning.*

The government not only has a duty to protect the local environment and maintain social order but is also responsible for setting reasonable administrative goals and adopting proper public policies to support the goals. Unreasonable goals will often face popular resentment and resistance and may even cause citizen protests. For example, the rise in acts of violence among citizens in response to land expropriation in recent years is also attributable to the failure of government to protect citizens' rights (Shao, 2004).

1.3.2 Corruption in the Justice System

As the state claims a monopoly over executive, the justice system should guarantee that citizens have access to remedies by due course of law. If the failure of the justice system to guarantee this "bottom line" will inevitably lead to social turmoil. Dissatisfaction of citizens over miscarriage of justice may prompt them to resort to informal social control or even escalate into retaliatory violence. The famous Yongxing County Case is a typical example of how a victim's indignation over miscarriage of justice could quickly spiral into violence.

Case 3: The Yongxing County Case

On February 25, 2005, Judge Cao Hua, who lived on the second floor of the No. 5 Dormitory Building of the People's Court of Yongxing County, Hunan Province, brought a package sent to him to a flower bed near the building because he suspected it was a homemade bomb. After he poured a bucket of water onto the package, the bomb went off, producing a 70 cm deep pit and shattering the windows of the two dormitory buildings nearby. Cao Hua was killed on the spot. If the explosion occurred on the second floor, the dormitory would collapse and put nearly one hundred lives at risk. Such an appalling retaliatory bomb attack against a court was very rare. The Public Security Department of the Hunan Provincial Government deployed a large number of police officers to form a task force investigating the case.

It was reported that police suspected it was a retaliatory attack by a party to a case the court had ruled over. The task force reviewed all the files of the cases that the judges living in the dormitory buildings had handled in recent years in the hope of finding a lead.

The bomb was first discovered at a place near Cao Hua's home. Cao used to serve as the chief magistrate at the court of Liyutan Town, Yongxing County. He was promoted a year ago to deputy director of the executive committee and the head of the executive chamber of the court of Yongxing County. The task force found a lead in a case file. Cao was responsible for handling a case involving child labor. A boy named Huang Hu became disabled in a work-related accident. "We all hold the opinion that the ruling was clearly unfair. The family of the victim blamed Cao for unfairness," an insider said. Huang Hu's father, Huang Yuncai, was ruled out as a possible suspect in the first round of investigation. The local police believed that Huang Yuncai was a well-recognized honest person. However, evidence collected at later stages of investigation all pointed to Huang Yuncai, an insider said. Huang Yuncai did not admit his guilt until two days and three nights later (Deng, 2005).

In this case, the legal system failed to deliver justice due to judicial corruption. After all legal remedies have been exhausted, Huang Yuncai took matters into his own hand (Deng, 2005). Instead of retaliating against the defender in the case, the honest man Huang Yuncai sent a bomb to the judge and the court because the real target of his anger was the corruption in the justice system. Judicial corruption often causes more public indignation than corruption in other branches of the state because it shatters people's hopes for the future, poses a major impediment to justice, and compels people to believe the state's promise of legal remedies is just a scam (Xiao, 2005). Huang Yuncai was forced to resort to vigilantism by no other than judicial corruption.

John Locke said, "where an appeal to the law, and constituted judges, lies open, but the remedy is denied by a manifest perverting of justice, and a barefaced wresting of the laws to protect or indemnify the violence or injuries of some men, or party of men [...] they are left to the only remedy in such cases, an appeal to heaven." (Locke, 1964, p. 15) In the case of judicial corruption, injured parties believe the court of heaven is on their side and gives them power to take matters into their own hands. Corruption in the justice system is a major impediment to access to legal remedies, thereby forcing people to resort to violence to redress their personal grievances.

1.3.3 Disconnect Among Different Dispute Resolution Mechanisms

In rural areas, it is not uncommon for the state to fail to perform its conflict resolution function. The law confers to autonomous village organizations and other social organizations the right to manage village affairs and mediate disputes within village limits, allowing these nonstate social control institutions to operate within the scope permitted by law. However, the *Notice of the Supreme People's Court on How to Handle Civil Disputes Transferred from Governments at Township/Town Level*, which came into force on September 3, 1993, established a very conservative and unreasonable mechanism for the collaboration between the government mediation system and the justice system. According to the notice, if the mediation does not settle, either side can file a lawsuit. However, the fourth article undermines the effectiveness of the mediation agreement reached by the parties on their own accord, which may increase the cost of dispute resolution.[6] The promulgation of *Several Rules of the Supreme People's Court on Civil Cases Involving Disputes over Mediation Agreements* on November 1, 2002 marked a substantial step in the direction of

[6] This article stipulates that, if a party applies for enforcement of an agreement reached through mediation by a judicial assistant or township/town government, the court may dismiss the application.

effective integration between the mediation system and the litigation system.[7] The following case is an example of a lack of linkage between different dispute resolution mechanisms.

Case 4: The Xiashuicao Village Case

In 1999, Villager A, Villager B, and Villager C from Niutang Village and Jiaobao Village pumped out the water in the fish pond of Villager D in Xiashuicao Village, causing the death of fish in the pond. The township government sent a mediator to sort out the dispute and requested Villager A, Villager B, and Villager C to compensate for the loss of Village D. However, Villager A, Villager B, and Villager C refused to pay for the damages. On the day following the Spring Festival of 2000, Villager D went to the homes of Villager A, Villager B, and Villager C and forcefully took their livestock in lieu of damages. (Kuang, 2000, p. 88).

In this case, the mediation agreement reached through the mediation presided over by the township government was unenforceable. If Villager D took the action to the court, it would mean that the energy, time, and money he had already invested in dispute settlement all went in vain. This dilemma eventually drove Villager D towards vigilantism.

The Xiashuicao Village case sheds light on an important issue. When talking about structure, we mean more than social and natural factors such as social structure, gender structure, and spatial structure. When a system is in full force and affects a society, the system constitutes a structural constraint on members of society and their actions. Members of society must behave within the framework of the system, which not only influences their decision making but also provides resources for their actions. Therefore, to reduce the costs and improve the efficiency of resolving disputes, it is necessary to establish effective mechanisms linking different dispute resolution mechanisms. If there is no such mechanism, structural failure of these dispute resolution mechanisms is inevitable. China's legislative authority has been pushing for the establishment and improvement of such linkage mechanisms. However, there are still many flaws in current linkage mechanisms, leading to structural failure of dispute resolution mechanisms and causing escalation of disputes or triggering incidents of vigilantism.

---

[7] The first article of this judicial interpretation writes: "An agreement document which is signed or sealed by both parties and embodies the main points agreed to by the parties in meditation presided over by the People's Mediation Committee is a contract. The parties shall perform their obligations in accordance with the contract and may not alter or terminate the mediation agreement without authorization." The second article writes: "If one party submits an application for enforcement to the court, the court shall issue a writ of execution." The tenth article writes: "For a notarized mediation agreement involving debt arrangement, the creditor may make an application to the court where the debtor's domicile is located or where the debtor's assets are located to enforce the mediation agreement."

1.3.4 Discussion: How to Prevent Violent Vigilantism

Judicial corruption, failure of government to provide protection to citizens, and the lack of linkage between different dispute resolution mechanisms can manifest themselves in more ways than discussed in this chapter. The three factors have one thing in common: all of them are impediment to citizens' access to legal remedies. If citizens are unable to access legal remedies, they will be forced to resort to violence as a means to redress their grievances. Therefore, the three factors are the structural causes of vigilantism. In the case of the existence of the three factors, vigilantism will become the only choice for people seeking justice. The individuals resorting to violence in all the cases mentioned in this chapter have shown profound disillusion with the justice system. They used physical forces to protect themselves, defend their values, and realize justice denied by the legal system.

However, vigilantism can be curbed and reined in.

Costs and benefits are always at the heart of vigilantism. The risks associated with vigilantism have deterrence effects on citizens. Not everyone has the capability or resources to use physical forces to redress grievances. There are compelling reasons to believe that if the government provides sufficient protection to citizens, the justice system fair, and the dispute resolution mechanisms effective and efficient, few people will choose vigilantism either in the form of vigilantism or retaliation. The case below shows the willingness of people to seek state-sponsored remedies.

Case 5: The Longzhupeng Village Case

Three villagers from Longzhupeng Village were abducted for stealing cows by a group of armed Burmese living near the China-Myanmar border. The kidnappers threatened to kill the victims within three days unless their families paid 120,000 yuan in ransom. One of the three victims was the younger brother of a prestigious Buddhist monk in a local temple. Burmese kidnappers threatened to abduct people and burn down houses. They shotgun into the air on the hills near Longzhupeng Village to scare villagers. In Longzhupeng Village, men picked up hoes and sticks to protect the village, and women and children hide in the woods near the village. The chief of Longzhupeng Village reported the incident to the village affairs office. After discussing with the local police, the village chief reported the incident to the government of Nuofu Township and the local foreign affairs office, hoping the foreign affairs office would come forward to settle the conflict. After negotiation between the foreign affairs office and the government of Myanmar, the Burmese kidnappers were ordered to release the three victims and pay compensation for injuries of villagers inflicted by them before the Spring Festival, whereas Longzhupeng villagers were ordered to pay five cows and 900 yuan in compensation before the Spring Festival. The two sides decided to obtain the rest of the details ironed out after the Spring Festival. The governments of the two sides successfully prevented the incident from escalating into a serious cross-border conflict (Wang, 2000, p. 121–122).

In this incident, the government efficiently provided protection to the villagers and properly handled the dispute. With the help of the government, the villagers did not have to use physical forces to protect themselves, thus avoiding possible tragedies and serious consequences that may result from the use of violence. As we can see from this case, vigilantism can be effectively curbed.

Based on the case analysis in this chapter, we have discovered that a weak justice system is the structural cause of vigilant*e* incidents.[8] Therefore, to curb vigilante incidents, the government needs to ensure access to judicial remedies, provide sufficient protection to citizens, fight corruption in the justice system, and improve dispute resolution mechanisms.

References

Daosheng, S. (2004). Use of force in demolition of illegal buildings and land expropriation. *China Land*, (7).

Delong, L., & Yang, Z. (2003). A tentative study on vigilante. *Journal of Tianjin Administrative Cadre Institution of Politics and Law,* (1).

Fei, D. (2005). The true story behind the explosion case in Yongxing County. *Phoenix Weekly*, (10).

Giddens, A. (2003). *New rules of sociological method.* Social Sciences Academic Press.

Hairen, H. (2004). From vigilante to state remedies—Modern discourse of remedies. *Studies in Law and Business*, (1).

Han, X. (2005). Protecting the final line of defense of justice. *Phoenix Weekly*, (10).

Hoebel, E. A. (1992). *The law of primitive man: A study in comparative legal dynamics* (Cunsheng, Y., et al., Trans.). Guizhou People's Publishing House.

Jinfan, Z. (1995). *Legal history of China.* Law Press.

Locke, J. (1964). *The second treatises of government* (Qifang, Y., & Junong, Q., trans.). The Commercial Press.

Nicholas, B. (2000). *An introduction to Roman law* (Feng, H., Trans.). Law Press.

Qiliang, W. (2007b). Meanings, values, and use of violence in Vigilante—Subjective dimension of human action. *Journal of Yunnan University (Law Edition)*, (3).

Qiliang, W. (2007c). Why does formal social control fail?—A field survey of trafficking of women in Ping County. *Journal of China Agricultural University (Social Sciences)*, (2).

Rigen, W. (2003). *Local society's order in the Ming-Qing dynasties.* Yuelu Press.

Yuan, S. (2005). The truth behind Dongyang environmental dispute. *Phoenix Weekly*, (13)

Spence, J. (2005). *The death of woman Wang* (Biyu, L., Trans.). Shanghai Yuandong Publishing House.

Xiaozhu, W. (Ed.). (2000). *The Lahu people—Nanduan Old Village of Nofu Township.* Yunnan University Press.

Xin, X. (2003). Order without Law—Study of a private debt collection case in South China. *Open Times*, (6).

Xin, X. (2004a). Is law important?--Study of a private debt collection case in South China. *Sociological Study*, (1).

[8] I have examined the subjective dimensions of vigilantism in another study. The causation of vigilante incidents is not only related to the objective dimension of society, such as rules, resources, and existing dispute resolution mechanisms, but also connected to the subjective dimension of society, such as beliefs, values, and worldviews. Violence as a form of vigilantism cannot be completely rooted out. It can only be curtailed. However, to rein in vigilante incidents, forcing changes in the subjective dimension would only lead nowhere. Instead, we should root out the objective causes by focusing on the reform of institutions and social structures (Wang, 2007b).

Xin, X. (2004b). Interaction between Vigilante and State Remedies—Legal interpretation. *Law and Social Development*, (4).
Xin, X. (2005). *On self-help remedy*. China University of Political Science and Law Press.
Yagang, L. (December 2001). Connotation and denotion of violent crimes. *Modern Law Science*, (6).
Zeqiang, G. (2005). A new interpretation of violence relating to infringement of the right to freedom of choice in marriage. *Journal of Yunnan University (Law Edition)*, (2).
Zhenglai, D. (2005). The future of legal studies in China. *Tribune of Political Science and Law*, (1–4).
Ziming, K. (Ed.). (2000). *The Yao people—Shuicao Village in Yaoshan Township*. Yunnan University Press.

Chapter 2
Suicide of Passion Among Nakhi People and Failure of Law

2.1 Problem: Informal Institutions and Failure of Law

Legal pluralists often deem as law all the rules and norms, either formal or informal, that govern a society, which makes the term particularly elusive. Because of this, some critics of "legal pluralism" have pointed out the folly of the concept in the field of social science (Tamanaha, 1993, p. 192–217). Undeniably, however, the world we live in does have different legal systems, as is widely agreed among scholars of legal anthropology (Engle, 1988, p. 869–896). The concept of "legal pluralism", at the very least, cautions us against legal centralists' one-sided argument that social order is maintained mainly by the state, law and other formal institutions.[1] Putting aside conceptual controversies and misunderstandings, the focus of legal pluralism in the area of legal anthropology is in fact on institutions and social control of different natures, including formal institutions of the state in modern society as well as their relationships with informal institutions. However, the existing literature on the interaction between institutions has not given sufficient attention to how formal institutions contribute to the birth of informal institutions.[2]

Basically, social institutions can be classified as either formal or informal. Formal institutions consist of laws, public policies, government regulations, etc. Informal institutions include taboos, habits, customs, practices, and customary laws. This classification not only distinguishes institutions based on their nature but also implies their different origins. In institutional economics, formal institutions are established by the state for such purposes as establishing social order. The state is empowered to

---

[1] See Robert C. Ellickson's commentary on legal centralism (Ellickson, 1998, p. 167).

[2] Mr. Liang Zhiping argues customary law was introduced to bypass the legislature. Liang's argument undoubtedly provides a new perspective to the relationship between formal and informal institutions (Liang, 1996, p. 59–60). If some of the institutionalized or quasi-institutionalized *vigilante* remedies can be regarded as informal institutions, Mr. Xu Xin's monograph on the relationship between formal and informal institutions in China is perhaps the most exhaustive study on this subject. Xu argues that there is an intrinsic connection between *vigilante* remedies and state-sponsored remedies. Problems and limits of formal state institutions give rise to the necessity of *vigilante* (Xu, 2005).

Q. Wang, *Sociology of Law*,
https://doi.org/10.1007/978-981-16-5509-8_2

create and enforce laws and policies in a well-planned manner. Although we cannot exclude the possibility that informal norms can also be established in a planned way, they are generally created through consultation and negotiation among members of a community with the intention of solving a specific problem, but the outcome of the consultation or negotiation is not foreseeable and may even divert from the intended goal. In general, informal institutions are the rules developed spontaneously from within a society; they are the result of long-term interactions of the society's members or they may originate from traditions. They are finally established as certain patterns of behavior have been accepted and recognized by the majority of the members. Some scholars of jurisprudence have also shown interest in the study of norms and institutions. For example, Professor Zhang Xiaohui writes, "We explore how the law emerges, evolves and gets enforced in a society without a written language by studying linguistic taboo of the Hani people. We believe that the primary form of social control evolves along the trajectory from taboos to customs to written laws in earlier forms of society". (Zhang & Lu, 1998, p. 182) Mr. Zhang Yonghe said: "The dominant form of social control has changed from taboos, habits, ethics, and customary law to written law [...] Introduction of written laws is a milestone in the development of a human society. It means that, in addition to modifying the natural environment around them, human beings began to realize that they could also create and modify institutions to benefit themselves" (Zhang, 2005, p. 5).

These studies all support the argument that formal institutions are established by the state, whereas informal institutions evolve spontaneously within a society. Moreover, informal institutions emerged earlier than formal institutions. Formal institutions evolve out of and are separate from taboos, customs, and other informal institutions. Formal and informal institutions can be distinguished based on way of emergence. Since these studies mainly focus on the development of institutions rather than the synchronization and interaction of formal and informal institutions, these arguments may lead to the misleading conclusion that the emergence of informal institutions has nothing to do with formal institutions. This conclusion is in fact true in earlier forms of human society, but after the formation of the state, formal state institutions have profound influence on all aspects of social life, and it becomes increasingly difficult for society to rid itself from the influence of the state. In this context, what are the connections between formal and informal institutions? Do the two types of institutions still have nothing to do with each other? This chapter will explain that the emergence of certain informal institutions is closely related to formal institutions such as state laws and that formal state institutions are an important factor in the development of informal institutions.

Another research topic in legal anthropology and sociology of law worthy of investigation is failure of law. As A. N. Allott puts it, ineffectiveness of law often arises from excessive ambition of a legislator or the failure to meet certain requirements, such as adequate preliminary investigation, communication, acceptance, and implementation mechanisms (Allott, 1980, p. 278). Is failure of law, a ubiquitous problem in justice systems around the world, related to informal institutions such as customs and customary laws? Previous studies have revealed many reasons for the failure of law, the most widely recognized reason being the departure of law from social reality, customs, and moral values (Rooij, 2004). However, these studies invoke the hypothesis that social customs, moral values, and other informal institutions that lead to failure of law emerge before the law. The second argument in this chapter is that law is capable of generating informal institutions and social norms, for example, that go against it. Since some informal institutions are created in the first place as a way of fighting against formal institutions, they will certainly become one of the factors that cause the failure of law.

This chapter takes an anthropological approach to studying law. While suicides of passion committed by lovelorn Nakhi people, or "*qing si*" in local dialect, were often understood as a social phenomenon peculiar to this ethnic community,[3] or the product of political changes, this chapter would shed new light on the issue, by looking at how the existene of informal institution might help us better understand the phenomenon. Observations of interactions and conflicts between institutions and subjective aspects of human societies are made to gain insight into the cause of this informal institution and to reveal the close relationship between the law and the informal institutions. The clash between law and local values, beliefs, worldviews, and other informal institutions may lead to the failure of law. At the end of the case study, its implications for the construct of the rule of law in a modern society. Unlike other legal anthropological studies, this chapter used historical materials and secondhand data on suicides of passion instead of first-hand data collected through fieldwork.[4]

2.2 Lovers' Suicide (*Qing Si*) as an Informal Institution

The famous Nakhi poem *Lubanlurao* tells a tragic story about a loving couple who killed themselves.

A long, long time ago, a group of enslaved shepherds living in an ancient Nakhi nomadic tribe were very unhappy about cruel treatment by slave masters. They decided to escape for freedom. On the journey, when they crossed the Jinsha River, they encountered a flood and were separated by the raging river. A part of the group successfully crossed the river, and the remaining stayed on the other side of the river. After repairing their boats, these brave shepherds successfully crossed the river and united with their families. Among the shepherds, there was a girl named Kaimeijiumingjin. She and her lover Zubuyulepan were separated on the road. She asked a crow to send a message to her lover. However, what the crow brought back was a curse from her lover's parents. They believed that she had affairs with three men and was not chaste. The girl sent a message to her lover again, asking him

[3] According to a local tale, the Nakhi lovers who committed suicide had been tempted by a spirit. Given this religious implication, I decided to use the ethnic group's dialectical expression "*qing si*" to refer to suicides of passion committed by Nakhi in this chapter.

[4] Fieldwork is not the only research method in legal anthropology. Nor is interpretation of legal phenomenon the only interest in legal anthropology. Some legal anthropologists have shown interest in legal history and published high-quality scholarly work on legal history (Qu, 1998; Moore, 1986).

to meet her. However, Zubuyulepan failed to arrive at the agreed meeting place in time due to obtrusion from a slave master. The heartbroken girl hanged herself from a tall mulberry tree. When Zubuyulepan discovered the death of his lover, he was devastated. After cremating his lover's body according to her will, grief-stricken Zubuyulepan ended his own life. The two were believed to ascend to a mysterious realm where lovers live happily ever after.[5]

The tradition of arranged marriage and Zubuyulepan's parents' strong stand for premarital chastity were what drove Kaimeijiumingjin to end her life. The two lovers committed suicide in defiance of this tradition and in pursuit of freedom promised by the local folk tale, according to which lovers who commit suicide will live happily ever after in another world.

The Han people also have similar stories. For example, the famous narrative poem "The Peacock Flies Southeast" (also known as "A Poem Written for the Wife of Jiao Zhongqing") tells a tragic love story of a man named Jiao Zhongqing and his wife Liu Lanzhi. The honest and hardworking young couple loved each other very much. However, Jiao's bigoted mother, who thought Liu ill-mannered and pervasive, forcefully separated the couple and sent Liu back to her maiden home. The story ends on a tragic note with the two ending their own lives and turning into butterflies.[6]

In this story, Liu and Jiao take their own life to fight against their despotic mother and brother who attempt to intervene in their marriage. For the desperate couple, suicide is the last-resort response to the feudal patriarchism that deprives them of freedom and dignity, as well as a way for them to proclaim their right and faith in love.

While the romance of Liu and Jiao is fictional, Lijiang, a city in Yunnan Province, was a popular choice among those contemplating suicide of passion. Countless young people of Nakhi ethnicity ended their own lives here in pursuit of freedom to love. Famous Nakhi scholar Mr. Yang Fuquan writes: "Peter Goullart, a Russian scholar who lived in Lijiang for many years in the 1940s, wrote in his book *Forgotten Kingdom* that Lijiang 'could really hold the doubtful honor of being the world's suicide capital. There was not a family that did not number a suicide or two among its members. 'British scholar Anthony Jackson also said that suicide was doubtlessly the most serious social problem of the Nakhi, and despite the efforts of many Han people governments, suicide remained popular among lovers until 1949. Many lovers, sometimes up to ten couples, committed ceremonial suicide together. The number of lovers committing suicide was staggering." (Yang, 2000).

Max Weber writes: "An actually existent probability of a regularity in the orientation of social action will be called 'usage', if the probability of its existence among a group of persons is conditioned entirely by its actual practice." He also writes, "Usage will be called 'custom' if the actual practice rests on long familiarity" (Weber, 2000:

---

[5] Lubanlurao is a famous folk tale of the Nakhi. Although the story has many versions, all versions end with Kaimeijiumingjin and Zubuyulepan killing themselves. Lubanlurao was chronicled by local priests called dongbas and became one of the must-read verses chanted by dongbas at funerals of lovers who committed double suicide. This section only presents the main thrust of this story based on Mr. He Zhiwu's translation and research works (He, 1991 & 1994, p. 75–94).

[6] For the interpretation of "The Peacock Flies Southeast", see Wu et al. (1992, p. 125–132).

48). The regularity of *qing si* has made it a custom of the Nakhi people rather than an individual occurrence, as in the story of "The Peacock Flies Southeast". Customs are by no means simple, repeated actions without any significance for legal researchers. Members of a social group conform, by their own free will, to customs that are a spontaneously developed component of social order and regularities of action among the group. *Qing si*, as a custom and informal institution through which young lovers express their defiance against forced marriage, was considered by the Nakhi a way to resolve the conflict between forced marriage and the freedom to love.

2.3 Law, Religion, and Suicides of Passion Among Nakhi People

The prevalence of *qingsi* in the history of the Nakhi was surely not caused by mental illness or personality disorder, nor was it an act driven by impulse.[7] It was a well-thought-out action of a normal person. The men and women who decided to die together in a suicide pact would often dress up and choose a secluded and beautiful site as their final resting place (Yang, 1999). Therefore, *qing si* is an act of rational choice. We cannot rule out imitation as a contributing factor to suicides of passion (Durkheim, 2001, p. 106–134), but imitation is by no means the chief reason. While suicides of passion also occurred among other ethnic groups in Lijiang and surrounding areas, none of these groups saw such a high rate of incidence as the Nakhi. It is neither hardship in life (Yang, 1999, p. 146) nor physical disability or illness that drove those young men and women to die by their own hands.

Since the above common causes of suicide were excluded, what caused the high rates of suicides of passion among the Nakhi? Some convincing research findings suggest that the high incidence of suicides was the product of social institutions. Some scholars blamed authoritarian rule for the tragedy in *Lubanlurao* (He, 1991, p. 275). It is worth noting *qing si* as an often observed phenomenon among the Nakhi people is not a custom from antiquity. Rather, it has been around for only a few centuries. It is believed that 1723 (the first year of Emperor Yongzheng's reign) is a milestone. In that year, the Qing government began to implement Han culture, especially Confucian values, among ethnic minorities, which had a tremendous impact on the social and cultural systems of the Nakhi people. Under the official legal system established with Confucian culture and ethical principles at its heart, many customs and values of the Nakhi became barbaric and illegal. Before the implantation of the Han culture, the Nakhi practiced free love and chose their marital partners of their own free will. After the cultural transformation, the Nakhi produced a large number of tragic love ballads and songs. "These songs criticized arranged marriage and other practices promoted by the feudal patriarchal system which suppressed the free spirit of young people[...]" (Yang, 1998, p. 110–111) However, despite the Qing government's efforts to promote Confucian ethics, the Nakhi's traditional values, such as respect for free love, still

[7] See Wasserman's analysis of the causes of suicide (Wasserman, 2003).

held sway. The two cultures therefore clashed violently. In some Nakhi communities where Confucian culture failed to penetrate, people enjoyed freedom of marriage, and lovers rarely chose suicide as a way of saying no to arranged marriages. On the other side of the spectrum, there were Nakhi communities largely assimilating into the Han culture. Readily accepting the Confucian ethics code, members of these communities did not resist arranged marriage; therefore, the incidence of suicides of passion in these communities was also low. The Nakhi communities most affected in this process were those that were forced to implement Confucian ethics but still preserved Nakhi's traditional views about free love. The strict Confucian code, which was advocated by the Qing government, clashed with Nakhi's traditional marriage system. In such a context, conflicts were bound to happen between people practicing different values. The clash of the two cultures led to many tragic love stories. As Mr. Yang Fuquan put it, the Nakhi had the freedom to pursue love, but marriage was a different story (Yang, 2005). Yang (2005) believes that the clash between the Confucian marriage code promoted by the Qing government and Nakhi's traditional values in relation to freedom of love eventually led to the prevalence of *qing si*.

Social institutional change and cultural clashes seem to be convincing viewpoints to explain the prevalence of *qing si* among Nakhi. Without cultural clash, Nakhi lovers would have no reason to commit suicide. How absurd it is that one has freedom to pursue love but has no say in whom to marry? Young men and women had no choice but to fight the absurd marriage system or run away. However, cultural clash alone was not enough to cause a large number of suicides.

In the history of China, many dynasties had attempted to assimilate ethnic minorities across the country, not just those living in Lijiang. Enforcing a uniform national legal system with Confucian values at its heart was an arduous task that required continuous efforts. Moreover, many other ethnic groups and communities also practiced free love before the implementation of Confucianism. Neither the concept of free love nor the clash between free love and the Confucian marriage code was unique to the Nakhi in Lijiang. Furthermore, even in societies where arranged marriage was already widely accepted, there were some individuals showing dissatisfaction with arranged marriage. Otherwise, there would not be stories like "The Peacock Flies Southeast". Why did *qing si* occur less frequently in ethnic groups other than the Nakhi? Why did it become customary among the Nakhi but not among other communities? Social institutions and cultural clashes alone are obviously not enough to explain this.

The Confucian marriage system was an institutional constraint on individual behavior. It was like a bird cage built to confine individuals. However, before the marriage was concluded, one was still free. The loss of freedom of an individual occurred after he or she entered an arranged marriage. Those who were dissatisfied with arranged marriage could still choose to fight it. Common actions in defiance of the arranged marriage system at the time included elopement, self-mutilation, and suicide. In any case, suicide was not the only way out. Why was it so popular among the Nakhi but not among other ethnic groups? Why did suicide, rather than elopement, become an institutionalized recourse to free love among the Nakhi?

To answer these questions, we need to examine the subjective world of those who chose to die by their own hands for freedom to love. Usually, a person who has a sound mind but never has any faith in life would not choose to commit suicide. Causes of suicide include but are not limited to hopelessness, loss of faith, pursuit of religious belief, and hope beyond despair. On the one hand, human beings are bound by structural factors, including the laws of nature and laws of human society (including marriage law). On the other hand, they are able to take actions and have their own ways of understanding and explaining the world. They make choices and respond to challenges based on their worldviews and available resources. Mencius said: "Life is what I want; righteousness is also what I want. If I cannot have both, I would rather take the righteousness than life." Mencius's value orientations decided how he would handle conflicts involving choice-making between life and righteousness. A person who believes life is more important than righteousness would make choices opposite to those made by Mencius. I think those who chose love over life must have firm religious beliefs that shaped their attitude towards life and death. This attitude gave them the strength and courage to commit suicide and conferred meaning on suicide.

Mr. He Limin believes that the Nakhi wind-worshipping ritual (that is, ritual of deliverance for lovers who died in a suicide pact) and the theory underpinning the practice appeared only at a time when social contradictions and tensions had become acute, of which suicides by lovers were a pronounced manifestation. [...] It was only after *qing si* became a prevalent that the wind-worshipping ritual and the idea of "love ghost" came into being. I partly agree with Mr. He's argument. However, he also writes: "So, those lovers who committed suicide were not tempted by the "love ghost" or the call from heaven. The custom of *qing si* was the result of an intense social contradiction. The answer to how this had happened among the Nakhi lies in the social and historical context. Religious beliefs related to *qing si* are merely an unreal and distorted reflection of this social contradiction." (He, 1991, p. 273–274) I do not agree with what Mr. He said about the relationship between religious beliefs and the *qing si* custom. I believe the interactions between the two should be much more complex than what was described by Mr. He.

The Nakhi people's religious belief and typical attitude towards death had already existed prior to the emergence of their wind-worshiping ritual. We cannot verify whether it was the local religious tradition and prevailing attitude towards death that gave lovers the courage to commit suicide in the first such incident. However, the high incidence of suicides of passion in the ethnic group was definitely related to their religious belief and attitude towards life and death. Nakhi believed that people would return to their ancestral home in the way they came in after death (Yang, 2001a, b), except for those who committed suicide. They believe those suicides would ascend to another beautiful realm where

> animals such as tigers, deer,
> and mountain donkeys work for humans, and people can connect the spirit of wind.
> It is a land in which there is an absence of suffering and evil.
> (Yang, 1997a, b)

Frustrated lovers who could not be together in their lifetime would be masters of their own destiny in this realm. Earthly existence is understood as a brief prelude to eternity. Since earthly life has become painful and meaningless due to loss of love, why not just enter blissful everlasting afterlife? After all, it is much easier than elopement.

Nakhi youngsters ended their own lives in defiance of the uncompromising Confucius marriage code with courage and strength from their religious belief in blissful afterlife. Of course, only true believers who have a firm religious faith would be able to draw strength from religion.

The connection between suicides of passion and the religion of the Nakhi is a complicated issue. On the one hand, religious belief gave young people spiritual strength to calmly end their own lives. On the other hand, as ceremonial suicide gained popularity, its status in the Dongba religion became increasingly prominent, and the description of the nether world in religious scriptures became increasingly beautiful, which in turn fueled the attraction of *qing si*.

For the Nakhi, *qing si* became a way for lovers to fight arranged marriage advocated by Confucianism.[8] This custom or informal institution arose from the clash between the external formal institutions (legal system) imposed by the state and Nakhi culture (values, beliefs, etc.). The combination of a formal institution such as a state law and the culture of a social group leads to the creation of a unique informal system.[9]

2.4 Implications of Love Suicide on the Introduction and Maintenance of Social Order

Suicides of passion among the Nakhi is a thing of the past. It has not only produced many tragic love stories but also offered fodder for thought to legislators and scholars of jurisprudence.

Such suicide arose from changes in social institutions (implantation of Han culture, including a legal system in compliance with Confucian values). Due to the implementation of Confucian culture, which was protected by state law, the Nakhi

[8] Mr. Yang Fuquan writes: "By the Qing Emperor Guangxu's reign, *qing si* had become a custom among the Nakhi in Lijiang. In the first year of the Republic of China, concerned about the high suicide rate, the local government of Lijiang banned the dafeng ritual (a religious ritual for lovers who committed suicide[…] At the time, the dafeng ritual was held almost at least every day in Lijiang[…]Apparently, *qing si* was very common in the region" (Yang, 1999, p. 13).

[9] Regarding the relationship between the religious beliefs and the *qing si* custom of the Nakhi, Yang argues that the ethnic group's culture, including belief in blissful afterlife, was the catalysis of *qing si* (Yang, 1998, p. 138). However, Yang believes that it is not religious belief but the emphasis of the Nakhi culture on courage, righteousness and love that was the most important factor in the emergence of the *qing si* custom (Yang, 1994). My opinion is different from that Mr. Yang Fuquan. I believe religion had a more important role. However, both of us hold the view that the *qing si* custom was a product of the interaction between formal state institutions and the Nakhi culture.

community had two contradictory value systems. Nakhi youngsters were in a weak position to fight the Confucian moral values and orthodox marriage system. In such a context, the objective dimension (i.e., formal institutions such as the law) and the subjective dimension (belief, values, etc.) of society became connected. On the one hand, the Qing government attempted to impose Confucianism on the Nakhi via formal institutions. On the other hand, the Nakhi never ceased to resist the intrusion of Confucianism. In this process, part of the dongba religion about the nether land began to grow. Religious belief in blissful afterlife undoubtedly fueled the attraction of suicide for frustrated Nakhi lovers.

The Qing imperial court attempted to use state law as a tool to instill orthodox Chinese values among the various ethnic groups in Lijiang. However, the high incidence of suicides of passion among Nakhi people indicates that this attempt encountered massive resistance. The law failed in the Nakhi community. The incidence of suicides of passion remained high until approximately 1949, which meant that the orthodox Confucian marriage code was never accepted by a large number of Nakhi people. The institutionalization of the *qing si* phenomenon was the root cause of the ineffectiveness of state law in Nakhi. As an informal institution, *qing si* showed strong defiance of the orthodox values and state law and drove up the suicide rate among the Nakhi.

Studies of *qing si* show that informal institutions are the product of interaction between formal institutions such as law and the subjective dimension of society (religion, beliefs, values, etc.). More importantly, the religious belief that accentuated the appeal of suicide for desperate Nakhi lovers would eventually become ineffective should the Qing imperial court not attempt to impose formal institutions in Lijiang. This is why, although the Nakhi had always believed in blissful afterlife, the suicide rate was low among lovers both before the implantation of the Confucian values in the Qing dynasty and after 1949.

Studies of suicides of passion among Nakhi people show that the law as a tool through which the sovereign state exercises its coercive power does not necessarily bring about the surrender of the people. Moreover, the effectiveness of state law, as a weapon used by the elite to rule over the rest of the people, is conditioned on human reason. How official state institutions will interact with local beliefs and values is unpredictable. No one had predicted that the interaction between the implanted Confucian system and the values and religious beliefs of the Nakhi would lead to the institutionalization of *qing si*. Enforcing an unpopular law may lead to the emergence of a contesting informal institution, which could in turn cause failure of law and catastrophic consequences.

Resistance is unavoidable in the implementation of a formal institution. We cannot abort reform efforts and formal institutions just because of popular resistance. However, we must recognize that law as the state's coercive weapon can cause disruptive shifts in society. Legislators should be aware of the risks and social consequences of ineffective law and put a bridle on their legislative ambition. An important reason for the popular resistance to the Qing government's law in Lijiang was that it attempted to promote Confucian values as the only "correct" values through formal institutions and denounced the lifestyle, beliefs, and values of other ethnic groups, including belief in personal autonomy and free love. However, the diversity of lifestyles, values and beliefs is unavoidable. People have the right to make choices regarding one's private life without interference by the state. The state must remain neutral with respect to values and beliefs and should not transform moral values of the elite into the law. Law as a formal institution should allow for the coexistence of different values and cultures on equal standing.

References

Allott, A. N. (1980). *The limits of law*. Butterworths.

Durkheim, É. (2001). *Suicide: A study in sociology* (Yunwen, F., trans.). The Commercial Press.

Ellickson, R. C. (1998). *Order without law: How neighbors settle disputes* (Li, S., trans.). Law Press.

Fuquan, Y. (1994). *The mystery of double suicides*. SDX Joint Publishing Company.

Fuquan, Y. (1997). The land of spirits in the Nakhi classical literature related to double suicides. *Ethnic Arts Quarterly*, (3).'

Fuquan, Y. (1998). *Multiculturalism and Nakhi society*. Yunnan People's Publishing House.

Fuquan, Y. (1999). *Double suicides*. Jiangxi Education Publishing House & Haitian Publishing House.

Fuquan, Y. (1999). The capital of double suicides. *Shancha Human Geography Magazine*, (4).

Fuquan, Y. (2000). The secret behind double suicides of the Nakhi people. *Ethnic Arts Quarterly*, (1).

Fuquan, Y. (2001). Influence of Tibetan culture on the Dongba religion of the Nakhi people—Interpretation of the road to heaven. *Social Sciences in Yunnan*, (5).

Fuquan, Y. (2005). Political changes and double suicide custom of the Nakhi people. *Journal of South-Central University for Nationalities (Humanities and Social Sciences)*, (5).

Guangwen, Y. (Ed.). (2001). *Almanac of Zhaotong prefecture*. Yunnan Fine Arts Publishing House.

Lin, Y. (1997). The customary law of the Yao people and the rule of law in socialist society. *Guangxi Ethnics Studies*, (1).

Merry, S. E. (1988). Legal pluralism. *Law and Society Review*, (5): 869–896.

Moore, S. F. (1986). *Social facts and fabrications: "customary" law on Kilimanjaro 1880–1980*. Cambridge University Press.

Rooij, B. V. (2004). The dimension of law—Legal failure from the perspective of spatial interpretation (Yan, Y., trans.). *The Ideological Front*, (4).

Tamanaha, B. Z. (1993). The folly of the "Social Scientific" concept of legal pluralism. *Journal of Law and Society, 20*, 192–217.

Tongzu, Q. (1998). *Collection of jurisprudence works by Qu Tongzu*. China University of Political Science and Law Press.

Wasserman, D. (2003). *Suicide: An unnecessary death* (Ming, L., et al., trans.). China Light Industry Press.

Weber, M. (2000). *Basic concepts in sociology* (Jingbei, H., trans.). Shanghai People's Publishing House.

Xiaoru, W., et al. (1992). *Encyclopedia of poetry in Han*. Shanghai Dictionary Press.

Xin, X. (2005). *On self-help remedy*. China University of Political Science and Law Press.

Yonghe, Z.. (2005). *Faith and authority—Swearing and law*. Law Press.

Xiaohui, Z., & Baohe, L. (1998). The Hani people's customary law and its cultural implications. In X. Zhongqi et al. (Eds). *Study of customary laws of ethnic minorities in China*. Yunnan University Press.

Zhiping, L. (1996). *The customary law of the Qing dynasty: Society and the state*. China University of Political Science and Law Press.
Zhiwu, H. (1991). On Lubanlurao. G. Dalie, & Y. Shiguang (Eds.). *Dongba culture*. Yunnan People's Publishing House.
Zhiwu, .H. (1994). *Translation of Dongba classics*. Yunnan People's Publishing House.
Zhonghua, H. (1991). Interesting philosophy—Elegy in Dongba scripture. G. Dalie, & Y. Shiguang (Eds.). *Dongba culture*. Yunnan People's Publishing House.

Chapter 3
Role of Religion in the Occurrence of and Resolution to Civil Disputes

3.1 Introduction

Chinese law protects freedom of religion[1] and provides for the separation of religion and government. The establishment of official state institutions is not affected by religion. This chapter examines the connection between religion and the causation and resolution of civil disputes. However, this does not mean that there is no connection between religion and formal institutions. In contrast, religion must be taken seriously in the operation of the legal system and other formal social controls, especially in regard to ethnic issues.

There are many religions in China, including Christianity, Catholicism, Buddhism, Islam, and Taoism. China is a multi-ethnic and multi-religious country. Believers of Christianity, Catholicism, Buddhism, Islam, and Taoism in China are unevenly distributed among the country's 56 ethnic groups.[2] The Han people have traditional folk religions (Watanabe, 1998). Most ethnic minorities in China, except those who believe in Islam, have their own religion (Yang, 1991). The interaction between Christianity, Catholicism, Buddhism, Islam, and Taoism and various folk religions has given rise to a variety of ethnic or regional religious traditions (Mo, 2005). Religious diversity and ethnic diversity lead to the complex relationship between order and law constructed or influenced by religion, which is partly reflected in the emergence and resolution of civil disputes.

This chapter takes an anthropological approach to the study of law. The data used in this chapter come from ethnographic materials. We will examine the relationship

[1] Protection of the Freedom of Religion. *The Voice of Dharma*, 2004 (1).

[2] Christianity, Islam, Catholicism, Buddhism and Taoism are the largest five religions in China. China has more than 100 million citizens who identify themselves with a religious group, more than 3000 religious organizations, and 300,000 religious workers. The General Office of the State Council. (2000). *The Gazette of the State Council of the People's Republic of China*, No. 10, p. 21. According to the recent official statistics, the numbers of religious believers, religious organizations, and venues are still rising in China. Wei Wu. *Practice of Freedom of Religion in China over the Past 60 Years.*

Q. Wang, *Sociology of Law*,
https://doi.org/10.1007/978-981-16-5509-8_3

between religion and civil disputes in a dynamic and legally pluralistic context by using the case study method and ethnographic data and understand disputes not simply as conflicts of interest but also in the dimension of values and meanings.

3.2 Religion and Occurrence of Civil Disputes

There are many ways in which religion can shape values and worldviews that might be directly reflected in religious norms, for example, the huge bunch of taboos observed by ethnic minority communities (Wang, 2006), internalized into the moral code, or embodied imperceptibly in certain rituals we may not easily know. In short, religion infiltrates every aspect of social life, shaping values, worldviews, social relationships, the relationship between man and nature, and notions of right and wrong. Of course, the extent to which religion affects values and worldviews of humanity depends on how religion is practiced, how well it is woven into the fabric of society and how complete its worldview system is.

Values and meanings are crucial for human beings. At the heart of any dispute is something that is valued and considered meaningful by the parties involved. No one will engage in argument over meaningless things. Disputes are interest-based, whether it is economic interest, material interest, or subjective interest. There are many universally accepted and recognized values in human society, such as justice and fairness. However, most disputes involve something very specific. We need to put such disputes back in their cultural background to fully comprehend them. Religion is part of the cultural background. The reason why there are connections between religion and disputes is that religion confers values and meanings on things that give rise to conflicts.

Religion not only confers values and meanings on things but also gives rise to material or sacred interests.[3] Conflicts may arise around these interests. For example, there was a dispute between two neighboring Dai villages in Xishuangbanna because a villager from one village where someone had just died visited the other village. The same behavior is unlikely to cause disputes in other cultural contexts. However, in the Dai community, the behavior of this villager was considered deviant by religious code. What is even more interesting is that in the process of resolving disputes, one of the focuses of the dispute was two plots of burial land that were of special cultural significance to the Dai people.[4]

Although the nature of conflicts is different, by studying the conflicts between religion and state law, we can still come to the conclusion that religion can give rise to disputes and conflicts. In Xishuangbanna, there lives an ethnic group called the Aini, which is a branch of the Hani. It is the custom of the Aini to use osmanthus trees to make coffins, which is why illegal logging is rampant among the Aini. The Aini people believe that osmanthus trees have something to do with the nether land.

---

[3] Because values and meanings are often conveyed through symbols and concrete objects.

[4] See Chapter Five of this book.

The following case also shows that religion as a tool for social control may be in conflict with formal social controls such as law and policy:

Family planning work in Shitoupo Village began in 1983. The Salar people living in Shitoupo believe in Islam. In Islam, abortion in the first four months of pregnancy is permissible. However, the fetus is believed to become a living soul after four months of gestation, and abortion after that point is generally viewed as impermissible. This religious belief hindered the implementation of the family planning policy in the village. The level of acceptance of ligation was very low among the villagers. By comparison, the family planning work proceeded much more smoothly among the Hui, Tibetan, and Han people in the nearby villages. (Zhu & Xie, 2004, p. 103).

This also shows that religion gives meaning to things that are otherwise considered insignificant and is a possible source of disputes.

3.3 Religion and Settlement of Civil Disputes

Religion is a possible source of disputes, but it can also help people resolve disputes arising in the same or similar cultural or religious context. This is because the spiritual and social aspects of religion contain elements that can facilitate dispute resolution: norms, organization, authority, and trust.

3.3.1 Norms

Religious norms indicate what kind of behavior should be displayed. Religion at least produces or influences the types of norms: (i) norms in relation to religious doctrines, rituals, communities, organizations and places; and (ii) norms related to the daily life of adherents.[5] The influence of religious norms depends on the status of the religion in people's lives. It varies from religion to religion. Usually, compared to folk religions of ethnic groups, highly rationalized religions such as Christianity and Catholicism produce fewer social norms that regulate everyday life. However, religious norms are definitely one of the components of social order in local communities.

Norms provide criteria and rules for people to judge right from wrong and settle disputes.

3.3.2 Organization

Religion is organized in one way or another (Ikeda & Wilson, 2003, p. 139). Some religions are highly organized, while others are loosely organized and only have

[5] See Chapter Five of this book.

temporary leaders. In addition to providing guidance on religious beliefs, religious organizations and authorities are also social control institutions. They are not only a possible source of disputes but also play a role in dispute resolution. Of course, the extent to which religious organizations and authorities play a role in resolving disputes depends on factors such as the influence of religion. For example, in the past, Buddhism and the Lahu people's folk religion occupied an important position in the village-level political system of the Lahu people.

> In a Lahu village, the head of the earliest village self-governing body was called "*ka xie*". After 1949, the power of *ka xie* was gradually weakened. The *ka xie* system was abolished during the Cultural Revolution. In 1986, at the request of the villagers, some Lahu villages restored the old *ka xie* system. The head of the village, called *ka xie*, *zhuo ba*, *jia li*, or *fo ye*, *was* elected by the villagers in accordance with traditional procedures.
>
> *Ka xie* was responsible for deciding punishment for minor offenses such as violation of ethnic code, theft, robbery, ill treatment of the elderly, and sexual misconduct and settling disputes between villagers or villages. In the event of a dispute over ethnic issues or between two villages, it will be resolved by the Kaxie of involved villages. If it could not be resolved by Kaxie, the dispute would be submitted to the village affairs office (*cun gong suo*). As mentioned before, Kaxie was also responsible for settling civil disputes between villagers. For example, a couple must notify *ka xie* before they can divorce, and *ka xie* would impose a fine of 20.5 yuan on the male and 19.5 yuan on the female (Wang, 2000, pp. 107–110).

Religious organizations and authorities can conduct informal social control in an unofficial capacity. This kind of informal social control is prevalent in small group settings in rural areas, especially ethnic minorities.

3.3.3 Authority

Whether the authority of the mediator is recognized by involved parties can determine whether a dispute can be efficiently resolved.

Religion not only carries out social control but also confers authority on religious organizations and workers to resolve disputes. Religious dispute resolution mechanisms work very differently from formal dispute resolution mechanisms. In theory, law provides the legitimacy of formal dispute resolution mechanisms. In practice, the legitimacy of formal dispute resolution mechanisms is not always recognized by people. The authority of a religious mediator is derived from his professional capacity in the religion and the influence of the religion. For example, the aforementioned example of the Lahu villages shows that it is the religion that gives *ka xie* the authority to settle disputes. For another example, in a village of the Hani people, there was a religious organization called *mi gu*. *Mi gu* was responsible for organizing religious activities and enforcing religious rules that were woven into the fabric of everyday life of the villagers. In other words, *mi gu* was not only a religious organization but also an important social control institution in the village and undertook the task of resolving disputes (He, 2000, p. 219–220 and p. 226–230). Tibetan Buddhism provides a typical example of a faith-based mediation approach for dispute resolution. Tibetan Buddhist monks were given the authority to preside over dispute mediation, including mediation of serious disputes involving man slaughter.

3.3.4 Trust

The fourth element that enables a religion to play a role in dispute resolution is adherents' trust or self-identification with the religious group. The key to dispute resolution is to find the common ground of the involved parties and prevent the dispute from escalating. This common ground may be related to the recognition of the subject of the dispute, a fact, or certain norms. The more elements that the parties agree with, the higher the probability that the dispute will be resolved smoothly.

In a society where religion is important, religion provides an alternative means to resolving disputes. If the involved parties believe in the same religion, they might agree that it is up to their god to make the judgment (Deng, 1991). For example, in some religions, people who are suspected of stealing were requested to put their hand in high-temperature oil. If their hands are not injured in the process, they will be believed to be innocent; otherwise, they will be considered guilty. Of course, such cruel religious rites have been banned. However, the faith-based dispute resolution approach has not completely disappeared. For example, in the Yi community in Liangshan, some people still resort to religious rituals to settle disputes. The Yi people could take an oath in front of the spirits of their ancestors to clear themselves of allegations. The ritual goes like this: a person accused of misconduct says he would die like the sacrificed animal if he has lied in front of the spirits of his ancestors and then kill the animal prepared in advance. The Yi people believe it would bring misfortune if one bets on his life, but since he is willing to risk his life, it should be enough to prove he is innocent.[6] The reason why this oath-taking ritual is an effective dispute resolution method among this Yi community is that the Yi people worship the ghosts of their ancestors. They believe that the ghosts of their ancestors are in charge of the fate of their descendants and that people would be unable to deceive the ghosts of their ancestors. A similar situation can also be found in the Dai community in Xishuangbanna, Yunnan.[7]

[6] (Hainailamo, Qumuyuezhi, and Liu, 1998, p. 39–41 and p. 56–57). The effectiveness of religious swearing as a form of social control in a society is closely related to the specific belief system in that society (Zhang, 2005).

[7] See Chapter Six of this book.

3.3.5 Interrelations Between the Four Elements and Conflicts Between Different Value Systems

These four elements can usually be observed in highly organized religions deeply embedded in daily life with well-accepted doctrines. They reinforce each other and provide conditions for religions to carry out social control and play a role in dispute resolution, as shown by the case of Dai village.[8]

However, this does not mean that a religion must have all four elements at the same time to be able to play a role in dispute resolution. In contrast, even poorly organized religions or those without a perfect system of doctrines could have an impact on dispute resolution among believers. For example, the Han people believe the spirits of their ancestors reside within a spirit tablet. The installation of a spirit tablet is symbolic. It "may not really have any effect on the deceased, but it is of great emotional significance to those alive", and this ancestor veneration practice resolving around identification with ancestors also plays a role in family dispute resolution among the Han people (Li, 1997, p. 279). An ancestral tablet is a symbol of lineage bonds. The common belief in spirits of ancestors shapes collective identity and thus can help prevent conflicts and stop fighting between clan members. By observing the ancestor veneration practices of the Han people, we can conclude that religions affect dispute resolution in many ways, not just through the participation of religious workers or organizations.

It must be noted that all the disputes discussed in the above case studies occurred between believers of the same religion. Differences in the system of value and world-view shaped by religion may give rise to religious disputes as well as contestation between religious norms and laws. Settling conflicts between different value systems is often an arduous task because of the lack of norms and authority accepted by both parties. For example, in the Aini case and the Shitoupo Village case mentioned above, state law could in fact be considered a foreign value system to local people. Whether conflicts between different value systems can be effectively resolved by informal institutions depends on whether there is a mechanism for cross-cultural communication and negotiation. In a culturally inclusive society, it is often easier to settle such conflicts. The effectiveness of formal institutions in resolving such conflicts depends on whether the authority of formal institutions such as law and government can override the influence of the value systems of ethnic and cultural groups.

Conflicts between religions and value systems, as an important aspect of social unrest, require special attention.

[8] See Chapter Six and Chapter Seven of this book.

3.4 Religion and Norms for Life

Religion is an important variable in studies of disputes. It influences the emergence and resolution of disputes in various ways. Fundamentally, this is because religion is designed and has the capacity to shape patterns of behaviors that conform to norms and values held by most members of a group. To understand this function of religion, we need to examine the influence of religion on the everyday life of adherents as well as the primary characteristics of religion.

Religion requires adherents to act in accordance with a certain set of norms and values. As mentioned earlier in this book, values are a component of the subjective dimension of society. Roger M. Keesing believes that human beings not only create various customs to regulate social life but also establish a larger structure to deal with the universe itself, the power that governs the universe, and the position of human beings in the universe, and religious beliefs and religious rituals are the foundation of this structure. He also believes that the interaction between things, the nature of time and space, how the world looks like, and how it should look are also the premises of the structure. (Keesing, 1993, p. 381). This means that a religion offers a way to its believers to come to grips with the world. This function of religion provides believers with appropriate attitudes toward nature, society, and others,[9] and patterns of behaviors consistent with such attitudes are considered to be "correct" by believers of the religion. If we say establishment of order is the prerequisite of socially accepted life, then the premise of this statement is that there is a set of commonly recognized standards of what is right and what is wrong. Since religion offers worldviews that help people tell right from wrong, it is not inappropriate to say that religion is one of the most important factors that shape socially accepted life. Of course, since human beings have other ways of coming to grips with the world, such as art and science (Niu, 2005), the extent to which religion can affect the formation of socially accepted patterns of behaviors depends on the influence of the religion on believers. For example, Islamic faith has a profound influence on the social and spiritual life of the Hui people in Yunnan; therefore, religion plays a dominant role in the formation of the code of conduct and moral values in this Hui community (Na, 2001, p. 172–174; Ma & Liu, 2009).

The pursuit of moral life links religion to the causation and resolution of disputes because religion not only defines but also maintains the right way of life.

3.5 Discussion: Understanding Disputes in Light of Values and Worldviews

Religion and law are similar in that they all aim to establish normative order. They are two different types of norms. Religion is one of the primary factors that causes

[9] In other words, religion defines secular/sacred, right/wrong, legal/illegal, and justice/injustice.

legal pluralism and may conflict with law. Despite some similarities, the faith-based dispute resolution approach and the dispute resolution mechanism designed by law are intrinsically different. Simply put, religion is associated with a particular world-view system. Thus, its role in triggering and settling disputes must be analyzed within a particular cultural context. In a society with multiple religions and cultures, the law must enforce scrupulous neutrality among religions and cultures. Religions require believers to follow a specific lifestyle, whereas the law must allow different lifestyles to coexist peacefully and prevent disputes caused by differences in lifestyle from escalating into violent conflicts. Examination of the connections between religion and disputes may help us to identify problems in formal dispute resolution mechanisms and gain insight into the law and culture of ethnic minorities.

Scholars study disputes with the goal of resolving disputes. It is difficult to identify the real root cause of a dispute in both theory and practice because the real cause is often hidden behind a complicated interest network. Sometimes conflicts may concern a value system, and the settlement of such conflicts requires a deep understanding of the cultural context in which conflicts occur.[10] The same behavior may have different meanings or consequences in different contexts. Therefore, the causes of similar disputes may be completely different.

As mentioned in another article of mine, I believe that the root cause of the high suicide rate and prevalence of vigilante violence in the Yi community in Liangshan is the synthesis of hero worship and the social structure of the Yi community (Wang, 2007b). Society provides a line of defense against our natural impotence by creating a hero system that convinces us that we can transcend death by engaging in something of lasting worth and therefore do not need to be afraid of death. The Yi people in Liangshan believe that deceased people will enter, after necessary rituals, the realm where the spirits of their deceased ancestors exist, and death is just the beginning of another existence (Mujeer, 2007). Due to the combination of this belief and heroism, the Yi people are not afraid of death. The world is a grand theater. Customary law of the Yi community in Liangshan, including suicidal attacks and the involvement of *de gu* mediation of clan conflicts, creates a theater for heroic dramas. The plot of these heroic dramas often begins to unfold with suicidal attacks, climaxed when two clans confronted each other in a violent way, and ended with the involvement of *de gu*. Therefore, I believe that it is not savageness of the people but excessive hero worship and belief in afterlife that have caused the institutionalization of suicidal attacks among this Yi community. State law often fails to address such disputes because state law cannot eliminate the root cause of the disputes. This is a problem frequently encountered by legal practitioners.

Another example of the role of religion in dispute resolution is the monetary compensation payment in a murder case in Tibetan society. The victim compensation payment in a murder case is of course a complicated issue. I believe one of the primary causes of this custom is the belief of Tibetans in karmic rebirth, which is why, contrary to expectations of national legislators, Tibetans believe death sentences are not the

---

[10] This is also why smooth dispute resolution in rural areas often requires involvement of village-level officials or authorities well versed in local knowledge (Chen & Guo, 2009, p. 40–42).

most severe punishment. Outsiders would argue that the death penalty is needed as a means of retributive justice, but Tibetan Buddhism prohibits killing. Many scholars have downplayed or even completely ignored the significance of this religious factor. Analysis from an outsider's standpoint of Tibetan society would often lead to the unnecessary criticism that this practice of Tibetans seriously undermines the authority of state law.

When mentioning disputes, we often think of interest disputes. Religion helps us better understand the internal logic of disputes from the perspective of values and worldviews. However, it should be noted that there is another type of dispute, such as religious disputes, that involve differences in values and worldviews. Moreover, we must realize that the connection between the subjective world (values and worldviews) and disputes does not only manifest in religious disputes or disputes resolved through the involvement of religious actors. Values and worldviews affect every aspect of our life–an important fact that we tend to overlook in discussion and resolution of disputes. We often focus only on the objective aspect of disputes and ignore their subjective aspect, resulting in failure of dispute resolution.

Another cause of disputes is the collapse of one's value system. Chen Baifeng and Guo Junxia point out in their research that a farmer's value system would complete collapse when he places personal interests over social connections or *mian zi* and believes pursuit of personal gains is the only thing that matters (Chen & Guo, 2009, p. 56). The study of Chen & Guo offers a new perspective on the causation and settlement of disputes in rural areas and invites us to look beyond interest-based conflicts. The collapse of the value system of a peasant or an entire society would lead to the occurrence of disputes that should not happen at all and the unnecessary escalation of some conflicts. From this perspective, if we only focus on disputes instead of rebuilding the value world, the incidence of conflicts and disputes will just grow, even if the dispute resolution procedures are improved.

Last but not least, I want to reemphasize the following points. First, China is a multiethnic country, and it needs more culturally neutral formal institutions to handle conflicts and disputes between different cultures. Such formal institutions should not only maintain authority and the influence of law in society but also help protect the diverse value systems of citizens, especially those of ethnic minorities. Second, as China strives to strengthen societal harmony, disputes and conflicts between different religions are an issue worth special attention. Third, in practice, dispute resolution institutions and authorities should pay attention to both the interests the involved parties claim and the values and worldviews behind the disputes. Otherwise, the disputes may not be resolved or may even escalate.

References

Baifeng, C., & Junxia, G. (2009). *Peasants and their subjective world*. Shandong People's Publishing House.

Hainailamo, Q., & Yaohan, L. (1998). *Customary laws of the Yi community in Liangshan—Case study*. Yunnan People's Publishing House.
Haiyun, M., & Ting, L. (2009). The Hui people's marriage and family customary law and state law. *Studies of the Hui People*, (1).
Heshuang, Z., & Zu, X. (Eds.). (2004). *The Salar people—Shitoupo Village field survey*. Yunnan University Press.
Ikeda, D., & Wilson, B. (2003). *Religion and society* (Hongfei, L., & Jian, W., Trans.). Sichuan People's Publishing House.
Keesing, R. M. (1993). *Cultural anthropology* (Gongqi, Z., & Jiayun, Y., trans.). Taiwan: Juliu Publishing House.
Lin, N. (2001). *Integration of tradition and modernity: An outline of the history, culture, and development of the Hui People in Yunnan*. Yunnan University Press.
Minwen, D. (1991). *Divine judgment*. Guizhou People's Publishing House.
Mujeer, J. (2007). On the Liangshan Yi's traditional practice of hospice care. *Journal of Social Sciences*, (9).
Qiliang, W. (2006). Normative system and social order in rural areas. *Journal of Guangxi University for Nationalities (Humanities and Social Sciences)*, (1).
Qiliang, W. (2007). Meanings, values, and use of violence in Vigilante—Subjective dimension of human action. *Journal of Yunnan University (Law Edition)*, (3).
Siqiang, H. (Ed.). (2000). *The Hani people—Luobie Village in Daxing Town*. Yunnan University Press.
Sulin, N. (2005). Religious worldviews. *Academic Journal of Zhongzhou*, (2).
The General Office of the State Council. (2000). *The Gazette of the State Council of the People's Republic of China*, (10).
Watanabe, S. (1998). *Folk religion of the Han Chinese* (Xing, Z., trans.). Tianjin People's Publishing House.
Xiaozhu, W. (Ed.). (2000). *The Lahu people—Nanduan Old Village of Nofu Township*. Yunnan University Press.
Xuezheng, Y. (1991). *On primitive religions*. Yunnan People's Publishing House.
Yiyuan, L. (1997). *Human vision*. Shanghai Literature and Art Press.
Yonghe, Z. (2005). *Faith and authority—Swearing and law*. Law Press.
Zhongjian, M. (2005). Folk religions of ethnic groups and social harmony. *China Religion*, (4).

Chapter 4
Causes of Corruption: "The Political Scene", Power in Everyday Life, and Individual Behaviors

4.1 Introduction: Power in Everyday Life

Professor He Xuefeng points out in his study of rural governance institutions that:

> From this perspective, institutions seem to operate in ways that transcend time and space, and there is no need for the analysis of specific scenarios [...] Since the 1980s, many Chinese sociologists, especially those with research interest in rural society, have placed excessive emphasis on institutions while ignoring the conditions for the establishment of institutions (He, 2008, p. 2).

An overemphasis on social institutions is also a common problem in academic circles interested in issues related to the problem of corruption. Corruption is often discussed in the context of criminal law. Therefore, the focus of anti-corruption efforts is often on how to prevent and control corruption as a criminal activity. However, corruption is not just a criminal activity. It is also a political process. It occurs in specific political situations. The notoriously corrupt public official Li Zhen wrote in his confession statement before his death:[1]

> At first, I also felt a little unease over accepting bribes [...] I still remember when I was a secretary, an official from the municipal government gave me two packs of cigarettes and

[1] Li Zhen was born in an ordinary government official's family in Zhangjiakou in May 1962. After graduating from a secondary vocational school in 1981, he worked in an orchard and later a paint factory in Zhangjiakou. In July 1989, he became a staff member of a construction investment company in Hebei Province. In November 1990, he became a secretary in the General Office of the Hebei Provincial Government. In June 1993, he was appointed secretary of the General Office of the Hebei Provincial Party Committee. In December 1994, he was appointed deputy director of the Hebei Provincial Party Committee. In December 1995, he became deputy secretary and deputy director of the Party Committee of the Taxation Department of the Hebei Provincial Government. In July 1997, he was promoted to director of the Party Committee of the Taxation Department of the Hebei Provincial Government. In April 1998, he became secretary and director of the Party Committee of the Taxation Department of the Hebei Provincial Government. On March 1, 2000, he was indicted. In April 2001, he was arrested and charged with corruption. On August 30, 2002, the Tangshan Intermediate People's Court sentenced Li Zhen to death for accepting bribes and deprived him of his political rights for life.

Q. Wang, *Sociology of Law*,
https://doi.org/10.1007/978-981-16-5509-8_4

> some other small items. I wanted to accept the gifts, but I was afraid that my boss would not be pleased. The official was unhappy over my hesitation. Just then, a driver came in and accepted the gifts without care. Seeing this, I recognized that I shouldn't overthink it and should just accept the gifts graciously. Once, I was in Beijing [...] I received a bribe, about 5,000 yuan [...] When I returned the money, Li was very angry and said with tears that I looked down on him [...]
>
> These two things changed my views on accepting gifts in official capacity. I began to believe I should accept a gift if it is from a powerful official or an old friend because refusal will not only affect our relationship, but more importantly, it may cost me political support [...] Gradually, I lost my grip on what to accept and what not to accept [...][2]

Li Zhen's confession gives us food for thought. It shows us how a young man who once dared not accept two packs of cigarettes became an infamous corrupt official. No one will suddenly become a criminal without any reason. Some place would turn good people into bad people. To understand corruption, we must dig deeper into its core: the daily operation of power.

The daily operation of power breeds corruption. The so-called political scene is at the heart of power. Several or dozens of corrupt public officials are not scary. What is really terrifying is when the written rules of the political scene penetrate into other aspects of social life and when the corruption of public power invades into the private sector. Corruption begins to reproduce itself in everyday life situations. Crony capitalism is eroding our society.

The political scene does not necessarily lead to corruption. However, without a proper formal supervision system, it will inevitably breed corruption. *The Water of Blue Waves* by Mr. Yan Zhen (2001) vividly[3] depicts the corruption and anti-corruption efforts in Chinese political scenes. Without demonizing or adding halos to people in the political circle, the novel reveals the interactions between humanity and the political scene in a straightforward and easy-to-understand manner. In fact, the scenes depicted in the novel are reminiscent of real-life politics. It makes us wonder: If I were Chi Dawei, would I make the same choices? When "relationships" become the most important part of everyday life and corruption becomes a daily practice, can law still control corruption? In a certain sense, it is more important to analyze the soil than to analyze what is growing in the soil. Here, "the political scene" is the soil, and corruption is what grows in the soil. As a special political and social phenomenon, the political scene is the platform or entire body of officials and the field where political activities take place.[4] It is the focus of anti-corruption efforts. To improve the efficiency of formal institutions, we must come to grips with problems in the bureaucratic system.

---

[2] Xiaoming (Ed.). (2003). Li Zhen's Confession. *Fangyuan Magazine*, No. 11.

[3] This book has won the 2001 Literature Award of the *Contemporary* (*dang dai*) magazine and the 2004 Mao Zedong Literature Award in the novel category.

[4] For further discussion of the political scene, see *An Invitation to Reflexive Sociology* by Bourdieu and Wacquant (1998, p. 19).

4.2 Definition of the Political Scene

The political scene is really a wonderful phrase. As an informal expression of bureaucracy and political circles, it unleashes our imagination of power. More importantly, it entails unwritten rules that determine the structure and play book of politicians and power brokers.[5] The political scene is a political field with power operation as its core. So, what kind of characteristics does this field have? First, the political scene is a cluster of relationships constructed with power operations as its core; second, the political scene constructs attitudes towards life; third, the interaction between bureaucratic structure and the attitude of the political scene enables the production and reproduction of unethical political relations.

4.2.1 The Political Scene as a Set of Relations

One of the characteristics of the political scene is exclusivity and lastingness. First, it is composed of a group of officials or civil servants who are about to become officials. They have powers more or less. People enter the political scene through formal systems (exams, selections, etc.), so this field is not accessible to everyone. Second, the so-called political scene is composed of large and small institutions or departments, which stably exist in the public power system. Third, the staff mobility in the bureaucratic system is relatively low.

The spatial attribute (i.e., exclusivity) and time attribute (i.e., lastingness) make the political scene a field for lasting group interactions between actors, which produces a cluster of social relations or connections centered on power operation.

Social relations form the basis of social life and are associated with actions, principles of behaviors, and social control. In China, social relations or *guanxi* are also a cultural concept and manifest informal norms (Yi, 2009).

It is precisely because relations encourage conformity that we can observe and understand how relations construct and influence the order of the political scene.

The reason why relations have normative social influence is that relations are derived from interactions between two or more individuals. Relations are shaped by power dynamics and allow us to define ourselves and others. A typical pattern of power dynamics manifested in social relations is what Xiaotong (1998, p. 24–25) called *chaxu geju* or differential modes of association. Relations, affiliative social ties, reciprocity, and face are key components of differential modes of association built on Confucian moral values. These components form a code of conduct that is incomprehensible to people outside the Chinese culture. This code of conduct has undoubtedly been woven into the fabric of daily life of Chinese people over the past thousands of years. When one is said to have no idea about how to 'zuo ren' (which literally means 'be human') in Chinese culture, it usually means that this person

[5] Mr. Wu Si believes that the term the political scene entails certain unspoken rules that govern political activities (Si, 2001).

has deviated from social norms. The political scene is a power allocation institution governing interactions between public officials based on authority, ability to rule, and status. In practice, public officials with common interests come together and form various connections as well as rules that govern interactions between members of the political scene. In the bureaucratic system, the nature of the relation determines the form of interaction. Relations accepted in the bureaucratic system help to entail accepted delegation of authority and duties and thus constitute constraints on human behavior, establishing an alternative normative order in the bureaucratic system other than the order created through law. From the perspective of legal pluralism in legal anthropology, relations can be considered "soft law" or unwritten rules (Wu, 2001) in the bureaucratic system. Every actor in the bureaucratic system is woven into a web of relationships rather than a single relation because of the multiple roles played by the actor.

There is already a pre-existing web of relationships in the political scene when any individual enters into it. He may choose to adapt to, change, or resist it. However, since the web of relationships is the product of group interactions, an individual's attempt to change or resist it signifies an intention to change or resist the group and often ends in failure. Therefore, the web of relationships in the bureaucratic system is a structure that stipulates how players in the political scene conduct themselves and interact with others and thus a form of social control. Of course, due to the complexity of the politicalecosystem, the web of relationships and unwritten rules vary from one political scene to another depending on the place, time, and creativity of those involved.

However, regardless of what form the political scene takes, individuals within it are often unable to control their own lives. The political scene and the web of relationships it produces form an external structure that constrains the behaviors of individuals within in. Every choice is made within the structure built on history and reality. Therefore, one's social status determines his thoughts.

4.2.2 The Political Scene in the Shaping of Worldviews

While the web of relationships, a kind of structure constructed by officials, represents the objective aspect of "the political scene", what is done in this particular field also shapes the attitudes of people there and therefore adds a subjective dimension to the word. Relations in the bureaucratic system change slowly but continuously and are passed down from generation to generation. The experience of past generations shapes the pattern in which one lives as a member of a group. Both the experience and the pattern of living are internalized and become part of our values and worldviews that guide our actions. The rules governing the relations in the bureaucratic system are perceived by heart and are manifest in officials' attitudes towards life.

In *the Water of Blue Waves*, Chi Dawei's father did not lose focus of his life because of some real-life predicaments. At the lowest point of his life, he said, "I have nothing left but my integrity. Wrap me in white cloth after I die. Don't forget." (Yan, 2001, p. 7) He remained faithful to his beliefs throughout his life.

Ding Xiaohuai, a supporting role in the novel, represents the majority of officials who quickly adapted themselves to the written rules of the political scene. Once, Ding Xiaohuai said after he was drunk:

> Dawei, my brother, to be frank, who doesn't want to be oneself? Who wants to kiss up to others? Sometimes even I look down on myself. I felt like a tail wagging dog kicked by its owner because he didn't like how it had wagged its tail. I have never kicked my dog. How could one kick his own dog? How could the lives of people be worse than dogs? If it were just for myself, I would bow to no one. But you know I have an entire family living in the countryside. They are dependent on me. I have to help them out. I cannot rely on anyone. My young siblings are getting closer to the legal age for working. They must hope I can at least help them get a job. Afraid of disappointing them, I dread the thought of disappointing them when going back to my hometown in the Spring Festival. Even if I only want to help them get a temporary job at the canteen or the job of doorman at our department, I will need to become a director to have such authority. Right? For this, I just have to swallow my pride. The world will not change just for you. We need to play by rules. I have to lower my head and follow the rules. What else could I do? Life is just not fair. All the fair talks are just lies fed to us by the TV. Don't you agree? (Yan, 2001, p. 52)

This shows that Ding Xiaohuai was not a bootlicker when he entered the political scene. However, after sobering up, Ding immediately returned to his groveling old self.

Like fathers such as sons, Chi Dawei entertained lofty ideals and was determined to be a person of moral integrity early in his life. He was inspired by those noble people, his father included, that he so admired. ButThere was a paragraph depicting what was on Chi Dawei's mind after the sudden death of his father:

> I carefully reached into it and pulled the thing out slowly. It was a very thin book: *Sketches of Famous Cultural Figures in the History of China.* On the first page was a portrait of Confucius, and an oft-quoted commentary on Confucius was penciled in at the lower left corner: A person of discipline and scruples, and an exemplar of virtues It was my father's handwriting [...] This was the picture of my father twenty years earlier. I was out of breath. The sound was magnified at night, as if it came from outside. The wind was howling and the dawn came. (Yan, 2001, p. 2–3)

The proud youth Chi Dawei once said to himself:

> The kind of thought chains oneself to mediocrity. It is really ridiculous. Others may be willing to choose this mediocre way of life. It is their choice. I will never be like them. There seems to be a mysterious voice coming from the depths of my soul, reminding me that I am destined to serve the world, not just to live for myself. This is my fate. I have no choice [...] (Yan, 2001: 9)

What a proud heart! He did not regret it when he could not stay in Beijing because he rejected a marriage proposal that seemed to be a good deal for most people. After work, he was marginalized in the political circle because of his frankness. He did not regret it either at least at first. However, a few years later, he completely betrayed his ideals and philosophy of life. There is one scene where he set fire to a book of his father's in front of the grave of his father:

> I closed my eyes, biting my lip. I kneel in front of the grave, pull out Sketches of Famous Cultural Figures in the History of China from the bag and gently put it on the ground. I have only read it twice in ten years. I don't have enough mental capacity to open the soul-searching book. I took out a lighter and ignited it. I hesitated. The fire cast light on the cover of the book. The heat burned my fingers. I relaxed my thumb. The fire went out[...] I ignited a fire again and took my father's portrait out of the book. I pluck up courage to take a closer look at it. It was as if my father were still alive, staring at me. I was unsettled by his gaze. My entire body was shaking, and my upper teeth hit my lower teeth. I picked up the book with my left hand. The paper was already crisp, and broke down when I touched it. I brought the fire closer. The book was ignited. The flame was dancing in the dark. The heat rushed to my face. I stared at the flame like I was going to engrave it in my brain. It was the only source of light in the boundless darkness[...] Wind blew over my shoulders, leaving me behind. The light of stars was swirling at an unfathomable distance (Yan, 2001, p. 523).

When Chi Dawei set the book left by his father on fire, he was carrying out a ritual to say goodbye to the past.

In the later years of his career life, Chi Dawei abandoned his belief and surrendered to the unwritten rules in the bureaucratic system. The reward he received in return was being appointed the head of the department. His mentality and attitude underwent profound changes. In the end, he placed power and self-interests above everything else.

In fact, in addition to the abovementioned three characters, other characters in *the Water of Blue Waves* also demonstrated different attitudes towards life. Whether it is Chi Dawei's father's lifelong devotion to his belief or Ding Xiaohuai's immediate surrender to unwritten rules, Chi Dawei's reluctant adaption, or Yan Zhihe's disillusionment and marginalization, they are all manifestations of human agency in response to unwritten rules and the structural constraints of the political scene.

4.2.3 Interactions Between Structure and Worldviews: Production and Reproduction of Relations in the Political Circle

The title of the book *The Water of Blue Waves* drew inspiration from Qu Yuan's poem *Yu Fu*, and it cleverly reflects a certain attitude towards life. For the majority of common people, whether the political scene is clean or dirty is something they cannot decide. People's reaction to the structural constraint of the political scene is different. Individuals are not completely at the mercy of society. They have the capacity to fight social structures. Some people may surrender to unwritten rules, but some would rather dance with fetters. Some may put personal gains above everything, but some would give up their lives for what they believe is right. Whatever their choice is, there must be meanings, reasons or intentions behind their actions unless they have lost basic reasoning capacity.

However, in any case, *The Water of Blue Waves* shows us that there are only a few people who have successfully freed themselves from the constraints of the environment. Confucius, Chuang Tsu, and Qu Yuan are among them. The political scene shapes the attitude of most people within it:

> When the River of Blue Waves is clean, I can use the water to clean my hat;
> When the River of Blue Waves is muddy, I can still use it to wash my feet.
> Most people in the bureaucratic system blindly follow the majority.

Of course, this does not mean that the political scene does not change. On the contrary, it is always changing. It is more like a fluid network. Relations within the network changes constantly. In our short life, we learn to interact and build rapport with others through socialization. Therefore, each generation inherits and produces "relationships". This means that everyone in the bureaucratic system is bound by and follows certain unwritten rules. In social activities, we conform to the unwritten rules of social relationships, seeking to maximize resources and benefits brought by social relationships and minimize their negative effects. Especially those who fail in the game of power competition, there will always be some attempts to use, confront, change the existing "relationship" rules, and constantly create conflicts. Power struggles and conflicts around power have always occurred in bureaucratic systems.

Therefore, in regard to the practice of law and dispute settlement, social relationships are existing structures that affect decision-making. However, at the same time, people will not completely succumb to constraints posed by existing relationships, especially when they are at a disadvantage. Human beings will try to seek external resources (state law, stronger relationships, etc.) to change the pattern of existing relationships. Therefore, people inherit the old "political scene" and create a new political scene. The political scene is constantly being reproduced in practice, thereby constructing a new structure and shaping a new attitude to life.

4.3 Causes of Bureaucracy and Corruption

The previous section aims to clarify the characteristics of the "political scene", and then what I want to examine is under what circumstances the "political scene" could become a hotbed for corruption? In the final analysis, the key to the breeding of corruption is that the "political scene" derives a set of informal institutions, and this informal system does not support the realization of the formal system but instead leads to the failure of the formal system. Then three consequences would ensue: first, power is concentrated in the hands of the few, and the exercise of it differs from person to person, with supervision inadequately provided; second, individuals in the administrative system must surrender to the political scene, "relationship", and power, and are deprived of ability to challenge unreasonable political decisions and exercise of power, which thus gives rise to a huge community of interests; third, the dynamic mechanism of corruption has formed, providing a "reasonable motive" for corruption. In the end, the political scene has two very different faces. One is associated with the formal system and national politics; it emphasizes values, ideals, integrity, and concern for people's well-being and is where our hope lies. The other face of the political scene is hideous; it involves a betrayal from values and ideals for the sake of pecuniary interests, positions, alliances, and personal futures."

4.3.1 Symbolism of Power

The political scene is like a fog which is everywhere and hangs over everyone who runs into it. In practice, the political scene produces a variety of power-using techniques. These techniques are different from formal political decision-making, from the hierarchy of a bureaucratic structure, and even more strikingly from what is prescribed by the formal political system. They involve the use of languages, behavior and symbols to express power relations and indicate certain positions; they convey political information by creating certain "scenes".

In *the Water of Blue Waves*, we also see a case involving the use of such symbols:

> I had to say: "Comrade, comrade, I am coming to report." He raised his eyelids slowly without lifting his head and said, "If you have something to say, just say it."[...] He squinted and smirked, ignoring me. He imitated my tone and said, "Comrade, did you not see that I'm writing something for Director Ma? Is your reporting more important than the request of Director Ma?" He held both of his hands up and made a fist. He swayed his head from side to side and said, "Which one is bigger? Which one is smaller?" (Yan, 2001, pp. 21–22)

This is the scene when Chi Dawei first met Ding Xiaohuai. Everything has a cause. So is Ding's behavior. What Ding tries to do is, first, put the new recruit in his place; second, convey the message that he himself is important as he is close to the person of real importance, Mr. Ma (that is why Ding asked, " Is your reporting more important than the request of Director Ma?").

If in the preceding paragraph, Ding explicitly shows Chi their respective position in the power structure, then in the paragraph below, he does it more implicitly.

> The arrangement of tables in the office is also meaningful. The space near the window is well ventilated and lighted. Of course, it belongs to Director Liu. Actually, tables are arranged according to the positions of staff members even though it is okay for people to sit down anywhere to work. Some think where they sit in the office makes them feel slightly different. How trivial this seems, the table arrangement can bring a lot of, or even huge differences, at least reminding people of their positions in the power hierarchy[...] (Yan, 2001, p. 26)

There is another scene:

> After entering the private room, Secretary Tong said, "Ma, have some wine. It would be just like those years in Lhasa. Wine can make you forget everything." Ding Xiaohuai said: "Choose mellower wine. Director Ma can no longer hold his liquor as well as before." Secretary Tong said: "Then, we will not order Maotai. How about Wuliangye." Director Yin said: "OK, two bottles of Wuliangye." The manager of the restaurant personally brought the wine to them. The waitress wanted to take over. The manager asked her to get the dishes. He took the wine out of the box and prepared to pour the wine. Director Yin said: "Let me pour wine for them." Director Yin picked up the bottle and poured wine for secretary tong and then for Director Ma. Deputy Director Wu grabbed the bottle of wine out of Director

> Yin's hand and said: "Let me." He poured a glass of wine for Mr. Yin, then for me and Ding Xiaohuai. Seeing how the bottle was passed around, I realized that even pouring wine is a sophisticated art. If only they would make this kind of effort in the workplace. When the dishes were served, Secretary Tong clinked his glass with Director Ma's and emptied his glass. He showed the bottom of the glass to Director Ma and said, "Bottom up!" They laughed together and said, "Nice."[...] Ding Xiaohuai stood up and said, "Director Ma's consumption of liquor is universally acknowledged, but it is too much for him to toast all of you. How about I drink this one for the director?" Deputy Director Wu was just about to empty his glass. After hearing Ding's words, he put his glass down and looked at Ding and then at the director. Director Ma banged the table and said, "What's the matter with you? Look who are sitting here. These are all my old friends. You want to drink on behalf of me? Hey! "[...] (Yan, 2001, p. 51)

Drinking is an art. What kind of wine is suitable for the occasion? Who is pouring wine? How to pour? How to drink? These are things one cannot be sloppy with because this is not just drinking wine. It is a political ritual and an exercise of power relations. Why did Director Ma deliberately let Ding Xiaohuai lose face? It is nothing more than to show that his relationship with several other directors is extraordinary.

In fact, this symbolic use of power through language and behavior can be observed everywhere in the political circle, including seating arrangements at meetings, the order of speech, and who walks in the front. These details remind people of their positions in the power hierarchy. Power is repeatedly stated in trivial matters. It is grossly wrong for us to think that the use of power is only symbolic or is nothing more than a political tactic. Behind these seemingly insignificant arrangements is a real power relationship, which is easier to understand. In addition, the symbolic use of power will lead to a series of reactions that will change the political landscape. For example, Deputy Director Sun wanted to report to the provincial party chief alone when Director Ma was in the hospital. However, Director Ma thwarted his attempt and appeared under the help of Chi Dawei and his wife and avoided a crisis that could lead to power reshuffling (Yan, 2001, p. 378–385).

4.3.2 The Art of Manipulation

The symbolic use of power alone is not enough for an official. He must also know how to use various political maneuvers to gain an advantage in the power structure, which is exactly why the "political scene" can become a bureaucratic structure that shapes the attitudes and views of people. These political tactics are ultimately implemented to achieve core purposes such as controlling the appointment and dismissal of public officials. The art of manipulation in the bureaucratic system comes partly from formal institutional arrangements, which must consider the smooth operation of bureaucratic organizations and thus pay close attention to ranking in the allocation of power, and partly from the informal system created by officials. More importantly, the art of manipulation is often veiled or masked, which makes it formal on the surface but informal in terms of the internal logic and operational details. It can also be said that the art of manipulation is using the informal system to counteract the formal system or to operate the formal system in an informal way. The ultimate goal is to invalidate the formal system or to make the formal system operate in line with the practical rules of bureaucracy and with the political interests of a specific group.

For a complex political system, its personnel and official selection, appointment, recall and other arrangements are crucial. These arrangements not only directly determine talent and human resource issues within the administrative system but also become part of the day-to-day operation of the bureaucracy. Whether these institutional arrangements are rationally designed and implemented is a matter of particular importance for political integrity, as it determines whether power will be excessively concentrated and abused. If a person can decide at will the appointment and removal of public officials, it means that he firmly controls the power as well as other individuals in the organization. In this way, he can finally have a firm grip on the organization.

One scene in *The Water of Blue Waves* depicts how Chi Dawei was marginalized because of some mistakes he made, and a senior official of the human resources department came to talk to him:

> [...] It seems that they want to transfer me to a position no one wants, but they say they want to know my own opinion. What a farce! As if they could promote me to the director of the department if I say so. I said: "It doesn't matter what I think. It all depends on the opinion of the organization." He said: "[...]You studied TCM at college and had a master's degree. A technical position will be perfect for great technical talent like you. There are few technical professionals in the department. We must make full use of your talent." When one says that you are a skilled talent in a government department, it means that you are a tool and not worthy of a position of leadership. However, who would slap a person who just paid you compliments by saying you are a great t talent? I said: "Has the department made a decision?" He said: "You can say that. It's the organization's decision."[...] I said: "Did I make any mistake? I hope that the organization could point it out for me." He smiled and said: "Who said that? We don't think so. The organization doesn't think so. We will criticize whoever said that." Who is the organization? When all is said, the fact remains that I pissed someone off. This someone is not happy, but he will never say that this is his decision. It was the decision of the organization. Who am I to complain? (Yan, 2001, p. 86–87).

Chi's experience was not uncommon. He was confronted with a long-standing problem in the Chinese political scene. As early as 1980, Deng Xiaoping pointed out in his speech on the reform of the party and state leadership system that power should not be excessively concentrated:

> It is not good to have an overconcentration of power. It hinders the practice of socialist democracy and of the Party's democratic centralism, impedes the progress of socialist construction and prevents us from taking full advantage of collective wisdom. Overconcentration of power is liable to give rise to arbitrary rule by individuals at the expense of collective leadership, and it is an important cause of bureaucracy under the present circumstances (Deng, 1994, p. 321).

Then Deng Xiaoping also pointed out:

> In addition to leading to overconcentration of power in the hands of individuals, patriarchal ways within the revolutionary ranks place individuals above the organization, which then becomes a tool in their hands [...] For example, when major issues are discussed inside the Party, very often there is insufficient democratic deliberation. Hasty decisions are made by

> one or a few individuals, and votes are seldom taken, as they should be under the principle of majority rule. This shows that democratic centralism has not yet become a strictly applied system (Xiaoping, 1994, p. 329–330)

What Deng Xiaoping pointed out is an important issue in China's political system and a hard nut to crack in political reform. In fact, the Communist Party of China has created a relatively mature cadre selection and appraisal system over the long years. Under the leadership of the party committee, party organizations draw strength from the masses and establish democratic mechanisms to select cadres. However, as Deng Xiaoping said, "Patriarchal ways are an antiquated social phenomenon which has existed from time immemorial and has had a very damaging influence on the Party. Chen Duxiu, Wang Ming and Zhang Guotao were all patriarchal in their ways. During the period from the Zunyi Meeting of the Political Bureau of the Central Committee [in 1935] to the socialist transformation [in the mid-50 s], the Central Committee and Comrade Mao Zedong invariably paid due attention to collective leadership and democratic centralism so that democratic life within our Party was quite normal. Unfortunately, this fine tradition has not been upheld, nor has it been incorporated into a strict and perfected system." (Deng, 1994, p. 329–330) As a result, it was not uncommon for self-interest to override the organization's interest in the Party. Democratic centralism became just a formality, and organizations became tools of individuals. Furthermore, power began to be concentrated in the hands of a few people. "Overconcentration of power means inappropriate and indiscriminate concentration of all power in Party committees in the name of strengthening centralized Party leadership. Moreover, the power of the Party committees themselves is often in the hands of a few secretaries, especially the first secretaries, who direct and decide everything. Thus, 'centralized Party leadership' often turns into leadership by individuals. This problem exists, to varying degrees, in leading bodies at all levels throughout the country." (Deng, 1994, p. 328–329).

Excessive centralization of power represents the core maneuver in the bureaucratic system. Whether it is about administrative matters or the appointment or removal of a cadre, the power to make decisions may be concentrated in a small clique.

Criticism and self-criticism are also among the many maneuvers in the bureaucratic system. Originally an important party-building mechanism of the CPC, criticism and self-criticism were important ways to ensure political integrity if the mechanism was fully respected and effectively implemented. However, when power was excessively concentrated, the mechanism would fail and become a weapon for retaliation. In *The Water of Blue Waves*, Chi Dawei, previously a promising young man, became a marginalized underdog after he made a mistake at a criticism and self-criticism session. All the people knew the unspoken rule that leaders could reprove themselves, but the subordinate officers should not criticize their leaders. All except for Chi Dawei. Almost every link in the process of the exercise of power, including voting and election, could be manipulated.

A result of the art of manipulation is that arbitrariness in decision-making is not effectively curbed, and people cannot effectively oversee officials.

4.3.3 The Art of Taming

How the "political scene" tames people within it has a close connection with the art of manipulation. If we say the ultimate goal of manipulation is to control the political situation, then the realization of this goal would depend on the taming of people within the bureaucratic system. While the art of manipulation targets a controlling position in the jungle of bureaucracy, the art of taming targets individuals—especially those who recalcitrate against people in power. Those who are in power often tame subordinate officials through political manipulation. If one doesn't know how to manipulate, he is also unable to keep his subordinates in check. Taming measures are used to ensure that individuals in the bureaucratic system surrender to its unwritten rules. Punishment is one of the most common taming measures in the bureaucratic system. For example, in *The Water of Blue Waves*, Chi Dawei was punished for his defiance of the unwritten rules, while Yan Zhihe was punished for life by the same token. It was not until the taming of Chi that his life underwent profound changes.

The unfortunate thing about Chi Dawei is that he wanted to be a dignified man. He once helped a villager who fell ill and had no money to seek treatment, which makes us believe he had a conscience. His integrity and trust in the organization drove him to unequivocally criticize the department head who spent money on luxury cars, which led to his marginalization in the organization.

Even after his girlfriend broke up with him because of "his lack of ambition", he still did not give in to Director-general Ma. He was not afraid of isolation or misunderstanding. He devoted himself entirely to his political ideal and conscience.

However, the cruelty of real life gradually eroded his conscience and shattered his belief. After Chi was married, he still lived in a dingy small room. At the beginning, his wife Dong Liu was able to tolerate it. Soon, his wife was pregnant. The fact that his pregnant wife had to catch a bus to commute between work and home tugged at his heartstrings. Chi wanted to transfer Dong to a municipal hospital and hoped she could take a break before giving birth. But he could do nothing because he had no authority. In the end, it was Deputy Director-general Sun who helped him solve the problem by putting in a good word for Dong. However, another problem soon ensued. His mother-in-law came to live with the couple temporarily to take care of Dong. The problem is how a house no more than a dozen square meters could accommodate three people. Chi paid a visit to Shen, Director of the Housing Management Department, and asked for a larger apartment. His request was rejected. "The day before my mother-in-law came, I cleaned the room and placed most furniture together so I could squeeze in another bed in the room for my mother-in-law. Her bed and our bed were only separated by a curtain." (Yan, 2001, pp. 119–120) It was difficult for the young couple to have a sexual life with Chi's mother-in-law in the house.

Chi Dawei was something of a loser after getting married. The Housing Management Division ignored his application. He could not even get his son into the kindergarten affiliated with the provincial government. In the end, it was his brother-in-law Ren Zhiqiang, someone given to boasting and who Chi had despised, that got it done for him. The most exasperating thing was the helplessness he felt when his son had his thigh burnt by hot water after the boy accidentally overturned a kettle. The panicked Chi asked a driver of the department to send them to the hospital but refused. It was after a few words of Director-general Ma that the driver agreed. After arriving at the hospital, Chi Dawei realized he didn't have any money on him. He pleaded with the doctor to treat his son. He nearly went down on this knees. The people in the hospital did not believe he was a government official. In fact, the doctor's request was simple—as long as any of his supervisors could verify his title, it would suffice. He called Director-general Ma and then Deputy Director-general Sun, but neither of them was available. In the end, it was his archenemy Deputy Director Ding Xiaohuai who helped him out.

This incident threw a bucket of cold water on Chi, who, at 34, was still a lowly clerk. He suddenly realized that his misery was due to his refusal to bend to the unspoken rules in the bureaucratic game. Clearly, he had nobody but himself to blame. Then, Chi began to worry whether his awakening had come too late. Finally, after taking the advice of Yan Zhihe, who had been irredeemably marginalized because of his disdain for the unspoken rules, Chi Dawei accelerated the "killing of his old self." The streak of good luck began with one small incident. Ma's granddaughter was hospitalized, and the doctors and nurses were so nervous that they kept botching the injection. Ding Xiaohuai, eager to suck up to Director-general Ma, then took a misstep. He introduced Chi's wife Dong Liu, who was known for her steady hand, to Director-general Ma's wife. Of course, Dong Liu did not disappoint. The little girl quickly recovered. Since then, Chi and Director-general Ma have become very close. Chi became a frequent visitor to Ma's house. The most crucial turnaround for Chi came soon. A group of stupid intellectuals attempted to start a "coup d'état" to overturn Director-general Ma, and Chi was invited to be a part of this political conspiracy. After listening to the advice of Yan Zhihe, Chi decisively exposed the conspiracy of this group of intellectuals. With the help of Chi, Director-general Ma put an end to the "coup d'état" and destroyed the political careers of these intellectuals. Generously rewarded for his loyalty, Chi quickly became a well-favored man in the department. He was promoted to division head, deputy director of the department, and then the director of the department in just a few years and was given the chance to study under a doctoral program. He now lived in a larger and better furnished apartment and making money in a "legal" way became easier for him. Chi began to enjoy the benefits of complying with unwritten rules.

After abandoning his ideal, Chi's life changed completely. Those who had looked down on him showed respect for him. In one sense, Chi finally got back his so-called dignity. Undoubtedly, his good luck was inseparable from his surrender to the unwritten rules of the political scene. He was completely tamed by the political scene.

The "political scene" controls, disciplines, and punishes its members in ways unbearable for humanity. People only live once. In the end, individuals tend to choose to surrender to the unwritten rules, among whom Chi is neither the first nor the last one to do so.

4.3.4 Causes of Corruption and Dissociation Between Corruption and Morality[6]

When we discuss the art of taming in the political scene, a question often comes up—why could these taming measures work? If an individual is unable to fight the control, discipline, or punishment by the political scene, why couldn't he just opt out, rather than hanging around despite the fact the political scene brings pain? And why does the political scene breed corruption? To answer these questions, we need to identify the causal mechanism of corruption.

The important mechanism that causes corruption to take place and to spread is related to not only the political scene itself but also private life. The malignant interaction between public and private life gives rise to the causal mechanism of corruption and disassociates corruption from morality.

To put this issue into perspective, let us review how Chi was being tamed by the political scene:

Even when Chi's life was a mess due to his defiance of unwritten rules, he still looked down on those who followed them. He despised Ding Xiaohuai, who became a division head and then deputy director by bootlicking. Nevertheless, Ding's house became increasingly larger and had the authority Chi didn't have. The changes in the attitudes of his friends also irritated Chi:

> Even Hu Yibing, the one who went with him to the countryside to conduct a survey, became a shameless hustler. They all lived a swinging life. Only I was suffocating. I shrugged my shoulders and sneered at myself. I used to laugh at these hustlers and suckers. Hustlers and suckers may have reasons to do what they have done after all. It makes sense. Who am I to laugh at them? To grab all those good things, they couldn't be soft-hearted. I suddenly realized that my father's life was too unworthy and his sacrifice was meaningless... (Yan, 2001, p. 211)

Recognizing he was a complete failure as husband and father became too painful for Chi to bear. After giving birth to the child, Dong Liu became a totally different person. She began to realize her husband was unable to improve their life despite the fact that he was the first person in his department with a master's degree. Chi could not do anything at the Chinese Medicine Association. He wanted to stick to his faith and be an upright man, but his life was a total disaster. He achieved nothing. No one respected him. In contrast, those "hustlers and suckers" he looked down on gained the respect of others and led a dignified life. Dong Liu often praised how clever their boy was. Yes, other parents provided their children with a superior material life. Chi's child had nothing but cleverness. The real world is cruel. Dong Liu once said: "What should we do with our life? We only live once." It is such a cruel question. Who does not want to enjoy glory and dignity in a time-limited life? In the face of such a question, Chi felt desperate and anxious. What did he do in the past six or seven years? Responsibility, conscience, integrity, and self-esteem are all large talks. The more one wants to talk about self-esteem, the less self-esteem one has.

---

[6] My thoughts about this matter are inspired by Ms. Li Na's advice and criticism. It could be said, for the most part, this section is to present Ms. Li's ideas.

In fact, Chi was a talented man. He had a good idea of how the political scene operates, at least in theory. He also knew how he had ended up in the current situation. He was simply unwilling to give up his belief. He couldn't let go of his self-esteem. In the end, the cruel reality forced him to surrender to the unspoken rules of the political scene and abandon his belief.

Chi realized that if you want to improve your private life, you must reach out and get resources from the political scene—only power can change one's life. Private life and public power become intertwined. In addition to manipulation and taming, corruption also stems from personal desires in relation to private life. The political scene controls and tames individuals, while individuals try to get their hands on power so they can enjoy unlimited possibilities in limited life. Once an individual gains power, he must maintain the rules of the political scene.

As a result, bureaucracy spreads from the political field to daily life, and corruption in the public sector becomes the most effective way to obtain resources to enrich private life. In such a scenario, corruption is no longer a purely moral or legal issue. It is justified to a large extent. In this sense, ordinary people's accusations of government corruption sounds like the pot calling the kettle black. It becomes local knowledge and a mentality that corruption can improve the quality of private life. As corruption digs its claws deeper into daily life, it would almost become an instinct of preservation for many. Disassociation of corruption from morality would further propagate corruption.

4.4 Direct Consequences of the Sprawling of the Political Scene

The mechanism for the exercise of power at the micro level centers on the political sphere and spreads like germs to other spheres of social life, leading to bureaucratization of both the political and the social life system.

4.4.1 The Sprawling of the Political Scene and Its Adverse Impact on Decision-Making

In the case of serious bureaucratization in the political system, the combination of the political scene structure and the pressure-based system will lead to the collapse of democracy and failure of communication in political decision-making (Rong et al., 1998). Without necessary supervision and sufficient communication, decision-making will also become bureaucratized. This kind of bureaucratization occurs in the daily exercise of power. There may be arbitrariness behind seemingly scientific decisions.

There are several scenes in *The Waters of Blue Waves* that reflect the perversion of decision-making by political calculus. Data tampering was a common practice in the health department when it came to the reporting of their work related to the prevention of porphyria. Before annual reporting, the department sent a working group to conduct surveys. However, regardless of the real situation, there was a tacit understanding between the rank and file and the department leadership that the incidence must always be lower than the previous year. The reported and disclosed figures were falsified by the staff to meet the expectations of the superiors (Yan, 2001, pp. 217–228). Figures were the result of the structure of the political scene, the pressure to meet performance targets and the official public performance evaluation system. One can't help but wonder how such figures could result in scientific decisions. Still more interestingly, even though the first floor of the new office building for the health department was ideal as rental space for retailers, and can potentially generate considerable revenue for the department, Chi suggested, eager as he was to curry favor with Director-general Ma, Chi proposed what even he himself felt ridiculous: converting the first floor into an exhibition hall of the health department or more accurately the hall of honor of Director-general Ma. Ma was very pleased to agree. (Yan, 2001, p. 282 and pp. 422–424).

In fact, there may be the influence of unreasonable unwritten rules behind every seemingly unreasonable political decision in real life. These unwritten rules may lead to undesirable consequences: "Through observation of others around me, I realized that many people lost the ability to sympathize with others. They can maintain an indifferent attitude towards the suffering of others" (Yan, 2001, p. 67).

Bureaucracy can clearly make public officials forget the benefits of the common people. The serious consequences of bureaucracy are ultimately borne by the general public.

4.4.2 *A Growing Political Alliance: When* Jiang Hu *Meets Bureaucracy*

Chi quickly learned the rules of the game on the political scene. He was also helped by other players who had the same place of origin as he did, as seen from the following scene:

> The three started speaking in their local dialect instead of Mandarin, which brought them closer. Common people may not understand it. Until one becomes part of the political scene, one cannot easily appreciate the importance of a shared place of origin. Why do the people in the circle flock together and take care of each other? If they are your fellow townsmen, then you have a reason. (Yan, 2001, p. 389)

Chi expanded his political alliance thanks to his connections with his fellow townsmen and gained political support in some important departments. The expansion of the alliance also brought insider knowledge to Chi. This was why Chi had situations well in hand in his subsequent career life.

In real life, officials often used geographical, family or other personal ties to build political alliances, but an even larger threat to good governance came from the notion of Jianghu (loyalty and brotherhood), which, when compounded by the practical rules of the political scene, would exacerbate already complex power dynamics in politics. The growing influence in politics of codes of conduct prevalent among banditry and sworn brotherhoods, which were built on the principle of *quid pro quo*, not only undermined the integrity of the government but also bred corruption. The most conspicuous manifestation of political maneuvers of such kind is endless hobnobbing among government officials at banquets and other functions that continued to grow in size. Beneath it all is an attempt to cultivate alliances with the powerful and the rich.

4.4.3 Interference by Government Officials in Microeconomic Activities: A Threat to the Market

The displacement of democratic and scientifically informed decision-making by political calculus leads to another serious problem, that is, interference by officials in the market. *The Water of Blue Waves* does not go to great lengths to discuss this problem, but there is a section depicting how Chi, after being promoted to the deputy director of the department, was trying to get his company Antai Pharmaceutical listed. There is a scene where Chi returned after attending the listing ceremony of the company:

> After I came back from the ribbon-cutting ceremony, Dong Liu had already asked Dong Hui to sell all the 40,000 shares she had received. She earned more than 300,000 yuan. It's like a dream. Although excited, Dong Liu still complained: "Yes. If you told me everything. I would have spent all the spare money to purchase the shares, and I would have been a millionaire." Many people would not be able to earn so much money even if they could live more than once. But I did it without any effort. I even didn't break the law. I couldn't believe it, but it was real. (Yan, 2001, p. 429).

In fact, since Chi got his hand on the levers of power, he became increasingly involved in economic activities. Of course, to be fair, given the many legal and political loopholes, Chi was more scrupulous than many other officials.

Mr. Wu Jinglian writes:

> At the turn of the century, governments at all levels were involved in microeconomic activities. Some officials abused their power to allocate land, loans and other important resources to vanity projects or emphasised strict regulation of project approval or stock listing approvals. This fueled corruption and allowed collusion between officials and businessmen (Wu, 2008, p. 5).

In the above case, corruption is a result of rampant intervention of bureaucrats in economic activities and of the lack of legal oversight over the highly bureaucratic political system.

4.4.4 Corruption in Everday Life

The encroachment of the political scene into everyday life is directly manifested in two ways. First, it affects the way people behave. The culture of the political scene seeps into daily life, and ordinary members of the public began to behave like politicians. Second, it shapes people’s values. Power and money become the only criteria for measuring success. People who are infected by these beliefs about what matter in life become restless chasers of quick fame, easy money and superficial power. This is because getting hold of just a little bit of power can turn the lives of otherwise ordinary people such as Ding Xiaohuai and Chi Dawei and their families completely around, bringing them social status, material benefits, and financial benefits. This is what people have learned by observing the political scene. It is a common understanding that, with power, people can improve the quality of their life. Power and profits thus become criteria for measuring the value of human life.

The permeation of bureaucratic culture into daily life has serious consequences. It allows the influence of corruption to go beyond the public domain and spread into private life.

4.5 Discussion: Strengthening the Rule of Law to Tackle Corruption

4.5.1 The Formation of Institutions and Morality

This chapter focuses on the operation of power in daily political situations, including the phenomenon of the political scene and relations, because the daily operation of power is at the heart of politics and the key to the formation of political landscape. Corruption has a direct connection with the operation of power in daily situations. The devil is in the details. We must pay attention to widespread minor corruption. Unbridled minor corruption can grow into major corruption. All high-ranking corrupt officials are once small corrupt officials. The spread of corruption harms social stability and hinders the development of a country. The collapse of the moral value system caused by the penetration of political power into citizens’ daily life is something we could not afford. The Chinese nation must rid themselves of power-worshiping and pro-corruption mentality to ensure sustainable development in the march forward.

We must ask ourselves the following questions:

> If we say that the logic of life is “an individual’s continuous efforts towards forecasting and realizing one’s own destiny,”[7] then *The Water of Blue Waves* tells a story of one person’s "continuous efforts towards forecasting and realizing their own destiny" after the collapse of his value system. What should we try to hold on to when following the logic of life? What is ethics? The ancients told us that it is benevolence, righteousness, and universal affirmation

[7] This definition of "logic of life" is suggested by Ms. Li Na.

> of life. The revolutionaries tell us that it is equality, justice, and the liberation of humankind. Currently, why do the things that we should stick to seem so vulnerable? Why is the past logic of life considered anti-logic now? The answer we can come up with is that the mentality of the political circle determines the mentality of the entire society.

If this is the case, then we must continue to ask: What causes the logic of the political scene (in relation to power, rank, possession, control, discipline, etc.) to penetrate into all corners of our life? Based on examination of the daily operation of power, the answer might be distorted institutions. This is because people do not necessarily become ethical animals and institutions with distorted details justify many unreasonable things. We have seen many individuals deviating from their ideals and moral values in the face of power and surrendering to or even defending those things that they once hated. They become machines of the political scene and a link of the reproduction process of bureaucracy.

4.5.2 The Uphill Struggle: Fighting Corruption with Legal Weapons

"Policy makers and researchers need to come to grips with the objectives of governance and the rationality of the policy itself. The inherent logic of the policy itself must be rational and the supporting measures must be effective." (He, 2008, p. 12) The current legal system in China fails to crack down on corruption because it fails to pinpoint the target.

Anti-corruption criminal law, which focuses on punishing work-related crimes, cannot directly prevent corruption. Its primary function is to post hoc punishment. Other anti-corruption mechanisms, including administrative supervision and financial auditing, also fail to effectively curb corruption because of the irrational design. The control target of anti-corruption mechanisms should be the daily operation of power that breeds corruption. Without pinpointing the correct control target, these mechanisms cannot effectively control and prevent problems within the political system. These mechanisms could only punish corruption that has become too enormous to be hidden. That is, with this kind of mechanism, the focus of anti-corruption is only to post hoc punishment rather than ex ante prevention. To a certain extent, discipline inspection departments of the Party may also be part of the political scene. Anti-corruption officials, especially those at lower levels of the discipline inspection system, may also be tied down by rules and the web of relationships in the bureaucratic system.

Therefore, the current predicament in the Chinese government's anti-corruption efforts stems from the inability to cut into the daily operation of power and put a bridle on rampant power abuse in the bureaucratic system.

4.5.3 Feasibility of Fighting Corruption with Legal Weapons

However, we have reasons to believe that the political scene that breeds corruption is constituted by a dynamic set of norms and structures in constant change. It can be changed and reshaped.

Whether the law can curb and reduce corruption depends on whether it has identified the correct control target and disrupted the causal mechanism. The causal mechanism of corruption has its roots in social background. Over the past three decades, the private sector in China has grown aggressively. People are paying increasing attention to the improvement of private life and have a growing desire to possess resources. In the era of a planned economy, power means easier access to resources. In the era of a market economy when everyone puts money above all, public power is still the best means to gain access to resources because we have failed to construct a fair system.[8] As a result, corruption is disassociated from morality, and its causal mechanism is strengthened, leading to the continuation of the political scene.

Wherever improper power practice prevails, whether it is in the court or in a village, at least one of the three factors can be observed: unfair distribution of resources, failure of formal institutions to protect individual rights (including rights of individuals in the political system), and unfair administrative procedures. Unfair distribution of resources forces individuals to seek connections with those in power to protect their legitimate interests and eventually makes corruption a common means to get rich. When individual rights are not protected by formal institutions, individuals are forced to seek protection from informal institutions or by leveraging their relations with others, which ultimately leads to unequal relations being constantly reproduced and strengthened. When administrative procedures are unfair, individuals must "grease" the rigid and unfair administrative system if they want to climb the ladder of power, which ultimately leads to corruption in both public and private life.

In this sense, the importance of law in controlling corruption lies in the fact that all moral pursuits must be supported by reasonable and effective institutions. Only by promoting the rule of law can we put a bridle on the bureaucratic culture that threatens justice and morality. Individuals are weak in the face of structures. The cultivation of honest and moral individuals requires the support of fair institutions. Only when the law can ensure effective configuration of government functions and the establishment of just institutions can we prevent malignant interactions between public and private life and break the causal mechanism of corruption.

At a more microscopic level, over the course of the history of the Party, we have seen some well-thought-out institutional designs that take into consideration

[8] Mr. Wang Shaoguang points out in one of his forward-looking studies: "The purpose of reform is not only to build a more effective system, but also to establish a more just system." (Wang, 2008a, b, p. 33) The Party reached a consensus on the establishment of a more effective system in its 14th National Congress in 1992. It reached a consensus on the establishment of a more just system in the Sixth Plenary Session of the 16th CPC Central Committee in 2006.

power operation in daily situations,[9] but these once effective institutions have become gradually distorted. Today, we need the legal system to reinterpret, strengthen and improve these institutions, supervise the daily operation of power, and shape positive attitudes towards fairness and justice. When following the instructions of the CPC Central Committee in the *Notice on the Establishment of a Sound Corruption Punishment and Prevention System*, we must not only pay attention to institutional building at the macro level but also recognize that how the law handles the daily operation of corruption will decide the effectiveness of the Party's anti-corruption strategy.

References

Bourdieu, P., & Loic, W. (1998). *An invitation to reflective sociology* (L. Meng, & L. Kang, Trans.). Central Compilation and Translation Press.
Jingben, R. et al. (1998). *The transition from a pressure-based system to a democratic cooperation system*. Central Compilation & Translation Press.
Jinglian, W. (2008) Reform and opening-up in the past three decades and outlook. In *Comparative studies* (Vol. 36). CITIC Publishing Group.
Jun, Y. (2009). *Connections, regulations, and dispute resolutions—Targeting the informal system in Chinese society*. Ningxia People's Publishing House.
Ming, X. (Ed.). (2003). Li Zhen's confession. *Fangyuan Magazine*, (11).
Shengjun, W. (2008). The justice system should keep up with the times. *Journal of Law Application*, (10).
Shaoguang, W. (2008). *The way to maintain social stability*. SDX Joint Publishing Company.
Si, W. (2001). *Unspoken rules—Real game in Chinese history*. Yunnan People's Publishing House.
Xiaoping, D. (1994). *Selected works of Deng Xiaoping* (Vol. 2, 2nd Ed. People's Publishing House.
Xiaotong, F. (1998). *From the soil and institutions for reproduction*. Peking University Press.
Xuefeng, H. (2008). *Problems in the countryside*. Law Press.
Zhen, Y. (2001). *The water of Canglang*. People's Literature Publishing House.

[9] For example, Mao Zedong repeatedly mentioned the operation of micro-level power mechanisms within the Party, such as organizational principles, the cadre system, and intra-party democracy. The leadership of the Party, including Mao, had adjusted the Party's guiding ideology of power operation from time to time to ensure clean governance.

Part II
Legal Pluralism, Social Control, and Social Order

Chapter 5
Law as a Classification System that Creates Order: An Anthropological Approach

> This passage quotes a "certain Chinese encyclopedia" in which it is written that "animals are divided into: (a) belonging to the Emperor, (b) embalmed, (c) tame, (d) sucking pigs, (e) sirens, (f) fabulous, (g) stray dogs, (h) included in the present classification, (i) frenzied, (j) innumerable, (k) cat drawn with a very fine camel hair brush, (l) et cetera, (m) having just broken the water pitcher, (n) that from a long way off "look like flies".
> —*The Order of Things: An Archaeology of the Human Sciences* by Michel Foucault (2001, p. 1)

Every philosopher, scholar of jurisprudence, or practitioner of law has their own views about law. For example, Aristotle believed that law can be defined as rationality that is not affected by emotions (Bodenheimer, 1999, p. 11); Donald Black (1994, p. 2) defined law as "governmental social control"; to the post-modern legal philosopher Boaventura De Sousa Santos (1987, pp. 297–302), law is "a map of misreading".

This chapter begins the discussion with a ridiculous taxonomy of animals, indicative of a unique answer to the question of "what is law". To us, who are outsiders of the then Chinese society depicted by this encyclopedia, this animal classification seems ridiculous. Why were animals divided into: (a) belonging to the Emperor, (b) fragrant, (c) tame, (d) piglets, (e) salamanders, (f) legendary, (g) stray dogs, etc. at that time? Did piglets and salamanders mean something special to people at the time? Did people treat animals that are "frenzied" differently from other animals? Although we cannot know why there was such a taxonomy, one thing is for sure: these animals occupied a place and were compartmentalized in the mind of the author and users (if there were any users). The taxonomy was not meaningless to these people regardless of how odd classification is to us. You might have had a chuckle looking at it, but has it not also provoked you to think more and perhaps differently about what implications this might have for our attempts to understand what law is?

Q. Wang, *Sociology of Law*,
https://doi.org/10.1007/978-981-16-5509-8_5

5.1 Significance of Classification to Human Beings

Although *primitive classification* (Durkheim & Mauss, 2005) contains many flaws, this classic work has still successfully drawn the attention of anthropologists to the importance of classification. Many anthropologists have developed their own important theories and ideas by drawing inspiration from this long essay (Needham, 2005). Classification therefore has become a topic of fundamental importance in the development of anthropological theories. However, it appears that classification has never been given the same kind of importance in the circle of jurisprudence scholars (at least in China).[1]

Classification is the most basic ability of human beings. Without the ability to classify, human beings will not be able to survive and take actions. Classification is an important indicator that we need to rely on when taking actions. It enables people to come to grips with their relations with others, gods, family members, the community, and so on and take corresponding actions in social life.

For example, a farmer must classify the land and crops that belong to him—what kind of land is suitable for growing crops; a worker must classify tools he has—the steel file is used to flatten the surface of metal and the wretch is used to screw the nut. Otherwise, they will not be able to carry out their work. The abovementioned classification systems are technical and not directly related to the development of social relations. The classification of social relations directly affects the behaviors and attitudes of people towards others.[2] For example, kinship terminology not only describes familial relationships but also conveys moral rights and obligations in the relationship (Zhuang, 2002, p. 277). Kinship terminology itself is a basic classification of social relations. It allows an individual to clarify whether a person is his relative or whether the person is a close relative or distant relative. Only when the relationship is clarified can the individual know how to interact with the other persons. Mr. Fei Xiaotong (1998) said that differential modes of association are shaped based on kinship terminology. Without kinship terminology, people cannot distinguish their relations with others, and therefore, there will be no differential modes of association. For example, when you call a person "father", it not only means he is biologically related to you in a certain way, it also means you should treat this person in certain ways, such as being respectful toward them. It means this is the person you can expect will pay for your schooling when you are young, who can be a listener when you are feeling sad, and whom you ought to support when they get old. Additionally, you may only

---

[1] Professor Su Li has mentioned or implicitly expressed the importance of classification system in his works. For example, in the famous *the Confusion of Qiuju and the Tragedy of Uncle Shan Gang*, Professor Su asserts that the justice Qiuju wanted is obviously different from the kind of justice offered by state law and the justice demanded by Qiuju was excluded from the classification system of state law (Su, 1996, p.23–37). In *Interpretation of Order*, Professor Su writes: "The social context determins that it is unlikely for the conflict to be resolved by means of law in its modern sense. The social context gives rise to an order established by unwritten rules which is more convenient to residents. These unwritten rules, in a sense, can also be called law." (Su, 1999, p. 381).

[2] The focus of this chapter is on classifications related to culture and social relations rather than technical classifications.

address him as “dad” or “father” when the society in which you live does not allow the younger generation to call the elders by their names. In short, the appropriateness of your actions and attitudes towards the person you call the “father” has been stipulated by the basic kinship classification of your society.

The appropriateness of an action often depends on whether the action complies with social norms in connection with the social relation classification widely accepted by members of society. For example, regarding the roles of an individual in social life (Popenoe, 1999, pp. 97–99), if a person acts the same way towards everyone around him regardless of what relation they are in, this person must be very bad at relationship or shifting social role. From the perspective of classification, his failure at shifting social roles is caused by failure to correctly classify his social relations. Every society has a basic classification system of relations with other people. Terms of references such as parents, classmates, teachers, friends, and neighbors all imply a relation (which is neither visible nor touchable). This classification system stipulates whether one’s behavior, language, and attitude towards another is appropriate or acceptable.

Classification also affects the way people handle things. Let us assume Person A decides to invite some of his friends over for dinner. However, after returning from grocery shopping, he finds that his pot is broken. Time does not allow him to go out and buy a new pot. At this moment, he suddenly remembers that there is a new cuspidor in the house. Therefore, Person A uses cuspidor to cook fish soup. Soon, his friends arrive. Person A serves the fish soup in the cuspidor. If you are one of the friends of Person A, what reaction would you have? Will you drink the fish soup? This kind of situation rarely happens. Even if it happens, it often occurs under special circumstances that make the situation justifiable. In any circumstances, a question worth reflecting is whether the fish soup is truly unsanitary. Will you really get sick if you drink the soup? In fact, a new cuspidor made of iron is not dirtier than a pot that has not been scrubbed for a long time. The reason why we do not use cuspidor to make soup is that cuspidors are classified as dirty things in our existing classification system. This is the same reason why we do not eat in the restroom even if the restroom is unused or sterilized every day.

There is no doubt that there is a close connection between judgment and classification. However, it needs to be pointed out that the two activities are not the same. Judgment is often a necessary but not the only premise of classification. Classification means creating a system. It is the process of categorizing and arranging things, phenomena, and people in our lives and minds. In the classificatory schemata mentioned at the beginning of this chapter, animals “(a) belonging to the Emperor… (n) that from a long way off 'look like flies'" are put into different categories. Even animals that do not meet any specified criterion are put under "(l) et cetera". The categorization put animals in order for the author. Judging does not create a system. In the process of classifying, people judge whether a specific object or phenomenon belongs to a certain category in a classification system. For example, an animal that looks like a fly from a long way is put into the category of animals "(n) that from a long way off 'look like flies'."

In fact, classification is the method by which we put things around us in order. As Rodney Needham puts it:

> When a person who has been blind since birth is operated upon and given sight,[3] he does not directly see the phenomenal world that we accept as normal. Instead, he is afflicted by a painful chaos of forms and colors and a gaudy confusion of visual impressions, none of which seems to bear any comprehensible relationship to the others. Only very slowly and with intense effort can he teach himself that this confusion does indeed manifest an order, and only by resolute application does he learn to distinguish and classify objects and acquire the meaning of terms such as 'space' and 'shape'." (Needham, 2005)

This passage conveys two points. First, after the person who has been blind since birth is given sight, he would find things around him, such as tables, the bed, books, sunshine, and rain, a "painful chaos of forms and colors" at first. Only when he learns to properly classify these things or, in other words, put things in the compartments where they belong in his mind that these things manifest an order. Second, to the blind person, learning the things around him through the eyes is not just a process of adapting to the regaining of sight but also a process of understanding the basic symbol system of society. As Rodney Needham puts it, he is acquiring "the meaning of terms such as 'space' and 'shape'." Therefore, we can also say that classification is a process of systematizing symbols such as language, art, behavior, and law. Society has a tendency to arrange things, phenomena, and behaviors in order. Nigel Rapport and Joanna Overing also emphasize the importance of classification in their book *Social and Cultural Anthropology: The Key Concepts*:

> The human practice of classifying the world into distinct objects and relations is a cognitive accomplishment: the means by which human beings create order and identity in an environment, making it sociocultural. It also embodies a paradox and tension. Classification is the activity of assigning people, things, concepts, relationships, forces and so on to different categories; human beings are perhaps unique among animals for the extent to which they manipulate the physical realities of their environs in terms of the categories they impose upon them and for the extent to which they depend upon such creative cognitive manipulations for the procuring of a stable environment in which to live. Classification is essential to our human ability to think about and know the world and to think about and know our own space and that of our activities within it. At the same time, as our classifying the world empowers us to act and to know, however, it also limits us because what we can know, what we anticipate, recognize, and intend, and regard as orderly and work towards, are in a way pregiven by classificatory schemata that we are employing.

5.2 Classification and Law

Human beings use classification to weave a huge web, on which people, things, phenomena, and meanings have their own place. Believing, with Max Weber, that

[3] This paragraph is from Rodney Needham's introduction to his translation of *Primitive Classification* by Emile Durkheim and Marcel Mauss.

man is an animal suspended in webs of significance he himself has spun, Clifford Geertz takes culture to be those webs (Geertz, 1973, p. 5). Classification is crucial to the weaving of these webs of significance. Without classification, how could we know where meanings should be placed? How could we make meanings into a web of significance?

Therefore, what is the relationship between classification and law?

My view is that if law is regarded as culture, classification is the core of the law, and the formation of a legal system is a process of classifying. Regarding the relationship between classification and law, Mr. Qu Tongzu points out in a case study of laws in imperial China:

> From the discussion in the above chapters, we can draw the conclusion that family and social classes were at the heart of laws in imperial China... In imperial China, the practice of concealing crimes of relatives was legitimized and the execution of a death or exile sentence could be delayed if a criminal was the only male bread-earner in the family and his parents were old or sick so that the criminal could stay at home to tend his parents. Apparently, the legal system in ancient China attached great importance to family ethics.
>
> The law of imperial China also recognized the different social statuses of nobles, bureaucrats, civilians and pariahs.
>
> The law attached great importance to identity. There were many provisions in relation to kinship and social status. These special provisions took precedence over general provisions. General provisions were employed only in situations where special provisions did not apply.
>
> The reason why the law placed special emphasis on kinship and social status is the strong influence of Confucianism. According to the moral code of Confucianism, family and social status are at the core of li (rites) and pillars of social order. It can be said that the law in imperial China was built upon the moral code of Confucianism. (Qu, 1998, p. 359)

Mr. Qu argues that the moral code of Confucianism had been at the heart of the law of imperial China since Confucianism became the mainstream ideology.[4] The complex legal system of imperial China was built around Confucian ethics.

How does Confucianism define *li* then? "The ideal social order advocated by Confucianism is molded around relationships that determine people's position with each other. Confucianism requires people to act in a way that is suitable for their social status and identities. *Li* is a concept that entails different rules of proper behavior for different social classes." "*Li* is a content-rich concept. It encompasses a wide range of human behaviors and state activities." (Qu, 1998, pp. 383–384) It, in fact, is a complex classification system involving people, social identities, and rules of proper behaviors. Only behaviors covered by this classification system fit into the ideal social order advocated by Confucianism. After Confucianism became the guiding ideology in the shaping of law, only acts covered by this classificatory schema were considered legal.

"The ideal social order advocated by Confucianism cannot be established and maintained without wide social acceptance of *li*." (Qu, 1998, p. 385) When *li* as a classificatory schema was accepted and internalized by society and became social

---

[4] Mr. Qu points out that Confucianism became the guiding ideology in the shaping of law in the Han Dynasty, but systematic modification of law in according with the thoughts of Confucianism began in the Cao-Wei Dynasty (Qu, 1998, p. 361–381).

norms, the ideal social order emerged. When *li* infiltrated into the law of imperial China, this classificatory schema became the logic of the law.

Li, the all-encompassing classification system of social identities and human behavior, replaced the classificatory schema of legalists to become the logic of law in imperial China. Chinese people were suspended in the massive web of significance (i.e., law) built upon the moral code of Confucianism for more than 1000 years.

Contemporary law, which is primarily a creation of ruling elites and legal experts (Cotterrell, 1992, p. 45), is also a massive classification system despite its striking difference from ancient Chinese law in content and form.

Before setting out to make law, the legislator must first identify exactly what this law is designed to handle and the scope of law. The legislator should first answer questions such as whether social issues such adultery should be solved by law, whether it is necessary to legalize euthanasia, and what issue falls under which branch of law. For example, if it is decided that adultery should be governed by law, then should the law handling adultery be classified into criminal or civil law? Issues governed by the same law must also be classified as necessary. For example, should the trafficking of women and the trafficking of children be distinguished under the law or combined into one crime, "trafficking of women or children"? In addition to the classification of behavior, the law also classifies people. It determines, for example, who has the qualifications to establish a company, who the anti-corruption law should apply to, and who may be defined as dependents and providers.

In short, law making is a process of constructing a classification system. It involves the classification of law branches, social relations, social issues, evidence, behavior, severity of violations, and so on. The process puts every element (event, relation, etc.) that the legislator considers should be dealt with by law in a proper place under the law, thereby establishing, although only in written form, the ideal normative order envisioned by the legislator. This kind of ideal normative order is a manifestation of the legislator's social classification views in the law.

5.3 Why is Law Deemed Local Knowledge?

Clifford Geertz, whose work is almost impossible to understand, believes law is local knowledge. He writes:

> Law, I have been saying, somewhat against the pretensions encoded in woolsack rhetoric, is local knowledge; local not just as to place, time, class, and variety of issue, but as to accent-vernacular characterizations of what happens connected to vernacular imaginings of what can. It is this complex of characterizations and imaginings, stories about events cast in imagery about principles, that I have been calling a legal sensibility.

If we treat the law as a classification system that arranges the order of things, behaviors, and meanings as previously discussed, then it may be easier to understand this passage written by Geertz.

Michel Foucault points out in his work *Nietszche, Freud, Marx* that there is a self-explanatory system in every culture (Sakurai, 2001, p. 107), and the classification system is a coproduct of many social factors or a local knowledge system (Foucault, 2001). It can be said that every society and every culture have its own different classification system, which inevitably leads to legal pluralism-local knowledge in pluralistic forms.

To the international community, the laws of each country could be considered local knowledge—the kind of local knowledge applied in a larger jurisdiction with higher authority. Lawmaking in each country is a process of classifying legal phenomena in the country. The classification views of the legislator are reflected in the text of law or the legal system. For example, the ancient Chinese legal system mentioned above undoubtedly demonstrates unique Chinese characteristics; the American judicial system has a "U.S." written all over it. However, in modern times, some countries, especially some developing countries, have borrowed extensive laws and classification systems from other countries. This kind of legal transplant leads to the weakening or loss of local characteristics of their national legal systems.[5]

The local characterizations of law are best demonstrated in local norms. Therefore, to demonstrate my point in a clear and vivid way, I will take an ethnographic approach in the discussion below.

Case 1: A Taboo in Mancun Village[6]

Mancun Village is a village of the Dai people in Xishuangbanna. There is a taboo in this area: if a resident of a village dies, people outside the village are not allowed to enter the village before his/her burial. Otherwise, the offender will be punished by *zhao man*. The penalty is a fine of fifteen yuan plus one chicken, ten packages of glutinous rice, and two sticks of candles that will be used in rituals to show respect for the Heart of Village or the God of Village.[7] An old man surnamed Yu in Mancun Village died at 9:00 a.m. on January 20, 2000. The village chief informed the villagers of his death through the village's broadcasting system. Yu's family members immediately set out to informed relatives. Yan, who was Yu's grandson-in-law, drove a motorcycle to the home of a family approximately 20 km away from Mancun Village, although he did not have a motorcycle license. To avoid being caught by traffic police, Yan detoured. When he passed Duancun Village, he was stopped by a villager who asked for a fine of 12 yuan for violation of the local taboo. Yan refused to pay the fine and continued to head to Menghun, where the relative lived. Later, Duancun Village asked Mancun Village to pay a fine of 500 yuan. This incident escalated into a dispute between the two villages. On January 27, the Mancun village chief convened cadres of the village party committee, party members, *zhao man*, and

---

[5] As De Soto puts it, developing countries have "plagiarized" the laws (property right law) of western capitalist countries, but in fact they do not know what kind of law they really need. The laws transplanted do not meet the economic needs in the third world (De Soto, 2000).

[6] This case study is based on the findings of fieldwork I participated in 2000. The field research project was headed by Professor Zhang Xiaohui of the Law School of Yunnan University. Other participants included Professor Xu Zhongqi, Dr. Zhang Liming, Mr. Chao Jianhua, and Ms. Liu Hong.

[7] *Zhao man* is responsible for presiding over primitive religious activities in a Dai village in Xishuangbanna, including caring for the Heart of Village and organizing religious rituals.

bu zhang to discuss how to handle the issue.[8] At 8:30 a.m. On January 28, a team made up by the village chief, Yan, cadres of the village party committee, a number of party members, two *zhao man*, *bu zhang*, and the chief accountant of the village affairs office of Mancun Village went to Duancun Village to negotiate. The negotiation team of Duancun Village was also composed of cadres of their village party committees, party members, *zhao man*, and *bu zhang*. The negotiation lasted nearly two hours. In addition to the fine imposed on Yan, Duancun Village imposed a fine of 500 yuan on Mancun Village, whereas Mancun Village, although agreeing with the fine on Yan, insisted that Duancun Village had no reason to fine Mancun Village. However, Duancun Village did not budge. The representatives of Mancun Village presented the cemetery shared by Duancun Village, Mancun Village, and Manen Village (known as *long lin* among the local people and located in Mancun Village) as a bargaining counter. Mancun Village proposed, if Mancun Village accepted the terms proposed by Duancun Village, then (i) Duancun Village should pay 1,000 yuan to Mancun Village for each body from Duancun Village cremated in *long lin* in the future; (ii) If a resident of Duancun Village passed away, any person of Duancun Village entering Mancun Village before the deceased is buried would be fined 1,000 yuan; and (iii) Duancun Village must return the land (four *mu*, Mancun Village's property) occupied by its Theravada Buddhist temple (a local tourist attraction) and the adjacent park lot and other buildings belonging to Duancun Village. These bargaining chips turned out to be quite useful. Between immediate and long-term interests, Duancun Village chose long-term interests. In the end, the dispute ended with only Yan being fined fifteen yuan plus one chicken, ten packages of glutinous rice, and two candles.

As seen from this case, entry prohibition is part of the local knowledge system. This is a religious taboo of the Dai people. They believe that such behavior violates the village god and will cost the villagers the god's blessings. The punishment for offenders is overseen by *Zhao man,* who are persons ordained to officiate religious ceremonies in the village. The penalty—fifteen yuan, one chicken, ten packages of glutinous rice, and two candles—is of symbolic significance to the Dai people. They believe that to regain the favor of the offended God, the offender must offer sacrifice to the Heart of Village and the God of Village. The causation and resolution of this dispute are undoubtedly indigenous.

This taboo is part of local knowledge. Its emergence is closely related to the local classification system. It is not possible for this sort of taboo and dispute to emerge in other areas where things such as death, village, chicken, the God, and cemetery are unrelated.

In another ethnographic study of law, the author writes:

> The customary law of Hua Dai (a subgroup of the Dai people) and contemporary Chinese law conflict with each other. Some acts considered crimes under contemporary Chinese law are not crimes under the customary law of Hua Dai. The differences are generally closely related to the means of production, lifestyle and religion of Hua Dai. For example, deforestation for farming purposes is tolerated by the customary law of Hua Dai but considered a crime under state law. For another example, according to China's state law, it is a criminal offense

[8] *Bu zhang* is responsible for supervising *fo ye* in a Dai village, and concurrently serves as the witch doctor of the village.

for anyone to have any kind of sexual contact with a girl under the age of 14. However, in the society of Hua Dai, the rites of passage into adulthood are held at the age of 12 or 14. Girls and boys who have held rites of passage are allowed to marry and have children. Therefore, underage sexual activity is considered acceptable in the society of Hua Dai. Regarding religious beliefs, the Hua Dai people believe in the existence of ghosts. Villagers will seize the property of people who are identified as *pi pa* ghosts (one category of ghosts in the culture of Hua Dai), evict them from the village or even assault or kill them. Such acts (trespass on property, damage to property of others, assault, battery, and homicide) are all considered criminal offenses under in the current law in China. The Hua Dai people believe such acts are justified because *pi pa* ghosts would bring harm to the village, and villagers who do not participate in this sort of exorcism rite (which usually involves collective violence) will be condemned.[9]

The aforementioned study shows that the justice views of the Hua Dai people are closely related to the local classification system, which is deeply rooted in the daily life of the ethnic group.

The Yi people living in Liangshan and Zhongdian in Yunnan also have their own customary legal system, which is built on their unique classification system:

Case 2: Customary Law and Classification System of the Yi People

To many of us, black and white are just two colors. However, for the Yi people living in Liangshan and Zhongdian in Yunnan, black and white were once used to refer to two castes. The caste system divides the Yi people into Black Yi (Hei Yi) and White Yi (Bai Yi).[10]The color classification system has evolved into a social classification system in the Yi community. Black, white, and hua are three words used to refer to the severity of an offense under the customary law of the Yi people. Ethnographer Lu Yumin writes: "The customary law of the Yi people living in Liangshan and Zhongdian uses 'black', 'hua' and 'white' to refer to the severity of an offense... For example, if a Black Yi woman has sexual contact, whether forced or consensual, with a commoner or slave, she would be considered to have engaged in adultery of the most serious nature, known as "black" adultery, and both the woman and the man engaging in black adultery will be sentenced to death; extramarital affair between a man and a woman, one of which is married to another person, from the same family clan would also be considered as "black" adultery... Sexual contact between cousins, both of whom are not married to another person, is considered a "hua" offense... Sexual contact between a male slave owner and a female slave is considered "white", but the male master will be subject to public humiliation or ridicule..." (Lu, 1986, p. 216) The black, white, and hua system is the most basic offense classification system. The offense classification systems of some Yi communities are much more complex. For example, some scholars believe that the customary law of the Yi community in

[9] In the article, the author points out that Hua Dai is an important branch of the Dai people living in Xinping County and Yuanjiang County of Yunnan Province, mainly in small valleys in the upper reaches of the Red River. The Hua Dai people are further divided into four sub-branches: Daiya, Daisa, Daika, and Daizhong. The language, culture, costumes, and architecture of the four sub-branches are similar (Yang, 2003).

[10] The Yi people that adhered to the white and black caste system were mainly distributed in Sichuan, Yunnan and Guizhou (You, 2001, pp. 373–374).

Liangshan divides criminal offenses and civil disputes into four severity levels and twelve categories. Based on severity, offenses are divided into "black", "hua-black", "hua-white", and "white", with "black" being the most serious and "white" being the least serious (Hainailamo & Liu, 1998, pp. 23–24). Punishment is determined based on the seriousness of the offense.

In Yi society, people employed the color classification schema in law practice. They associated colors with the severity of offenses.[11] I don't know how this unique offense classification schema was produced. However, one thing is certain: it is a unique cultural phenomenon in Yi society.[12]

Classifications of people, social relations, and social phenomena evolve over time. The development of customary and statutory law is a manifestation of 'the evolution of the social classification in a society. As a society applies its social classification system to the legal field, the legal system is gradually perfected. Differences in living environment, culture, and mentality lead to different classification systems and legal systems. The law exists and operates in the form of local knowledge; different societies have different laws.

5.4 An Interpretation of Conflicts Between Local Norms and State Law

People may experience cultural shock when they visit another place. For example, if we visit Mancun Village, we will be puzzled by their customs and may even offend the villagers because of ignorance. Conflicts may arise from differences in local knowledge or legal systems. Regarding conflicts of laws, there is so much to

---

[11] For more information on the use of colors to distinguish the severity of offenses in the Yi society, see Hainailamo et al. (1998, p. 23–34), Zhou (1998), and Zhang and Fang (2005, p. 295–302).

[12] Dr. Mujeer of the Anthropology Department at Yunnan University writes: "The offense severity scale is not directly related to the classification of Black Yi and White Yi. The former is a trichotomy and the latter is a dichotomy. For example, rape can be divided into three levels: black, hua and white. Even the same offense can be divided into black, *hua* and white based on the offender's attitude and the degree of intentionality. The offense severity scale is very flexible. It is not a codified rule. As for why black is the most serious, white the least serious, and *hua* in-between, there has been no widely accepted conclusion so far. I personally believe that this is related to the primitive religion of the Yi people. The Yi people believe there are three paths in afterlife, the black path leading to the hell, the yellow one leading to the land of spirits, and the white one leading to the ancestral land. As for the caste system, different scholars have different interpretations because the language of the Yi people is different from that of the Han people. In fact, Black Yi and *nuo* (the noble class in the Yi language) are not fully equivalent. Neither are White Yi and *qu nuo* (the commoner in the Yi language). Furthermore, the caste system of the Yi people appeared after the Yuan Dynasty whereas the offense severity scale appeared much earlier than the caste system. Therefore, the influence of the caste system on the offense severity classification is disputable. The symbolic meanings of black (sins or devils), white (goodness), and hua/yellow (evilness) may have their roots in the primitive religion of the Yi people. In fact, white offenses refer to offenses that are not committed intentionally. That is, lack of bad intention is good.".

be discussed, but it is not the focus of this chapter. The focus of this chapter is the conflict between local norms and state law.

Roger Cotterrell points out that the majority of the general public does not understand the large part of the legislation, and many people do not even know the existence of some laws (Cotterrell, 1992, p. 45). This is a major contributor to the conflict between local norms and state law. Whether in Western society or China, modern law is mainly the creation of ruling elites and legal experts. Modern law is a manifestation of the classification views of elites who rule the legal life (rather than social life) of the state regardless of whether their classification views are derived from their own experience, the study of legal profession, or foreign legal systems. In short, this large and exquisite classification system is no longer part of a particular local knowledge system. Conflict may arise due to the difference between local culture and the mainstream culture of a country. Let us look at the findings of some ethnographic studies on ethnic minorities:

Case 3: *Pi pa*Ghosts[13]

There was an old widow in Mancun Village who was rumored to be a *pi pa* ghost and to have sent out ghosts to hurt people. Many people from the neighboring village, it was alleged, had been victims. In 1998, a resident of a neighboring village (Village B) who had been ill died, and residents of Village B blamed this *pi pa* ghost of Mancun Village for death. As a result, dozens of residents of Village B went to Mancun Village, destroyed the old woman's house and beat her up, which resulted in injuries. Not only did the other residents of Mancun Village do nothing to intervene, they did not even consider such action either unlawful or harmful to Mancun. In fact, they believed the old woman deserved it. In the end, when all other options ran out, the residents of Mancun Village built a bamboo hut in the bamboo forest by the sid of the road for the old woman to live in. Since then, this 80-plus-year-old woman has lived in isolation. When I visited her in February 2000, she had lost her sight and hearing.

On February 14, 2000, a few days before I was scheduled to leave Mancun Village, another "expulsion" event broke out. The house of a woman in a different neighboring village (Village C) accused of being a *pi pa* ghost was destroyed by other village residents who threw bricks and stones at it. Both the woman and her husband were chased out of the village. Later, faced with the other residents' refusal to let the couple return to the village, the county government resorted to offering them to settle down near a reservoir far away from Village C and to work as reservoir watchmen.

At the beginning of 2000, there were several similar violent incidents in Xishuangbanna.

For a long time, I was unable to make sense of these incidents. On the one hand, I found that most Dai people generally quite friendly and gentle in nature and that their culture was rich and fascinating. On the other hand, their cruelty towards those rumored to be *pi pa* ghost were seared into my memory. I balked at drawing the simplistic conclusion, either on the emotional or the rational level, that the residents

---

[13] This case study is based on the findings of my field research in 2000.

of Mancun Village or the Dai people are cruel and ruthless in nature, or that they are ignorant and superstitious. My conflicting emotions about the Dai people propelled me to pursue the underlying causes of these violent incidents.

In addition to Theravada Buddhism, the Dai people have their own primitive religion and generally believe in the existence of spirits. The residents of Mancun Village believe that there are seven kinds of ghosts, namely, *pi ya* (devil), *pi bao* (*pi pa* ghost) s, *pi ga* (flying ghosts that are more fearsome than *pi pa*), *pi she* (the ghosts of drowned prisoners), *pi hong* (ghosts of persons who die in tragic accidents), *pi wang* (collective term used to refer to the group of ghosts in the village), and *pi meng* (collective term used to refer to the group of ghosts in the entire settlement area). *Pi pa* ghosts are believed to be one of the most difficult to expel. *Bu zhang* of Mancun Village once told me that[14] he could expel four kinds of ghosts in addition to *pi ya, pi bao* and *pi ga.* In fact, the intense animosity toward *pi pa* ghosts has its root in the ethnic group's primitive religion. The Dai people believe *pi pa* ghosts are no longer human, so in harming them, they are not harming a person but are performing a ritual. Both real-life practices and folk tales of the Dai people (Yan & Yan, 1981) show that the social classification schema of the Dai people classifies persons who are considered to be *pi pa* as ghosts, which explains why moral norms do not apply to whatever is done to them. If anything, exorcising the *pi pa* ghosts is justified, righteous and necessary. What we may think of as cruelty, therefore, is, from their point of view, perfectly reasonable.

Of course, there are underlying causes behind the Dai people's belief in ghosts. Studies have revealed that there is a connection between the Dai people's practice of classifying certain people into the ghost category and the real-world social problems they are faced with. Mr. Wang Lianfang, a senior government official overseeing matters related to ethnic minorities, recalled, "Expelling *pi pa* ghosts was considered by the Dai people as a way to rid themselves of disease.... They believed disease was brought by *pi pa.* After the medical team treated many patients whom local people believed were bitten by *pi pa* ghosts. After the recovery of these patients, rumors were circulating that the Communist Party could save the people who were bitten by *pi pa.* Patients who used to believe only prayers by the Buddha began to come to us for medical care. The movie *Moyatai* in the 1960s was based on a true story." (Wang, 1998). Indeed, in the past, many Dai people believed their disease was brought by *pi pa* ghosts, and the only way to cure disease was to expel ghosts. This belief reduced their panic and anxiety over incurable or unexplainable disease, making them believe that life is still under control. Obviously, their belief in the rite of exorcism was derived from their confusion and helplessness in the face of disease. Therefore, before the establishment of a modern medical system in the 1960s, exorcism was a common practice in the settlement areas of ethnic minorities such as the Yi people.[15] After access to essential medicines was improved, cases of exorcism began to decrease.

[14] *Bu zhang* is a monk who acts as a chanter in a Buddhist temple and concurrently serves as medicine man in a Dai village and is believed to have the ability to expel ghosts, demons or other spiritual entities.

[15] For example, the "War Against Smallpox" episode of *Exploration and Discovery* broadcast by CCTV10 on the evening of May 4, 2005 also illustrates this point. In the 1950s and 1960s, there

However, in the past 20 years, the lack of access to health care in rural areas near the southern border has led to the resurgence of the exorcism rite in the settlement areas of ethnic minorities.[16] It is not difficult to understand that people, tormented by illness, try to look for comfort in supernatural beliefs.[17]

Studying the classification systems and culture of the Dai people from the outsider's point of view is conducive to objective and detached observation of a culture different from ours. Although we can understand that the expulsion of *pi pa* ghosts has its roots in the culture of the Dai community, we cannot deny the cruelty behind this practice. The outsider's point of view is also conducive to the identification of the root cause of the problem—we aim to find answers to problems rather than cast the entire culture of the ethnic group in a negative light. Only in this way can we find a solution to conflicts of law or culture of this sort. Simply attributing all problems to feudalism, superstition, and ignorance is not helpful. We should identify the root causes of conflicts by pinpointing problems in the classification system as part of a local knowledge system and find a solution to problems by changing or improving the local classification system.[18] For example, the *pi pa* ghost exorcism

---

were still no effective smallpox control measures in Yunnan Province. Local people didn't know how to cure the disease. They could only regard it as test coming from the God. Such supernatural beliefs led to the rise of exorcism rituals. After the medical team sent by the Communist Party brought the smallpox vaccine to Yunnan, exorcism rituals disappeared with smallpox.

[16] Information on health care in the settlement areas of ethnic minorities.

[17] Bronislaw Malinowski believes the insecurity and uncertainty caused by uncontrollable happenings are the fundamental causes for the emergence of religious faith and supernatural beliefs (Malinowski, 2002, p. 340–367). The resurgence of exorcism rituals was fueled by fear and anxiety caused by the lack of access to the modern health care system. Qu (1999) writes in *the Ever-Changing Religious Landscape in the Modern Society of the Dai People in Xishuangbanna:* "In the past, the Dai people often drove people who were believed to be possessed by evil *pi bao* ghosts out of village. This custom has basically died out due to a ban imposed by the government. Although many Dai people are still afraid of *pi bao* ghosts, they no longer treat people who are considered to be possessed by *pi bao* with cruelty. People from other villages are allowed to marry people from villages once 'haunted" by *pi bao*." He also writes:"The above facts show that, as a result of the interaction between various internal and external factors, including the government's democratic reform efforts in the past several decades, it is impossible for the primitive religion of the Dai people in Xishuangbanna to return to its former glory. Their primitive beliefs are weakening." (Qu, 1999) The conclusion I draw from my field research in Mancun Village is the opposite of Mr. Qu's conclusion. I believe primitive religions, although weakening, remain important knowledge that guides people's behaviors, and *pi bao* ghosts still exist in people's mind. The reason why the primitive religion is weakening is because the external environment has become increasingly diversified in terms of culture and the knowledge system has become more complicated. As a result, the status of primitive religion in the residents' daily life is not as prominent as before. But when the society is once again faced with unsolvable problems, members of the society will once again seek comfort in supernatural beliefs and thus the primitive religion will regain force.

[18] Some scholars believe that: "In the settlement areas of ethnic minorities, due to the lack of advanced science, superstitious practices are common and have led to many cases of intentional assault and voluntary manslaughter. Some communities of ethnic minority groups, such as the Miao community in Rongjiang County of Guizhou Province and the Dai community in Jinghong County of Yunnan Province, believe in supernatural existences such as *gu*, ghosts, and *long mai* (a dragon's vein). People who are believed to have released *gu,* or be haunted by ghosts, or have damaged *long mai* will be treated by residents with contempt. There are cases where such people were

rites become obsolete in the Dai community because their access to modern health care has improved. Of course, this solution depends first and foremost on people's interpretation of phenomena. If Mr. Wang Lianfang and his colleagues did not adopt a modest and pragmatic attitude, they would not be able to identify the root cause of the problem, let alone take appropriate measures to solve it. Using forceful means would only exacerbate the problem. However, the event that took place in Xishuangbanna in 2000 showed that officials did not find the crux of the problem and that the system was in trouble.

There are two more cases worth mentioning:

Before the liberation, the Yi people and the Blang people in Xishuangbanna regarded elephants as divine creatures and did not dare to hunt them. However, after the famous documentary *Capture of Elephant* (*bu xiang ji*) filmed in Xishuangbanna was released, they no longer thought harming elephants would bring misfortune and began to hunt elephants (Zhang & Wang, 2002).

In this case, in the classification system of the Yi and Blang ethnic groups before the founding of the People's Republic of China, elephants belonged to the category of divine existences with supernatural power, so the Yi and Blang people did not dare to hunt them. However, the compelling documentary where the elephant was killed but the person who killed the elephant was not punished by the god completely changed the position of elephants in the two ethnic groups' classification systems. Elephants were no longer treated as divine animals and became targets for hunting. This change cost the state expensively because the state was forced to take legal measures to crack down on elephant hunting. This case shows that local knowledge is not cast in stone. The classification system of a society and the way of thinking are changeable-it may only take one movie. The key question is whether they are changing for the better or the worse.

The above case is an example of an unexpected change in the local knowledge system leading to unwanted consequences. The following case shows the positive side of changes in local knowledge.

Case 4: The Tree Planting Project in Mannalan Village

In 1999, the Xishuangbanna Nature Reserve Administration launched a tree plant project ("Grow Up with the Tree I Plant") with a grant from the UNEP-GEF Project. The project not only achieved the purpose of protecting the forest but also allowed the Hani people to preserve their burial custom. The Hani people conventionally use Paramichelia baillonii to make coffins, and one tree can only be used to make one

assaulted or even killed by residents…Therefore, criminal law should divide intentional killings and intentional injuries into several categories (for example, intentional killings/injuries driven by superstitions or intentional killings/injuries driven by conflicts between ethnic groups) and stipulate punishment for each category of criminal offenses. For example, punishment of intentional killing/assault driven by superstition or conflicts between ethnic groups should be lighter than aggravated manslaughter/assault…" (Liang & Shi, 2001). These scholars of course take note of the particularity of ethnic minorities and attempt to solve the problem by adjusting state law. However, I believe changing state law cannot fundamentally solve conflicts between local norms and state law.

coffin. Paramichelia baillonii is a state-listed species and can only be found deep in the mountains of the reserve. The Hani people living in this area often disregard the law and cut down Paramichelia baillonii in the nature reserve, posing a major challenge to the Nature Reserve Administration Bureau. To protect Paramichelia baillonii in the conservation area and help the Hani people preserve their burial customs, with support from the UNEP-GEF Project, the village launched a tree planting project. Each schoolchild living in the village was asked to plant a Paramichelia baillonii tree in a land plot of 60 mu on a barren hill and put a name plate on the tree. More than 400 trees planted in 1999 survived, and the children involved also became more aware of the importance of forests through this project. (Zhang & Wang, 2003).

The project not only protects Paramichelia baillonii trees in the reserve but also helps the Hani people preserve their burial customs and improve the environment. This case also shows that local classification systems are changeable, or there could be communications between formal state institutions and a local classification system. The state could leverage local customs in a creative way to facilitate social changes. However, the premise of this change, communication, or leverage is to show respect for local knowledge and to gain insight into local classification systems. Imagine what would happen if the Nature Reserve Administration Bureau imposed a fine on Hani people who harvested Paramichelia baillonii or handed them over to the judiciary. I think it would only lead to conflicts and there would be an increase in the cost of law enforcement and unnecessary lawsuits.

Military strategists say psychological warfare is superior to any other type of warfare. Similarly, the key to resolving the conflict between state law and local norms is not to suppress either side by force but to facilitate communications between, or change of either of, the two different classification systems-state law and local norms. Legislators, law enforcers, and local officials must suspend condescending judgments to understand local norms. It would be much better to treat conflicts of law in a modest and pragmatic manner and pinpoint the crux of the problem, either in state law or local knowledge or both.

5.5 Conclusion

Modern state laws and local norms are classification systems designed to solve real-world problems. However, the two classification systems have huge differences. Local social norms, as a classification system, encompass a wide range of nontechnical content, including local people's way of thinking, worldviews, attitudes towards divine existences, imagination of the universe, and way to interact with others, similar to the abovementioned nonentering taboo in Dai village. This taboo has its root in the Dai people's belief in divine existences. By contrast, state law is a classification system that is considered to be rationally constructed. This system also contains values, such as "justice" and "human happiness". However, the values and meanings expressed and contained in state law are abstract concepts to the public. State law is a general, more technical classification system that does not encompass thoughts on the meaning of life, worldviews and so on. On this huge and exquisite website, there is no place reserved for local knowledge and worldviews.

Therefore, diversity is important for people who do not wish the world to have only one language, men to smoke the same brand of cigarettes, women to wear the same kind of clothing, or children to play the same toys. Likewise, for those who are unwilling to use law only as a tool and for those who hope to live in a world with diverse values and worldviews, recognition of legal pluralism is necessary—local norms could provide values and worldviews that are not encompassed in state law. For those who work to promote the rule of law, the key question is not how to eliminate the difference between normative orders (between state law and local norms or between local norms) but how to deal with the difference because normative orders are modifiable and coordination between the two is possible.

By analyzing and studying law as a classification system, we are trying to explain law and real-world problems in a more versatile manner instead of simply using the paradigm of state law to judge informal social norms or attributing all diverse social and legal phenomena to conflicts between informal norms and state law. Before setting out to handle differences and conflicts, we must be aware of the complex factors behind differences and conflicts. Emile Durkheim writes: "Logicians and even psychologists commonly regard the procedure which consists in classifying things, events, and facts about the world into kinds and species, subsuming them one under the other, and determining their relations of inclusion or exclusion, as being simple…" (Durkheim & Mauss, 2005, p. 2) Based on Durkheim's view, in addition to handling differences, more importantly, state law must effectively and reasonably distinguish between areas and interests, such as common areas/discrete areas, public domain/private sector, and public interest/personal interests. Only in this way can we reduce the conflicts caused by differences while preserving cultural diversity and establishing a unified normative order.

When seeing law as a classification system, we adopt a relatively value-neutral methodology to avoid a priori assumptions of overstating the importance of law (both state law and local norms) or understating its rationality. Value neutrality is crucial for comparative research.[19]

While any law is designed to solve specific problems, the world we live in is fraught with problems. Every discourse has boundaries, and any explanation is just one among many. There is no master key in the academic world. Classification is only one of the many discourses, explanations, and keys. Thus, it depends on you to decide which key to use and to answer the question "what is law".

---

[19] As Geertz says, "it is unacceptable to think that law is only a tool, indicating that law concerns only means rather than ends and that law is only a simple agency to realize social values, which are set elsewhere—probably in religion, or in philosophy, or designed by ordinary people."

Of course, adoption of this research pathway often means that the researcher is also one of those supporting legal pluralism.

References

Black, D. J. (1994). *The behavior of Law* (Y. Tang & L. Su, Trans.). China University of Political Science and Law Press.

Bodenheimer, E. (1999). *Jurisprudence: The philosophy and method of the law* (D. Zhenglai, Trans.). China University of Political Science and Law Press.

Cotterrell, R. (1992). *The Sociology of law: An introduction.* Butterworths.

De Soto, H. (2000). the mystery of capital, why capitalism triumphs in the west and fails everywhere else. Black Swan.

Durkheim, E. & Mauss, M. (2005). *Primitive Classification* (Z. Ji, Trans.). Shanghai Century Publishing Group.

Fei Xiaotong. (1998). *From the soil and institutions for reproduction.* Peking University Press.

Foucault, M. (2001). *The order of things: An archaeology of the human sciences* (W. Mo, Trans.). Shanghai Sanlian Publishing House.

Geertz, C. (1973). *The interpretation of culture.* Basic Books.

Hainailamo, Q., & Liu, Y. (1998). *Customary laws of the Yi Community in Liangshan—Case Study.* Yunnan People's Publishing House.

Liang, H. & Shi, Y. (2001). On the Adaptation of Criminal Law in Settlement Areas of Ethnic Minorities. *Tribune of Political Science and Law, 2.*

Lu, Y. (1986). Field survey of the Yi Community in Zhongdian. In Yunnan Editorial Group. *History of the Yi People in Sichuan, Guangxi, and Yunnan.* Yunnan People's Publishing House.

Malinowski, B. (2002). *Crime and custom in savage society* (J. Y, Trans.). Yunnan Shandong People's Publishing House.

Needham, R. (2005). Introduction. In *Primitive Classification*, by Emile Durkheim & Marcel Mauss (Z. Ji, Trans.). Shanghai Century Publishing Group.

Popenoe, D. (1999). *Sociology.* China Renmin University Press.

Qu, T. (1998). *Collection of Jurisprudence works by Qu Tongzu.* China University of Political Science and Law Press.

Qu, M. (1999). The ever-changing religious landscape in the modern society of the Dai People in Xishuangbanna. *Studies in World Religions 1*

Sakurai, T. (2001). *Foucault: knowledge and power* (Z. Jiang, Trans.). Hebei Education Press.

Santos, Boaventura de Sousa. (1987). Law: a map of misreading. Toward a postmodern conception of law. *Journal of Law and Society 14*(3).

Su, L. (1996). *The rule of law in the Chinese context.* China University of Political Science and Law Press.

Su, L. (1999). *Interpreting order.* Shandong People's Publishing House.

Wang, L. (1998). Wang Lianfang's memoirs on his work related to Ethnic Affairs (Part 7). *Ethnic Relations 2.*

Yan, W. & Yan, W. (Eds.). (1981). The origin of Pi Pa Ghosts. *Ban Na 2.*

Yang, L. (2003). Genealogical study of reciprocity in anthropology. *Guangxi Ethnics Studies 4.*

You, Z. (2001). *Ethnic history of Yunnan.* Yunnan University Press.

Zhang, X. & Wang, Q. (2002). Environmental protection in ethnic minority autonomous areas—a case study of Xishuangbanna Dai Autonomous Prefecture. *Journal of Southwest Minzu University 7.*

Zhang, X. & Wang, Q. (2003). The interaction between man and nature—environmental protection law and law enforcement in Xishuangbanna Dai Autonomous Prefecture. In Report of China-Norway Regional Ethnic Autonomy System Research Project.

Zhang Xiaohui & Fang Hui (Eds.). (2005). *Legal Culture of the Yi People.* Ethnic Publishing House.

Zhou, X. (1998). Suicide and Liangshan Community. In R. Ma, & X. Zhou (Eds.). *Field work and cultural consciousness (Vol. 2).* Qunyan Press.

Zhuang, K. (Ed.). (2002). *Basic theories of anthropology.* Shanxi People's Publishing House.

Chapter 6
Religion as an Instrument for Social Control and Its Connections with Village-Level Social Order and Law: A Case Study in Mancun Village (I)

> What kind of life and behavior is the "right" or "justified" is determined by the ends of human life. The question "what is justice" is entailed in the question "what is the meaning of human life." In other words, justice is undefinable without first discussing the meaning of origin vs. future and human life vs. death. Here, science cannot provide all the answers. In this sense, law is unavoidably based on religions or worldviews (Rüthers, Bernd. (2003). Rechtstheorie (Ding Xiaochun & Wu Yue, Trans.). Law Press., p. 189).
> —Bernd Rüthers

6.1 Introduction

The reason why we examine religion and law in the context of social order is that both of them are sources of order. Religion and law produce order through the control of people. The difference is that law primarily controls human behaviors, while religion mainly applies psychological control methods.[1] The relationships between religion, law, and order are a question of interest for legal anthropologists and legal sociologists. The inquiry into this question often draws inspiration from several different fields of study. From a sociological or anthropological perspective, religion is considered a subsystem of social order because it binds people together (social cohesion), promotes behavior consistency (social control), and offers mental strength to people (Sun, 2003: 119–154; Li, 1980, pp. 239–246). Religion, family, and law are often regarded as key contributors to social cohesion (Stroup, 1945, pp. 104–110). The multiple dimensions of religion, especially the legal and political dimensions, have never been overlooked (Smart, 1996). The relationship between religion and law is almost an unavoidable problem by every jurisprudential work (Horn, 2005, p. 58). Legal anthropologists and sociologists have also shown interest in connections between religion and law, especially the influence of religion on the operation of law

[1] Another study of mine shows that religion, as one of the sources of values and meaning of life, like all other subjective dimensions of society, provide motivation for human actions and thereby drives actions related to law and social control. (Wang, 2007).

Q. Wang, *Sociology of Law*,
https://doi.org/10.1007/978-981-16-5509-8_6

and dispute resolution (Reynolds, 1994, pp. 433–451). In short, why religion deserves the attention of so many academic fields, especially legal anthropology, may be best explained by the words of Clifford Geertz: "Religion is sociologically interesting not because, as a vulgar positivism would have it, it describes the social order (which, in so far as it does, it does, it does not only very obliquely but very incompletely) but because, like environment, political power, wealth, jural obligation, personal affection, and a sense of beauty, it shapes it." (Geertz, 1999, p. 135) This ability of religion to shape social order is enough to spark the interest of legal theorists. For legal researchers, religion points to faith and faith groups (Horn, 2005, p. 58), but more importantly, it is highly probable that law exists in religion (Rüthers, 2003, p. 189). If we are not discussing "law" in its strict (and narrow) sense as defined by state-centered legal positivists, religion itself is law or a source of law.[2] Therefore, for any society that is not theocratic or has multiple religions, religion will inevitably lead to legal pluralism.[3] Religion thus constitutes another force, other than the law of state, that shapes social order.

The influence of religion on social order has long been noticed by scholars. The explanations for the problem of why religion can shape and influence social order and thus affect the operation of law in the social life of a village are scattered in the literature of multiple fields. As a result, there is a lack of systematic exposition of this subject. This chapter is centered around the case study analysis of Mancun Village, which is a Dai village, and investigates religion from the perspective of social control in its narrow sense. In other words, we will discuss why religion is a form of social control from the perspective of norms, social control agents, and dispute resolution. At the end of this chapter, we will analyze the relationship between religion and local legal culture.[4] I believe that although observation of religion in Mancun Village in isolation can shed light on why religion is a form of social control, it cannot lead to findings regarding whether religion has positive or negative effects on the formation of the village-level social order or what position religion occupies in the village-level social order. Only by putting religion back in the village-level social control system can we determine its influence on the formation of social order in the village. Religion and other social controls, such as village-level political organizations, families, and economy, together constitute the social control system within the village. At the same time, we must also see that in a contemporary society, the social control system of a village is not entirely self-sufficient or closed off from other parts of society. The religion in Mancun Village, like other forms of social control in the village, is

[2] In his study on the history of law, Mr. Liang Zhiping (2003, p.5–8) posits that the religious customary law was a contributor to the pluralistic pattern of law in imperial China.

[3] To put it simply, legal pluralism means the existence of multiple legal systems in a society. According the definition of legal pluralists, the law includes the norms formulated by state institutions and informal norms that govern human conduct. So, the "law" here is a concept of sociology of law and legal anthropology.

[4] The majority of existing studies, such as the studies of Sun and Li mentioned in the introduction, investigate the social control function of religion from the perspective of broad-sense social control. This is an obvious sociological and anthropological approach to religion. The approach adopted in this chapter is more suitable for scholarly interests in norms, control agents, and dispute resolution.

subject to the influence of the state. The law as a formal social control and religion as an informal social control influence each other. Therefore, my study of religion as a social control is carried out in the context of a pluralistic social control system. Of course, Mancun Village cannot represent every village, but the field research in Mancun Village can provide insights into why religion shapes village-level social order and what kind of relationship it might have with the law.

Mancun Village, the subject of my field research, is one of the fourteen natural villages (villager groups) under the villagers committee of Menghai County, Xishuangbanna Dai Autonomous Prefecture, Yunnan Province.[5] In December 2004, there were 96 households in the village with a total population of 511. Located on Kunluo Road, Mancun Village is approximately 10 km from Menghai County. The area is located in a famous grain production area in Xishuangbanna. In 2000, I stayed in the village for one month. In the spring of 2001, I went to Xishuangbanna for another field research project and made a short stay in Mancun Village. In November 2004, I visited Mancun Village for the third time and lived there for over one month (from November to December). In March 2005, I visited Mancun Village for the fourth time and stayed in the village for the short term.[6]

6.2 Religious Beliefs in Mancun Village

Political changes and economic reforms have not weakened the religious beliefs of the residents of Mancun Village. The village has a well-developed belief system that is influenced by Theravada Buddhism and the folk religion of the Dai people, providing the meaning of life and worldviews for the villagers.

In addition to the folk religion of the Dai people, the villagers also believe in Theravada Buddhism. The Theravada Buddhist temple is located at the back of the village. It is the highest building in Mancun Village, overlooking the entire village. The temple is managed by *da fo ye*. *Bu zhang* is responsible for leading worshipers in chants at the temple and supervising *fo ye*. Five of the villagers used to serve as *fo ye* at the temple. After returning to secular life, they are called "*kang langs*" by villagers. *Kang Lang* could marry and have children like other villagers. In the eyes of the villagers, *kang langs* are a group of knowledgeable people. By tradition, all boys of Dai families who believe in Theravada Buddhism, aged between 8 and 18 years, will be sent to a Theravada Buddhist temple and become monks. *Dan fo* is a regular Buddhist ritual during which believers pay homage to Buddha and make donations to a temple. *Dan fo* is divided into *da dan fo* and *xiao dan fo*. *Da dan fo* is usually held on New Year's Day of the Dai calendar, the Gate Closing Festival, and the Gate Opening Festival. *Xiao dan fo* is held twice a month. In addition to collective *dan fo* rituals, individuals can also conduct *dan fo* at any time. *Fo ye* and the monks of the Theravada Buddhist temple are often invited by villagers to chant

[5] The names of places and people in this chapter are all pseudonyms.

[6] Information used in this chapter comes from my field research unless otherwise specified.

healing mantras for patients or perform the rite of exorcism. They also visit homes of the recently departed or *long lin* (cemetery of the village) to recite sutras to help the soul of the departed go to a higher realm. Villagers will tie pieces of cloth that have sutras written on them on *sao zhao* and *sao nan* (which literally means the prince column and the princess column) of their house, which is also part of the end-of-life ritual. *Fo ye* also chant sutras for patients suffering from lingering illness as well as those who are believed to be haunted by ghosts. In addition to these activities, villagers also carry out many other religious activities on festivals, such as the New Year's Day of the Dai calendar, the Gate Closing Festival, and the Gate Opening Festival.

Ancestor worship practices are also prevalent in Mancun Village. Villagers regard their ancestors as gods. Symbols of ancestor gods are omnipresent in villagers' daily lives. They are also all-pervasive in villagers' mind. In Mancun Village and other Dai villages in this area, ancestor gods are divided into three categories: family gods, village gods and regional gods. Family gods are called *diu la hen* in Dai language. The house of every family has an altar where offerings (candles, food, etc.) are made to ancestor-gods. In addition to the altar, other symbols of ancestor gods in their houses include *sao zhao* (symbol of male ancestors, located in the bedroom) and *sao nan* (symbol of female ancestors, located outside the bedroom). Village gods, *diu la man*, are the founding gods of Dai villages. Mancun Village has two village gods. *Zhao man* is the person taking charge of rituals relating to village gods. Mancun Village has two *zhao man*. The altars of village gods are located in the houses of *Zhao man*. The position of *Zhao man* is usually hereditary, but there may be exceptions. *Ning man* refers to the sacrificial ritual for village gods. Mancun Village holds two grand sacrificial rituals for village gods every year, one in June (March in the Dai calendar) and the other in October (June in the Dai calender). For *zhao men*, their family gods (*diu la hen*) and village gods (*diu la man*) are the same. For the other Dai people in Mancun Village, *diu la man* is superior to *diu la hen*. Another important duty of *Zhao man* is to maintain the "Hearts of Village". Mancun Village has two "Hearts". They are wooden piles shaped like male genitals, with a diameter of approximately 20 cm. The bottom is buried in the soil. The exposed part is about 40 cm high. The Hearts are maintained by the two *zhao man*. The sacrificial ritual for the Hearts of Village is held once every three years. The ceremony, hosted by *zhao man*, is usually very magnificent. In addition to *ning man*, a grand sacrificial ceremony for the regional god, which is called *ning meng*, is held once every year in Jingzhen Village. According to residents of Mancun Village, all one hundred villages originally ruled by Jingzhen Tusi will participate in the ceremony. The Dai people also believe in natural deities, such as mountain deities, tree deities, and water deities. These deities are in charge of forces of nature or naturally occurring phenomena. However, nature gods are rarely mentioned in Mancun Village.

The residents of Mancun Village believe in the existence of ghosts. They told me that ghosts are the spirit of the deceased. According to them, ghosts are able to cause a living person to fall ill or even die. They wander around and may even visit the Theravada Buddhist temple. The villagers often used the words "gods" and "ghosts" interchangeably. However, after conducting an investigation, I found that the villagers could clearly distinguish between gods and ghosts. They believe ghosts are "bad", and gods are "good" and protect people. Both *bu zhang* and *fo ye* have the ability to banish ghosts. However, in general, the rite of exorcism is performed by *bu zhang*. It is rarely performed by *fo ye*. Villagers often believe they are haunted by ghosts when they fall ill suddenly or are suffering from a lingering illness. At such times, they will invite *bu zhang* over to banish ghosts at a price of 10 yuan, 20 yuan, or 30 yuan. *Bu zhang* will use divination to gain knowledge of the ghosts haunting the villagers (what types of ghosts, where they are now, etc.) and perform the rite of exorcism accordingly.

Bu zhang are important figures in the discourse of ghosts and exorcism in the society of the Dai people. The primary responsibilities of *bu zhang* are to lead worshipers in chants at the Theravada Buddhist temple, to manage the temple and to supervise and provide help to *fo ye*. Additionally, in the folk religion of the Dai people, *bu zhang* also has the ability to banish ghosts. They serve as the liaison between folk religion and Buddhism, which is why rituals and activities of the two religions are often interlocked in Dai villages.

In fact, in Mancun Village and other Dai villages, after thousands of years of contending, blending and compromise, Theravada Buddhism and the folk religion of the Dai people have influenced and intertwined with each other to such an extent that they are almost indistinguishable from one another. The Dai people have a long history of rice cultivation. Its complex farming customs and culture have been influenced by both Theravada Buddhism and the Dai people's folk religion (Guo, 1998, pp. 105–131; Huang, 1995, pp. 290–307). The influence of Buddhism on Dai society has also manifested in ancestral worship rituals. The purpose of this chapter is not to clarify the relationship between Theravada Buddhism and the folk religion of the Dai people in Mancun Village but to discover the relationship between religion as social control, village-level social order, and law.

6.3 Religion as an Instrument for Social Control

6.3.1 The Emergence of Religion and Norms

Why religion deserves a place in discussion of law and social order is that it is a social activity (Ikeda & Wilson, 2003, p. 138). Religion is a term used to describe a group's way of thinking and life. Religious norms indicate what kind of behavior should be displayed. Religion at least produces or influences (i) norms in relation to religious doctrines, rituals, communities, organizations and places and (ii) norms related to the daily life of adherents.

Religious norms arise from the needs of a faith-based group to uphold doctrines or creeds, explain religious procedures and rituals, and protect the purity of the community's faith. There are many such religious norms in Mancun Village:

Here are some of the norms arising from doctrines and beliefs of Theravada Buddhism:

The code of conduct in the temple: (1) Men must take off their shoes before entering the hall of the Theravada Buddhist temple. (2) Women must take off their shoes at the entrance of the Theravada Buddhist temple before entering the temple. (3) The death of laymen in the Theravada Buddhist temple is a taboo, so people who are too old usually do not enter the temple.

Norms relating to who fund the temple and monks: The Theravada Buddhist temple is financed by donations from the villagers. In addition to dozens of *dan fo* every year, villagers, divided by the villagers committee (now the villager group) into groups, take turns to send meals to the temple. The current *fo ye* in Mancun Village has decided not to return to a secular life. His costs in all his future life will be funded collectively by residents of Mancun Village.

The code of conduct for monks: (1) follow the Ten Commandments: (i) do not kill; (ii) do not steal; (iii) abstain from impurity and lead a life of chastity; (iv) do not lie; (v) avoid alcohol; (vi) abstain from eating after noon; (vii) do not gamble; (viii) do not wear makeup; (ix) do not wear long sleeves or high heels; and (x) do not wear a watch or necklace. (2) If any property of the temple is lost, it will be compensated by *fo ye*. (3) Monks should not gossip about or intervene in village affairs. (4) Should a monk die at home, *fo ye* and other monks should be invited to send his ghost away, and the expenses of the ritual should be borne by the parents of the deceased. (5) A monk cannot stay at home overnight.

Norms relating to how laymen should treat monks: (1) Do not touch the head of a monk. (2) Parents are not allowed to beat the son if he is a monk. If the son made a serious mistake, the parents could use a stick wrapped with yellow cloth to beat him.

The following norms are based on the beliefs of the folk religion of the Dai people:

Norms relating to the maintenance of sacred symbols and religious rituals: (1) Do not touch the Hearts of Village. (2) Maintenance of the Hearts of Village: Before the villagers committee was changed into the villager group, the villagers committee (now the villager group) would set aside 100 yuan from the reservation fund each year and give the 100 yuan to *zhao man* to cover the costs of maintaining and making offerings to the Hearts of Village. (3) During the *ning man* ritual (where offerings are made to the village gods), outsiders are not allowed to enter or leave the village. When the village is carrying out the ritual, a bamboo and grass-made warning sign with "*da liao ha xiu*" (phonetic transcription of the original Dai words) written on it will be placed at the entryway of the village. Outsiders who violate this rule will be asked to pay a fine of fifteen yuan and one chicken, ten packages of glutinous rice, and two candles, which will be used in a sacrificial ritual to gain forgiveness from the village gods.

In Mancun Village, because the two belief systems are intricately intertwined in the social life and spiritual world of the villagers, norms about dealing with conflicts between the two religions are created. There is a clear division of labor between the key figures in the Buddhist system and the folk religion in the village.

Religion provides a way of understanding and interpreting the world for its believers. In this sense, religion is an important source of information for believers.

It helps people cope with phenomena and events that occur in social life, thereby guiding people's behavior. This kind of guidance will penetrate into the daily life of the community and give rise to the norms that govern the daily life of believers. In Mancun Village, religious beliefs occupy an important position in villagers' spiritual life. In addition to norms related to doctrines, creeds, sacred places of worship, rituals, and religious figures, religion also creates norms that are woven into the fabrics of daily life.

Norms about houses: (1) A villager's house must have two doors, the front door and the back door, so that the spirits of the ancestors can return home. (2) Firewood cannot be placed in front of the three-legged stand sitting over the fire pit, and only male elders can sit in front of the stand. (3) Outsiders cannot enter the master bedroom. (4) There are two columns in the house of each villager, *sao zhao* and *sao nan* (which literally means the prince column and the princess column). Villagers believe the two columns are where the spirits of their male and female ancestors live after their death. They are sacred, and people are not allowed to lean against the two columns. (5) The house warming ceremony must be held before 12:00 noon. (6) Cremation of a body can only be carried out after 12:00 noon (except when it is a full moon day). If the deceased does not die a natural death, the body must be cremated on the day it dies. Otherwise, it can be cremated on the next day. The bodies of villagers who do not die naturally are cremated at a different cemetery (*long lin*).

Norms related to public life in the village include the following: (1) Before the cremation of the body of a recently deceased villager, people in the village are not allowed to work or enter other villages. Disputes arising from violation of this rule should be handled by the *zhao man*. (2) If someone from another village where the body of a recently deceased villager has not yet been cremated enters Mancun Village, an act of disrespect towards the village gods, they will be asked by the *zhao man* of Mancun Village to pay a fine of 15 yuan and offer a chicken, 10 packages of glutinous rice, and two sticks of candles to the village gods. (3) Outsiders are not allowed to pass through the village when transporting or carrying firewood, which is associated with cremation of bodies. Violators are required to pay a fine of 1 yuan and offer one *jin* (1/2 kg) of edible oil, one *jin* of rice, and two candles to the village gods. (4) If a village other than Mancun has too many deaths in a year, people of the village will not be allowed to enter Mancun Village to avoid offending the village gods. Violators of this rule will be fined by *Zhao Man*, and the amount of fine will be determined by *Zhao Man*.

The following are norms related to the travel and purchase of livestock: (1) Farm animals bought by villagers must be checked by *Zhao man*. Only after *Zhao man* determines they are disease-free and prays for the health of these animals can villagers keep the animals. (2) Villagers must pray for the blessings of the family gods, the village gods and the regional gods before embarking on a journey.

Norms of giving birth in Mancun Village include the following: (1) A married woman cannot give birth at her parents' home. (2) When a woman dies during pregnancy, the fetus must be removed from the uterus and cut into pieces. The mother and the fetus must be cremated separately. (3) After giving birth to a child, the mother cannot go out of the house or enter other people's homes until the baby is one month old. If she has to leave the house, she has to carry a sickle in the waistband. (5) Babies who die before they reach six months must be thrown into the river.

The following norms are in connection with the moon: (1) In the event of a lunar eclipse, villagers are required to set off firearms and firecrackers. If there is a pillar at the center of the house, the villager should use a knife to hit the pillar or splash it with wine. (2) Do not drink up all the wine on a full moon day. Leave some so it can be used to splash the pillar at the center of the house in the event of a lunar eclipse. (3) At the time of a lunar eclipse, if a boy is in the house of her girlfriend, the girl's parents should ask the boy to stay for the night, and the two will be considered a married couple after the night. (4) If a person dies on the 15th lunar day, his/her family must hold a funeral for the person immediately. (5) If a villager dies at his/her home during a lunar eclipse, his/her body may not be carried out of the house through the door. Instead, the family should cut an opening on the wall of the house and move the body out of the house through the opening. If the dead body swells, it must be cremated immediately. (6) Villagers are forbidden to go on a date, build new houses, or hold a house warming ceremony during the period from the Gate Closing Festival (July 15 of the Dai calendar) and the Gate Opening Festival (October 15 of the Dai calendar).

Why religion can create a normative order is that it defines what deviant behavior is and stipulates how deviant behavior should be remedied. The following is an incomplete list of religious norms in Mancun Village (Table 6.1):

It can be seen that the religious definition of deviance has penetrated many aspects of the social life in the village. In addition, a religious definition of anomie/deviance is connected with people's observation of life. Phenomena defined as anomie/deviance are less likely to occur and are contrary to the general experiences of the villagers. For example, full moon and lunar eclipse are opposed to waning moon, monks opposed to laymen, and profanity opposed to sacredness. These binary oppositions conjured up by religion have influenced social norms that govern human behaviors.

6.3.2 Religion and Social Control Agents

The influence of religion on social order is also derived from its organization (Ikeda & Wilson, 2003, p. 139). Religion is generally organized in one way or another. The difference is that some religions are highly organized, while others are loosely organized and only have temporary leaders. However, no matter how organized a religion is, religious authority is bound to emerge. In addition to providing guidance on religious beliefs, religious organizations and authorities are also social control agents. Of course, the extent to which religious organizations and religious authorities play a role as social control agents and their relationship with other social control agents depend on the influence of religion and the number of believers.

Both Theravada Buddhism and the folk religion of the Dai people are well organized.

Table 6.1 Deviant behavior defined by Religion in Mancun Village

Compliant situation/behavior	Deviant situation/behavior	Avoidance of deviance and remedy
The temple is a sacred place	Wear shoes into the temple	Take off shoes before entering the temple
	Death of a layman in the temple	Older people generally do not enter the temple
Monks should have virtues	Violation of the the Ten Commandments	Comply with the "Ten Commandments"
Monks are keepers of the spiritual world	Asking about or intervene in secular affairs	Monks can't ask about or intervene in village affairs
Monks should live in the temple	Death of a monk at home	Monks should not stay at home overnight; should a monk die at home, *fo ye* and other monks should be invited to send his ghost away and the expenses of the ritual should be borne by the parents of the deceased
The sacredness of monks	Touch the head of a monk	Villagers are not allowed to touch the head of monks
	Beat monks	Parents are not allowed to beat the son if he is a monk
		Exception: If the son did make a serious mistake, the parents could use a stick wrapped with yellow cloth to beat him
The sacredness of the Hearts of Village	Offend the village gods	Do not touch the Hearts of Village
		The Hearts of Village are maintained by *zhao man*
	Offend the village gods; during the *ning man* ritual, outsiders are not allowed to enter or leave the village	The violators will be punished by *zhao man*
Return of the spirits of the deceased	The spirit of the deceased will not be able to return home if the house does not have a back door	There must be a back door when building a house
The family gods must not be disturbed (purity of home, good fortune for the family)	Firewood can not be placed in front of the three-legged stand sitting over the fire pit	Firewood can not be placed in front of the three-legged stand sitting over the fire pit and only male elders can sit in front of the three-legged stand at the fire pit

(continued)

Table 6.1 (continued)

Compliant situation/behavior	Deviant situation/behavior	Avoidance of deviance and remedy
	An outsider enters the master bedroom of a villager	Outsiders may not enter the master bedroom of a villager. Remedy: Invite monks to chant mantras
	Lean against *sao zhao* or *sao nan*	People are not allowed to lean against the two columns. Remedy: Invite monks to chant mantras
	Violation of the rule regarding house warming	The house warming ceremony must be held before 12:00 noon
Do not disturb gods	Unnatural death	Cremate the body in the designated *long lin* on the day the person dies
Do not disturb or offend the family gods	Sick farm animals	Farm animals bought by villagers must be inspected by *zhao man*
	A married woman gives birth at her parents' house	A married woman should not give birth at her parents' house
Smooth birth	Death of a pregnant woman	Cremate the mother and the fetus separately
Avoid being haunted	Encounters with evil spirits	After giving birth to a child, the mother can not go out of the house or enter other people's home until the baby is one month old. If she has to leave the house, she has to carry a sickle in the waistband
Moon	Lunar eclipse	Don't drink the wine up. Villagers are required to set off firearms and firecrackers. If there is a pillar at the center of the house, the villager should use a knife to hit the pillar or splash it with wine
		At the time of a lunar eclipse, if a boy is in the house of her girlfriend, the girl's parents should ask the boy to stay for the night and the two will be considered a married couple after the night
		If a villager dies at his/her home during a lunar eclipse, his/her body may not be carried out of the house through the door. Instead, the family should cut an opening on the wall of the house and move the body out of the house through the opening. If the dead body swells, it must be cremated immediately

(continued)

Table 6.1 (continued)

Compliant situation/behavior	Deviant situation/behavior	Avoidance of deviance and remedy
Lunar eclipse	Full moon	If a person dies on the 15th lunar day, his/her family must hold a funeral for the person immediately

In addition to government regulation of religion, Theravada Buddhism itself has an internal management mechanism. Theravada Buddhist temples are divided into several levels. Temples closely related to the temple in Mancun Village are the Central Theravada Buddhist Temple, the Duancun Village Temple, and the Jingzhen Temple, ranked from low to high in terms of authority. There are regular or irregular meetings between these temples to discuss matters such as temple management and the organization of religious activities. *Da fo ye* is in charge of the daily affairs of the temple in Mancun Village. The current *fo ye* of Mancun Village, named Yan La, was appointed in 1998. He is now more than 60 years old. Yan La is responsible for the management of the temple, educating young monks, and hosting and participating in various Buddhist rituals and ceremonies. On the 15th day and the 30th day of each lunar month, *fo ye* of Mancun Village will attend the *fo ye* meeting held in Duancun Village. The meeting is hosted by *da fo ye* of the Duancun Village. Topics discussed at the meeting include (i) how to promote the self-development of *fo ye*; (ii) how to educate young monks; and (iii) how to manage the temple. *Bu zhang* is responsible for assessing whether *fo ye* has faithfully performed his duties. Obviously, there is a hierarchy of controls among abbots of Theravada Buddhism temples at different levels. In every Theravada Buddhist temple, *da fo ye* (the abbot) is responsible for educating and managing other monks. He must ensure that the monks comply with Buddhist norms and basic social etiquette rules. In summary, *da fo ye* is a social control agent in the temple. Therefore, as a bureaucratic organization, Xishuangbanna's temple system constitutes a social control institution, and this social control extends to the social life of villagers in this area.

Another important authority figure in the Theravada Buddhist temple of Mancun Village is *bu zhang*, who is primarily responsible for leading worshipers in chants at the temple. *Bu Zhang* is also responsible for presiding over various Buddhist activities in the village. The first sentence of the sutra to be chanted by *fo ye* at a Buddhist ceremony must be recited by *bu zhang*. Without *bu zhang*, the chanting ceremony will not commence. In addition to presiding over Buddhist rituals, *bu zhang* is also responsible for assisting *da fo ye* in managing the monks and finances of the temple. Another duty of *bu zhang* is to supervise the behavior of *fo ye* and keep an eye on whether *fo ye* is obeying the rules of the temple, whether he has provided adequate education to the young monks and so on. In addition to leading worshipers in chants, *bu zhang* has a special ability. He is said to know all types of ghosts and how to banish them. *Bu zhang* can claim to be representative of witchcraft culture in the folk religion of the Dai people. In a sense, *bu zhang* is the liasion between Buddhism and the folk religion in Mancun Village. *Bu zhang* not only provides guidance to *fo ye* on how to behave in the secular world. More importantly, he is also a social control agent. Bu zhang is tasked with superivising the behaviors of *fo ye*, meeting the religious needs of the villagers, and maintaining the order within the temple. In some cases, *bu zhang* is also the teacher and mentor of *fo ye*. For example, the current *fo ye* Yan La became the abbot of the temple in 1998 under the circumstance that there was no worthy successor to the original abbot. At first, he knew neither how to chant sutras nor the rules of the temple. After two years, with the help of *bu zhang*, he had basically learned all important sutras, basic etiquette rules of *fo ye*, and regulations of the temple by heart. When I visited Mancun Village in 2004, Yan La was already familiar with the scriptures. The villagers said that he was a qualified *fo ye*.

In the folk religion of Mancun Village, the aforementioned *zhao man* is also a key social control agent. The *zhao man*, also known as "*long ba tou*", translates literally into English as the head of the village. However, in fact, the *zhao man* is a hereditary priest in the village. As an important authority figure in the folk religion of the Dai people, he presides over the sacrificial rituals aimed to please the Hearts of Village and the village gods. He is also responsible for handling matters related to family gods, village gods, and regional gods. Due to the villagers' respect and firm belief in the existence of gods, the *zhao man* has high social status in the village. The beliefs in family gods, village gods, and regional gods have given rise to many norms, part of which have been listed in the previous section, and the *zhao man* is the person who supervises the enforcement of these norms. For another example, one of the rules arising from the folk religion is that when the village is holding sacrificial rituals for the village gods (approximately 2–3 h), *bu zhang* will place a warning sign made of bamboo and grass at the entryway of the village. This sign means that the village is holding a grand ceremony, outsiders may not enter and people inside the village may not go out. Outsiders disregarding this rule will be punished by *Zhao man*. The offender will be required to pay a fine of 15 yuan (five yuan for each direction: east, west, north, south, and middle) and offer one chicken, two candles, and 10 bags of glutinous rice to the village to gain their forgiveness.

6.3.3 Religion and Disputes

Case 1 from Chap. 5 illustrates well the relevance of religion to disputes. As we saw in that case, when Yan breached the prohibition regarding the deceased, such behavior was believed by residents of Duncun Village to have upset the latter's village God and would cost them the God's blessings. To get back into the God's good graces, Duancun Village residents asked Yan to offer sacrifice to the Hearts of Village and the village gods. Another piece of background information worth mentioning is that the two villages had frictions over the local barbecue market prior to this incident, which was another contributor to the rapid escalation of this dispute. The prior clash of economic interests led Duancun Village to take advantage of its position in this incident to punish Mancun Village. This was why they imposed an additional fine of 500 yuan not mentioned in local customs. This request was eventually rescinded largely because (i) this customary law arising from religion has a high level of authority among local people and provides legitimacy for Mancun Village's refusal to Duancun Village's requirement that is not supported by the customary law; and (ii) a *long lin* is of great significance to both villages. Although the Dai people in Mancun Village believe in Buddhism, they also think that the Buddha is only in charge of the afterlife, and happiness in this life depends on the blessing of their ancestor gods. The cemetery "*long lin*" is the place where their ancestors are buried. Losing *long lin* is equivalent to losing the blessing of their ancestor gods, which can be further translated into misfortune in this life. The folk religion of the Dai people stipulates the importance and significance of *long lin*, making it a useful bargain chip for Mancun Village in the negotiation with Duancun Village.

This dispute between the two villages arose from the violation of customary law, which is deeply rooted in the folk religion of the Dai people. More importantly, this case demonstrates how religion defines deviance (behavior that offends gods) and how to deal with deviance (punish the offender to appease the offended gods). It is the folk religion that links death, entry into a village, *zhao man*, fine, sacrifice of chicken, Hearts of Village, village gods, and cemetery, which are otherwise unrelated and give rise to customary law. On the one hand, violations of such customary law lead to disputes. On the other hand, customary law arising from religion provides the basis for the resolution of religious disputes.

The relationships between religion, disputes, and dispute resolution have been reflected in many real-world cases. For example, Case 3, which will be discussed later, is also a typical example of conflict arising from religion. Furthermore, if the parties involved in the dispute believe in the same religion, they might agree that it is up to their gods to make the judgment. During my stay in Mancun Village, I did not observe examples of villagers relying on divine judgment as a way to resolve disputes. However, a local police officer and a villager told me that people in Mancun Village and nearby Dai villages sometimes appeal to the court of gods for justice.

For example, if a person is suspected of stealing something or doing something bad and there is no conclusive evidence to prove that the person is innocent, any party involved in this dispute may ask the other party to take an oath before a god statue in the temple. If the accused party takes an oath, he will be considered innocent, thus bringing an end to the dispute.

Such a dispute resolution method has its roots in religion. The existence of such dispute resolution methods also shows that religion can give rise to a variety of dispute resolution methods.

In Mancun Village and nearby Dai villages, religion creates norms that define what is "right", what is "wrong", and what is deviant behavior. Religion itself may be the source of disputes, but religion also provides ways to resolve disputes. To put it simply, religion shapes or influences the way disputes are resolved.

6.4 Religion in Mancun Village's Pluralistic Social Control System

6.4.1 Religion as a Form of Social Control

Mancun Village is a harmonious village. Villagers are friendly to each other. This is of course largely attributed to the fact that the villagers share the same religious beliefs. However, religion is not the only "glue" that holds this society together. Another study of mines in Mancun Village shows the impact of the market economy on village life. There is a growing desire for material wealth among villagers, and their lifestyles are also becoming more diverse. People see things differently; thus, religion is not the only social structure that offers ways to resolute disputes and conflicts. For example, consultation is also an important mechanism for dispute resolution in the village.[7] There are primarily two factors behind the positive effects of religion on the maintenance of social order in Mancun Village: (i) the harmonious relations between Theravada Buddhism and the folk religion in Mancun Village; and (ii) the harmonious relations between religion and other forms of social control.

In Mancun Village, Theravada Buddhism and folk religion coexist in a harmonious way, and there is a clear division of labor between them.[8] In the case study concerning the dispute between Mancun Village and Duancun Village, we discovered that there is a tacit agreement between the religious authority and the village governance body. This division of labor and tacit understanding can be observed in every aspect of the public life of the villagers.[9] My field research findings indicate that there is a division of labor and cooperation between the religious authority and the political authority in the village and that the religious system is integrated by the political system and is not the only form of social control in the village.

Religion as a social control is subject to its own internal constraints as well as external constraints from the political authority of the village. In the Theravada Buddhist temple, as mentioned above, *fo ye* was supervised by *bu zhang*, and *bu zhang* was elected by the elders in the village. Suffice to say, authority of *bu zhang* rests on the villagers' support. The villagers supervise the behaviors of *bu zhang*. If *bu zhang* wants to maintain his reputation and social status, he must act in accordance with social norms in the village. This is how villagers exercise control over *bu zhang*. In 1998, the former *da fo ye* of Mancun Village decided to return to secular life, and the villagers invited a *fo ye* from Bulang Mountain to manage the temple. But this *fo ye* was lazy; what's more, he was a smoker. He was driven away by the villagers in less than a year. Apparently, the villagers also have control over *da fo ye*. That is, there is a continuity of social control among the villagers, *bu zhang*, and *fo ye*. By comparison, the control of the villagers on authority figures of the folk religion is weaker. Generally, *Zhao man* is a hereditary position, so the primary way for

[7] See Chap. 7 of this book.

[8] See Chap. 7 of this book.

[9] See Chap. 7 of this book.

villagers to influence the behaviors of *Zhao man* is through public opinion. Based on my research in Mancun Village, public opinion is a strong force that molds and influences the behaviors of *Zhao man*. The heirs of *Zhao man* in the village were still very young at the time. They once complained to me that becoming *zhao man* would cost them freedom because the duty of *zhao man* was to handle religious affairs in the village, which meant that they cannot leave the village as they wished or for a long time. However, the two young men also told me that they would become *zhao man* as demanded by the villagers.[10]

In social life in Mancun Village, religion as a social control has no dominance over other forms of social control. It is only part of the social control system in the village and has harmonious relations with other forms of social control. This is why religion has played a positive role in the formation of social order in Mancun Village.

6.4.2 Interrelation Between Religion and Law

To gain insight into the influence of religion as a social control on the enforcement of state law in Mancun Village, we can proceed from two perspectives: support and obstruction of state law enforcement from religion.

Law enforcement does not entirely depend on the use of coercive power by the state. The resources and power of the state are limited. Therefore, social support is crucial for law enforcement. As a form of social control, religion has an important influence on the stability of social order. For state law, support from a religion means support from the believers of the religion. For Mancun Village, religion is a contributor to the construction and maintenance of social order. The collaboration between religion and other forms of social control has contributed to the stability of social order in the village, which is in line with the purpose of state law. The role of religion in maintaining social order helps the state pay less price for law enforcement. Therefore, religion has important implications for the realization of the goal of law in Mancun Village.

In the following case, we will see the influence and control of government on religion:

Case 2: Temple or School?

According to local customs, boys aged seven or so in Mancun Village and other Dai villages will be sent to the Buddhist temple to live as monks and learn Buddhist sutras and the Dai language. In the past, there was no school in this region, and Buddhist temples served as centers of religious activities and important places for young people to learn the Dai language and culture. Therefore, Buddhist temples play an important role in the preservation of the Dai language and culture. However, training to become a

[10] Of course, there is no way for me to predict whether they will really assume their responsibilities in the future. But one thing is certain: the two young men obviously are faced with huge pressure from the traditions and the residents.

monk starts at the same age as that of compulsory education. To ensure that children receive adequate formal education, Meng Township, which has jurisdiction over Mancun Village, launched a special program at local schools for little monks. The program taught both the Chinese language and the Dai language and made special accommodations for little monks. However, this move of the government to keep children at school was not successful. In 1998, the enrollment rate of school-age monks in the township was 98 percent, but the dropout rate among school-age monks was also high. In recent years, the living conditions at local temples have been good. There are TVs and VCD players. For children, the temple is a more interesting place than the school where they have to sit through 45-min boring lectures. Therefore, many small monks escaped school or dropped out. According to the religious norms of the Dai people, parents are not allowed to beat the son if the son is a monk. Therefore, many teachers do not dare to discipline these young monks at school. Overall, it is very difficult to keep school-age monks at full-time school.

The people in Mancun Village have conflicting views on this issue. Some elderly people think that the Theravada Buddhist temple provides good education and that boys should be sent to there. Many middle-aged villagers take a cavalier attitude, but since other families have sent their boys to the temple, it must be reasonable to send their own boys there. Monk education at the temple cost a few thousand yuan. If they do not send their boys to the temple, they believe they will be ridiculed for poverty. A small number of villagers have clearly expressed concerns over monk education. They believe the experience at the temple has a very bad influence on these boys. They have become lazy and sloppy after being sent to the temple. For example, a villager had a 14-year-old daughter who was in the second grade of middle school and an 11-year-old son who was in the fifth grade of primary school and studied at the temple as a monk at the same time. He wanted his son to receive formal education and asked his son to return to secular life to focus on school life.

In 2000, the government of the township where Mancun Village is located rolled out the *Meng Township Compulsory Education Management Rules (Provisional, 1999)*, which stipulates that religion must not interfere in school education and, if a school-age boy is sent to live as monk at a temple, his guardian, *bu zhang*, *fo ye* of the temple, and officials of the village will be fined 3,000 to 5,000 yuan. This provision means that Dai boys can only become monks after completing compulsory education. Therefore, when I returned to Mancun Village in 2001, there were no little monks in the temple of the village. All the school-age children went to school. Later, the temple of the village borrowed three small monks from a neighboring village.

Here, we will not discuss whether the regulation of the township government is appropriate[24]. However, it is obvious that this regulation is based on the government's understanding of education law. The township government was merely performing law enforcement duty, hoping to change a religious norm, that is, the starting age of monk education. Although this regulation sparked complaints among Buddhist monks, *bu zhang*, and villagers, it has effectively improved student enrollment and retention rates. This case shows that law (more specifically law enforcement by the state) has an influence on religion and directs religion towards a desired direction.

As we already saw in the *pi pa* ghost expulsion cases discussed in the Chap. 5 (case 3), studying religion as a cultural system in Mancun Village can shed light on the root cause of this seemingly unreasonable social phenomenon concerning *pi pa* ghosts, which are extremely cruel in the eyes of outsiders. Studies of this sort can support informed decision making of policymakers and assist the government in eliminating or controlling religious risk factors that undermine social order envisioned by the legislator.

6.5 Discussion

6.5.1 Religion and Local Legal Culture

In Mancun Village, religion is clearly a form of social control, as it gives rise to norms, social control agents, and dispute settlement procedures. Fundamentally speaking, the key reason behind religion as a form of social control is that it shapes or influences the formation of local legal culture. To understand this function of religion, we need to examine the influence of religion on the everyday life of adherents as well as the primary characteristics of religion. Roger M. Keesing believes that human beings not only create various customs to regulate social life but also establish a larger structure to deal with the universe itself, the power that governs the universe, and the position of people in the universe, and religious beliefs and religious rituals are the foundation of this structure. He also believes that the interaction between things, the nature of time and space, how the world looks like, and how it should look are also the premises of the structure (Keesing, 1993, p. 381). This means that a religion offers a way to its believers to come to grips with the world. The core issue to be dealt with by law is how to lead citizens to live and act in the "right" and "just" ways, whereas what is "right" and "just" is determined by religious beliefs or worldviews (Rüthers, 2003, p. 189). This function of religion provides believers with appropriate attitudes toward nature, society, and others,[11] and patterns of behavior consistent with such attitudes are considered to be "correct" by believers of the religion. If culture does have a tendency to arrange the world in order and tells people what is right and what is justice, then religion has one of the factors that influence the direction of this tendency, so it is safe to say religion is a basic element of local legal culture. Of course, since human beings have other ways of coming to grips with the world, such as art and science (Niu, 2005), the extent to which religion can affect the formation of socially accepted patterns of behavior depends on the influence of the religion on believers. The influence of religious norms depends on the status of the religion in people's lives. It varies from religion to religion. Usually, compared to folk religions of ethnic groups, highly rationalized religions such as Christianity and Catholicism

[11] In other words, religion defines what is secular/sacred, right/wrong, legal/illegal, and justice/injustice.

produce fewer social norms that regulate everyday life. However, one thing is certain: religion is an important force that shapes local legal culture.

Therefore, the most important way that religion contributes to the construction of grassroots-level social order and the formation of a pluralistic legal pattern is building a religious legal culture. Religious legal culture dominates the social control function of religion. It influences the formation of local legal culture to varying degrees. Religion is part of the local social control system. Due to ethnic and religious diversity, such a local legal culture molded by religion also exhibits characteristics of pluralism. Such pluralism is reflected not only in the diverse religious legal cultures produced by different religions but also in the fact that one religion may create different legal cultures in different places or ethnic communities. Therefore, localities and ethnic groups have different ways to put the world in order. For example, Islamic faiths have a profound influence on the social and spiritual life of the Hui people in Yunnan and therefore play a dominant role in the formation of the legal culture in this Hui community. Family education of the Hui people mainly entails beliefs, how to conduct oneself, and how to make a living. The first two items have close connections with the creed of Islam (Na lin, 2001, pp. 172–174). In particular, social norms regarding how to conduct oneself and the right way of life in this Hui community are basically derived from the Koran, the holy book of Islam. These social norms are at the core of local legal culture.

6.5.2 How Should Law Treat Religion

Although religion, as an informal way of social control, may conflict with formal social control of the state, this does not mean that the law should prohibit religious practices. How the law should treat religion is a matter concerning social stability and citizens' spiritual world.

Take Mancun Village for example. Although some religious norms clash with state law or formal social control, religion generally has positive effects on the maintenance of social order in Mancun Village. This is primarily because religion is well integrated into the political and public life of the village and has harmonious relations with other social controls, forming a system of checks and balances that effectively prevent religion or any other forms of social control from becoming a hegemonic power.[12] In the meantime, religion has played a supportive role in the maintenance of social order in Mancun Village in most circumstances.

Moreover, the law can exercise control over religion and direct religion to generate desired behaviors. Of course, such control must be exercised prudently. Religion is a very important part of the culture of ethnic groups and village-level societies. It is a cultural expression. The collapse of religion as a form of traditional social control will

[12] See Chap. 7 of this book.

leave a blank space in the social order system and thus make the system vulnerable, which is one of the important lessons we have drawn from history.[13]

Regarding the conflict between religious norms and state law, we must recognize that religion answers the question of the meaning of life and the way of life. Religion is and will remain, at least in the foreseeable future, a common cultural phenomenon. Therefore, the law needs to deal with problems arising from religion in a strategic fashion. If the law stipulates the only "correct" lifestyle and set of values in areas where it should not, its encounters with local values, beliefs, and meanings may give rise to unexpected informal institutions. Therefore, the law must maintain neutrality and give space to different values, beliefs, and lifestyles in society.[14] Conflicts between religion and law, such as conflicts between any other informal social control and formal social control, are solvable.

Although folk religions are often intricately intertwined with secular life and generate norms that guide behaviors in the secular world, folk religions as belief systems also demonstrate instrumental rationality. The superstitious elements in folk religions are most likely to clash with the state law. These elements often arise from helpless or hopeless feelings of human beings in the face of real-life problems. Once the real-life problems are solved, these elements will lose value and simply disappear. For example, in the case of *pi pa* ghosts, villages did not intentionally violate state law but only acted in an appropriate way according to religious norms. Their acts were driven by their religious worldviews. If such worldviews do not change, conflicts will continue to occur. Luckily, worldviews are moldable. The belief of the people in Mancun Village in *pi pa* ghosts has its roots in reality—lack of access to health care. As long as access to adequate health care is guaranteed, such belief and behavior generated will disappear. Therefore, the state cannot always use coercive power to solve conflicts between religious norms and state law. First, it should be determined whether it is the flaw in formal institutions, such as failure to provide social welfare or adequate health care, that leads people to seek help from religion, including superstitious beliefs and practices, to cope with real-life problems. On this issue, Karl Marx has given us some food for thought: "To abolish religion as the illusory happiness of the people is to demand their real happiness. The demand to give up illusions about the existing state of affairs is the demand to give up a state of affairs that needs illusions. The criticism of religion is therefore the criticism of the vale of tears, the halo of which is religion" (Marx, 1965a,b, p. 453). Therefore, conflicts between religion and law can often be resolved using nonlegal methods, especially by strengthening the government's ability to provide protection to citizens and adjusting public policies, as shown in Mr. Li Yiyuan's study (1997, p. 279) of the native religious movement in Taiwan.

---

[13] See Chap. 8 of this book.

[14] See Chap. 2 of this book.

References

Geertz, C. (1999). *The Interpretation of Cultures* (Naribilige et al., Trans.). Shanghai People's Publishing House.
Guo, J. (1998). *Rice culture of the Dai people in Xishuangbanna* (W. Zhang, Trans.). Yunnan University Press.
Horn, N. (2005). *Einführung In Die Rechtswissenschaft Und Rechtsphilosophie* (L. Luoi, Trans.). Law Press.
Huang, Z. (1995). *Festivals of ethnic minority groups in southwestern China.* Yunnan Education Publishing House.
Ikeda, D. & Wilson, B. (2003). *Religion and society* (H. Liang & J. Wang, Trans.). Sichuan People's Publishing House.
Keesing, R. M. (1993). *Cultural anthropology* (G. Zhang & J. Yu, Trans.). Taiwan: Juliu Publishing House.
Li, Y. (1997). *Human vision.* Shanghai Literature and Art Press.
Li, Y. (Eds.). (1980) *Selected readings in cultural anthropology.* Shihuo Publishing House.
Liang, Z. (2003). *Thinking at the margins.* Law Press.
Marx., Engels. (1965a).*Marx and Engels Collected Works* (Vol. 1). People's Publishing House.
Marx., Engels. (1965b).*Marx and Engels Collected Works* (Vol. 13). People's Publishing House.
Na, L. (2001). *Integration of tradition and modernity: An outline of the history, culture, and development of the Hui People in Yunnan.* Yunnan University Press.
Niu, S. (2005). Religious Worldviews. *Academic Journal of Zhongzhou, 2.*
Reynolds, F. E. (1994). Dhamma in dispute: The interactions of religion and law in Thailand. *Law and Society Review, 28,* 3.
Rüthers, B. (2003). *Rechtstheorie* (X. Ding & Y. Wu, Trans.). Law Press.
Smart, N. (1996). *Dimensions of the sacred: An anatomy of the world's beliefs.* HarperCollins.
Stroup, H. H. (1945). The family, law, and religion as cohesive factors in society. *Journal of Educational Sociology, 19*(2).
Sun, L. (2003). *Cleavage: Chinese society since 1990s.* Social Sciences Academic Press.
Wang, Q. (2007). Meanings, values, and use of violence in vigilante—subjective dimension of human action. *Journal of Yunnan University (Law Edition) 3.*

Chapter 7
Pluralistic Social Control and Village-Level Endogenous Social Order: A Case Study in Mancun Village (II)

With the shifts in the country's political landscape, the political system of Mancun Village also underwent profound changes. After the launch of democratic reforms in the 1950s, the power of the state started to penetrate Mancun Village. The ensuing political movements created conditions for the state to gain full control over every aspect of social life in Mancun Village. At a time, state law suppressed organizations and practices of folk religions, leading to the collapse of the traditional social control system in the village, especially during the Cultural Revolution when all religious activities were banned by the state. The temple in the village stopped religious activities, and *fo ye* and monks returned to secular life. The authority figures of the folk religion in the village, *bu zhang* and *kang lang*, also stopped participating in public activities; religious ceremonies such as *dan fo* and *ning man* were all banned; folk rituals presided over by *fo ye*, *bu zhang*, or *zhao man* were canceled. Many folk beliefs, customs, rituals, and norms were banned and criticized as superstitions. State law leaved no space for self-governance in the village. The government's decision to relax control over religion in 1979 and the rural economic reform in the early 1980s allowed villages to repossess autonomy. The social life in Mancun Village therefore underwent profound changes once again. While the villagers were busy resuming family-based agricultural production, they did not forget their traditional beliefs, customs, and social order. Folk rituals and ceremonies, which had been put on hiatus for more than 20 years, made a big comeback. The villagers invited *zhao man* to start performing their religious duties and then elected *bu zhang*. When the Theravada Buddhist temple reopened, many families sent their boys to the temple to live as monks.[1] Mutual support groups regained popularity and penetrated more fields. This speed of restoration of traditional culture was quite amazing. In the meantime, the new village-level political organizations and authorities began to function, and a new political pattern gradually took form in the villagers' mind. In 2000, Yunnan

[1] The Buddhist temples in Xishuangbanna are modeled after temples in Myanmar so they are also called Burmese-style temples.

Q. Wang, *Sociology of Law*,
https://doi.org/10.1007/978-981-16-5509-8_7

Province revoked the village affairs office system, and villages in the province established villagers' committees and village-level self-governance bodies, which was a major step towards village autonomy.

From the national perspective, the political changes experienced by Mancun Village over the past 50 years were not unique. Almost all villages across the country underwent the same kind of changes due to adjustment in formal institutions. On the one hand, many traditional customs in Mancun Village have changed or disappeared in the process of modernization. On several occasions, the village found itself on the brink of anomie. On the other hand, new ideas, new norms, and new interpretations of traditional culture continuously emerged. Adaption of culture, continuity in social controls, harmony in human relations, and orderly village life are the main features of Mancun Village. During my stay in Mancun Village in 2000 and 2004, I lived in a villager's house. I rarely locked my room, but I never lost anything. Villagers also rarely locked their houses. In the past 20 years, there were only three criminal cases and few public safety cases in Mancun Village. In 2004, I visited the police station in the township where Mancun Village was located. The local police said Mancun Village was a safe and orderly village. The orderly social life in Mancun Village aroused my interest.

Many Dai villages, including Mancun Village, believe in Buddhism and the folk religion of the Dai people. Sharing the same set of beliefs is an important factor in the formation of the village order, but this does not mean faith is the only "glue" that binds the villagers together. Neither is religion the only form of social control in the village. Signs of pluralism could be observed in the social life of the village. Market-based economic reform has greatly changed the lives of villagers. Villagers are more likely than before to express different views about the same issue. The good social order in Mancun Village is not simply a continuation of the traditional social control system but the result of the balanced and effective operation of pluralistic social controls (including the formal social controls of the state) in political and public life of the village. Moreover, external agents with coercive power are not the primary source of social control in Mancun Village. Instead, the primary source lies inside the individual. The maintenance of social order in Mancun Village largely depends on the individual's willingness to maintain order and stability through cooperation and consultation. Cooperation and consultation are the key to the formation of the order in political and public life in Mancun Village. Cooperation and consultation have enabled villagers to continuously establish effective norms and social controls to solve emerging issues. The social order in Mancun Village is therefore endogenous. The endogeneity of this order allows villagers to effectively adapt to the challenges in the external environment and address the internal problems of the village. The norms and social controls are slowly but constantly changing. The village-level social order is thus created and maintained in this dynamic process.

Endogenous social order is vital to village life. It helps villagers overcome the difficulties brought about by social changes. In the absence of such endogeneity, the village's worldview system and social control system would face the risk of collapse, and the village would be on the brink of anomie, as demonstrated in another village field study of mine. The case study on Mancun Village will help us understand how the endogenous social order is constructed in the village and what are the contributors behind a good village-level social order?

7.1 Different Social Control Agents in Public Life of Mancun Village

Let us not consider the influence of the state on Mancun Village for the time being. We will find that there are different social control agents active in the public life of Mancun Village. The interactions between these social control agents have a direct impact on the basic power structure in the village. These agents can be broadly divided into three categories by nature: village self-governing organizations, religious authorities, and social groups, as shown in Table 7.1.

These organizations and social groups are in fact social control agents in the village (Zhang & Wang, 2005). For example, in the religious system, *fo ye* at the Theravada Buddhist temple is responsible for educating young monks, including disciplining those who violate rules; *bu zhang* is responsible for supervising the behaviors of *fo ye*; *zhao man* is responsible for punishing villagers who violate folk religious norms. These semiorganized social groups also implement social control. For example, family clans (*ha gun*) often serve as mediators of family disputes. Non-organized groups such as elders (see "Case 1: A Dispute over the Roof Type of House") also exercise control over the behaviours of villagers. These diverse social control agents coexist in the public life of Mancun Village, and their relationships determine the social order in the village.

7.2 Relationships Between Different Social Control Agents

The standings and interests of different social control agents are not always the same. If such differences are not properly handled, conflicts will be sure to ensue. One of the reasons why Mancun Village has maintained a relatively stable social order for such a long time is the harmonious relationships between the multiple social control agents. These agents are in collaborative relationships and form a system of checks and balances.

Neither the village affairs office nor the villagers committee was in a rigid command relationship before the village-level organization reform. They acted in their respective capacities and showed respect for the authority of each other. For example, if a villager brought a dispute to the villagers committee, the villagers affairs office would not directly intervene in the resolution of the dispute even if the villagers committee asked for advice of the village affairs office. Only when the dispute could not be resolved by the villager committee would the dispute be handed over to the village affairs office.

Table 7.1 Social control agents in Mancun Village

Type of organization	Name	Description
Village self-governance organization	Villagers committee	In 2000, the village affairs office in the settlement area of the Dai people was abolished and a villagers committee was set up to manage the nine natural villages (villager teams) in the area. The villagers committee of Biancun Village was merged into the villagers committee of the Dai people at the end of 2003. Since then, there are 14 villager teams under jurisdiction of the villagers committee of the Dai people. Mancun Village is one of the 14 villager teams
	Villagers' team	Before the village-level organization reform in November 2000, Mancun Village was a villagers committee. After the reform in November 2000, it was changed to a villager team. The head and the accountant of the villager team are the only two public servants in the village
	Partisan group	The partisan group of Mancun Village has one team leader and nine party members. It was established before the village-level organization reform. In addition to regular party affairs, the partisan group also participates in decision-making concerning village affairs
	Religious affairs management team	Established in 1995. Before the village-level organization reform in 2000, the religious affairs management team had five members. After the reform, it only has three members. All of them are male elders in the village and one of them is the team leader. The team is mainly responsible for conveying religious policies of the state and managing the finance of the Theravada Buddhist temple in the village: financing *dan fo* rituals, managing the property of the temple, and financing and supervising the repairs and maintenance of the temple
Religious authorities	*Fo ye* at the Theravada Buddhist temple	The residents of Mancun Village believe in Theravada Buddhism, and there is a Theravada Buddhist temple in the village. The temple is a place of great significance in the social life of Mancun Village. *Da fo ye* is the head of the Theravada Buddhist temple. As the abbot of the temple, he prays for the villagers. He also serves as the preacher of Buddhist teachings in Mancun Village and is highly respected by the villagers

(continued)

Table 7.1 (continued)

Type of organization	Name	Description
	Bu zhang	*Bu zhang* is a monk who leads worshipers in chants in a Theravada Buddhist temple. *Bu zhang* provides guidance for *fo ye* on how to behave in the secular world. Other duties of *bu zhang* include managing the temple and supervising the behaviors of *fo ye*. For example, he must keep an eye on whether *fo ye* is obeying the rules of the temple and whether he has provided adequate education to the young monks. In addition to leading worshipers in chants, *bu zhang* has a special ability. He is said to know all types of ghosts and how to banish them. In a sense, *bu zhang* is the liasion between Buddhism and the folk religion in Mancun Village
	Zhao man	*Zhao man*, also known as "long ba tou", translates literally into English as the head of the village. But in fact, *zhao man* is a hereditary priest in the village. As an important authority figure in the folk religion of the Dai people, he presides over the sacrificial rituals aimed to please the Hearts of Village and the village gods. He is also responsible for handling matters related to the family gods, the village gods, and the regional gods. Due to the villagers' respect and firm belief in the existence of gods, *zhao man* has high social status in the village
Social groups	*Ha gun*	A family clan is called *ha gun* in the Dai language. For a married couple, the clan of the wife is called *mu la ha gun* and the clan of the husband is called *ji la ha gun*
	Kang lang	*Kang lang* refers to men who used to be *fo ye* at a Buddhist temple. *Kang lang* understand Buddhist scriptures as well as the language, culture, and folk customs of the Dai people. They are responsible for helping *bu zhang* exorcise ghosts and helping *zhao man* protect the Hearts of Village. They are among the few people who can touch the Hearts of Village. These distinguish them from ordinary villagers. They are also highly respected among villagers
	Elders	In Mancun Village, mainly villagers who have become grandparents are considered elders. Elders are highly respected in Mancun Village. Village officials often seek advice from elders on how to handle village affairs

(continued)

Table 7.1 (continued)

Type of organization	Name	Description
	Lao geng	*Lao geng* means peers of the same age group. Mancun Village is a community with low mobility. Therefore, *lao geng* often means a group of friends growing up together. *Lao geng* trust and help each other. *Lao geng* are the main participants of many folk activities, such as folk song singing events and mutual support programs
	Youth groups	Unmarried young people in Mancun Village often spontaneously form groups after reaching a certain age. Such a youth group is made up of young men and young women (almost 20 members) around the same age. The proportion of men and women in the group is basically the same. They often organize leisure activities together. The leader of the group, called *huo zi tou*, is responsible for assisting the villagers' team to handle matters concerning the young people in the village. He is also responsible for handling matters concerning the young people on folk festivals

After the village-level organization reform, this collaborative relationship was inherited by the villagers committee and the villagers' teams. However, there was a difference between the villager committee and the village affairs office. The latter was a formal institution established by the state and received direct support from the government. The former is a village self-governing organization and does not receive much support from the government. Therefore, to make its work easier, the villager committee needs to establish a collaborative relationship with the villager team. For example, the government of Menghai County decided to promote a type of flax seedling in 2004. The county government assigned production quotas to townships, and then township governments assigned quotas to villagers' committees. Mancun Village was required to grow 1500 *mu* of this type of flax crop. The officials of the villagers committee were very clear headed that if they directly imposed the quotas, it might cause resentment among the villagers' teams. Therefore, they convened a meeting among the leaders of the villagers' teams and asked them to apply for a quota. The village officials informed the villagers of the news. And then the villagers applied for quotas. In the end, Mancun Village applied for 150 *mu*. Through this kind of quota allocation method, all villages of the Dai people met allocated quotas. There was another important event in Mancun Village in 2004. Mancun Village and nearby villages have been using water wells for years. As the villagers' income increased, they wanted tap water. Macun Village, a neighboring village of Mancun Village, first proposed the idea of building a water supply plant. The villagers committee convened its members as well as the members of the CPC branch in this area to discuss this matter. Macun Village, Mancun Village, and Duancun Village used the same water source, and the three villages were connected to each other and had similar economic conditions. If they wanted to build a water supply plant, they should do it together. The three villages were recommended to hold village-level meetings to ask for the opinions of their own villagers. From November to December 2004, the three villages held several village-level meetings to discuss the construction of the tap water project. At the time, the villagers committee only made some preliminary preparations for the project and had not decided whether to build a tap water plant in any village.

Various social control agents in Mancun Village also demonstrate a spirit of cooperation and consultation.

The villagers' team and other social control agents act in a spirit of cooperation for the good of the village. Before the village-level organization reform, the partisan group of the Communist Party was responsible for nominating candidates for seats of the villagers committee. If villagers were dissatisfied with the work of the villagers committee or any member of the committee, they may voice their opinions to the leader of the partisan group. There was a supervisor-supervisee relationship between the partisan group and the villagers committee, but this relationship did not affect the cooperation between the two. According to my investigation findings in 2000, most matters and disputes in the village were handled by the villagers committee and the partisan group together. For example, the villagers committee would submit its accounts to the economic commission of the partisan group for inspection. The villagers committee was very supportive of the work of the economic commission. After the village-level organization reform, the economic commission was abolished, but the collaborative relationship between the villagers' team and the partisan group continued.

The people in Mancun Village believe in Theravada Buddhism and the folk religion of the Dai people. Based on my observations, religious beliefs have infiltrated every aspect of village life. Religious beliefs and secular life are intricately intertwined in this village. It is the religious beliefs and worldviews rather than religious authorities or organizations that achieved this level of infiltration. There is a clear division of labor and cooperative relationships between secular social control agents and religious social control agents. For example, in November 2004, the Theravada Buddhist temple gate was about to be repaired. After some discussions among *Fo Ye*, *Bu Zhang*, the religious affairs management team, the villagers' team and the partisan group, it was decided that the fishpond in the Theravada Buddhist temple should be rented out to a villager. I was there when they signed the rental agreement. Three villagers bid on the pond. After discussion between village officials, *bu zhang*, and bidders, the bid was awarded to the highest bidder. The rental agreement was signed by the religious affairs management team, the villagers' team, the partisan group, and *bu zhang* on the owner side. This case is a typical example of collaboration between religious social control agents and secular social control agents in the village. In this case, *fo ye*, as a religious authority figure, cannot directly intervene in the secular life of villagers. Therefore, he participated in the decision-making process but not the conclusion of the contract. Below are a few more examples that show the collaborative relationships between the villagers committee (now the villagers' team), the partisan group, *zhao man,* and b*u zhang*.

The dispute between Mancun Village and Duancun Village mentioned in the previous chapter could have been handled by the religious authority of Duancun Village. However, the dispute escalated into a conflict between the two villages because the villager who violated the religious norms did not pay the fine according to local customs. This conflict concerned both religious norms and relations between the two villages. Therefore, to handle this dispute, the two villages set up their respective negotiation teams led by their political authority figures. Religious authority figures (*zhao man* and *bu zhang*) served as assistants/consultants to political authority figures. They explained the source and significance of religious norms that might be evoked in negotiations. In the negotiations with Duancun Village, the political authorities of Mancun Village and the religious authorities worked as a team for the good of the village. After deliberation, they proposed a negotiation strategy that was later proven to be very effective.

This case shows that there is a tacit understanding between political and religious authorities of Mancun Village regarding their respective responsibilities. This understanding is manifested in every aspect of the public life of the village. First, let us examine the relationship between the villager group and the religious authority figures *bu zhang* and *zhao man*. The village self-governing body does not intervene in the activities of *bu zhang*, including exorcism and representation of *fo ye*. Village officials participate as ordinary villagers in the rituals and ceremonies hosted by *Zhao man*. Before the tax reform in 2004, *Zhao man* received 100 yuan every year from the villager group as a fund for event organization. When handling village-related disputes arising from local customs, village officials will consult *bu zhang* and *zhao man*, but *bu zhang* and *zhao man* will not interfere in matters within the scope of duties of the villagers' team (formerly the villagers committee). There is a natural transfer of power between religious and secular social control agents. For example, in the past, matters such as fight between villagers and unweded pregnancies were handled by *Zhao man*. In the 1990s, they were handled by village officials. This indicates the changes in the social status and authority of *Zhao men* in village life. In the past, *Zhao man* was not only an authority figure of the folk religion but also had considerable influence on the secular life of the villagers. *Currently, Zhao man*'s influence on secular village life has been weakened and largely transferred to the village self-governing body. The second relationship worthy of attention is the relationship between the villagers' team and the religious authority figures at the Theravada Buddhist temple, that is, *fo ye* and *bu zhang*. *Da fo ye* and *bu zhang* are in charge of the internal affairs of the Theravada Buddhist temple. The villagers' team finances and provides materials and supplies to the temple. However, since 1999, the villagers' team has also been responsible for supervising the temple. In 1999, the township government stipulated that boys must finish elementary school before they can become monks at the temple. The admission of new monks must be approved by the township government. In case of violation of the regulation, *bu zhang*, village officials, and the guardians of the boys who violate the rule will be fined. The villagers' team (formerly the villagers committee) therefore has a responsibility to supervise the recruitment of monks at the temple. Although unhappy about such arrangement, *fo ye* and *bu zhang* still followed the rules. The third relationship worth discussion is the relationship between the religious affairs management team and the Theravada Buddhist temple. The religious affairs management team does not interfere with religious activities organized by *fo ye* and *bu zhang*, but it is responsible for managing the finance of the temple to avoid unnecessary financial burden on the villagers.

The religious authorities under different belief systems also have different responsibilities. In house warming ceremonies, marriage and other major folk cultural activities, *fo ye*, *bu zhang*, and *zhao man* are all indispensable. There is a certain competition between them, but generally, they have different roles to play. For example, in the traditional house warming ceremonies in Mancun Village, *bu zhang* is responsible for organizing the entire ritual, which contains elements of both Buddhism and the folk religion, including the chanting ritual of *fo ye*. *Zhao man* is responsible for offering sacrifices to the family god. *Zhao man* makes arrangement for his own activities. The housing warming ceremony becomes a gathering for ancestral gods and Buddhist gods where *bu zhang*, *fo ye*, and *zhao man* pray for the peace and happiness for the villagers. This is a typical example of how *bu zhang*, *fo ye*, and *zhao man* act within their respective spheres of service and keep village life in perfect order. The relationships between the three are harmonious. *Fo ye* and *bu zhang* sometimes participate in rituals organized by *zhao man*. *Kang* Lang serves as a liaison between the different religious authorities in Mancun Village. For example, in the rite of exorcism, after *bu zhang* gains knowledge through divination methods about what kind of ghost is haunting the villager and where the ghost is, *kang lang* will be invited to banish the ghost; *kang lang* also serve as assistant to *zhao man* in the maintenance of the Hearts of Village; *kang lang* are often the most devout believers in Buddhist rituals. *Kang langs* are a special group of residents of Mancun Village. They represent neither Buddhist gods nor ghosts, but they can communicate with ghosts and gods. They unite the worlds of the unseen and seen and become a vehicle of communication between *bu zhang*, *zhao man*, *fo ye* and villagers.

The following social groups also have different levels of influence on the public life of Mancun Village. They play an important role in the maintenance of social order in the village. (i) Clans (*ha gun*): In Mancun Village, mediation by family clans is usually the first resort when there is a dispute. Only when the clans could not resolve the dispute to the satisfaction of the involved parties would villagers seek help from village officials. Although the clans do not directly interfere in the decision-making of village officials, village officials take the opinions of the clans seriously for fear of losing support from villagers. (ii) Youngsters. The wisdom of the villagers is also manifested in the handling of intergenerational relationships. Village officials generally do not directly intervene in the activities of young people. Instead, they communicate with the head of the youth group (*huo zi tou*) to manage the behaviors of young people. *Huo zi tou*, if literally translated, means the head of a militia squad. In fact, there was no militia squad after the village-level organization reform in 2000, but still a *huo zi tou* was elected to take charge of matters concerning young people. In 2002, the then *huo zi tou* left the village to do barbecue business. He was absent in the village all the year round. Therefore, the young people in Mancun re-elected their head. In 2002, the villagers' team provided an activity venue, especially for young people, according to their requirements and bought a set of drums for them. (iii) Elders. In Mancun Village, elderly people are generally held in esteem by villagers. Their words have an important influence on community affairs. Usually, elderly people are not village officials or the ones who make decisions in regard to public affairs, but village officials often consult elderly people when dealing with major disputes or important village matters. *Bu zhang* and members of the religious affairs management team are also elected by the elderly. In 2003, some villagers wanted to remodel their houses and build toilets at home. However, because the elderly suggested that the toilets would pollute the wells in the village, these villagers abandoned this idea. This incident shows the influence of the elderly as a social control agent in the villager.

Generally, the relationships between different social control agents in Mancun Village are harmonious, indicating that there are certain normative guidelines for the behaviors of these agents and that these norms are faithfully observed. The village self-governing organization shows respect for the religious authorities and social groups, while the religious authorities and social groups also recognize the village self-governing organization as the political authority in the village. These organizations and authorities all act in their respective spheres of service and maintain harmonious relationships with each other, leading to orderly village life in Mancun Village.

7.3 Consensus-Based Decision-Making and Codified Norms

In Mancun Village, there are two sets of written norms: *Rules and Regulations of the Villagers Committee of the Dai People* and *Rules and Regulations of Mancun Village.*

After the election at the end of 2000, the first villagers committee of the Dai people and the branch of the Communist Party stationed in the Dai villages community drafted and issued *Ordinances of the Villagers Committee of the Dai People.*

7.3.1 *Ordinances of the Villagers Committee of the Dai People*

Article 1: Every villager should learn the law, abide by the law, safeguard the authority of the law, and report illegal and criminal activities.

Article 2: Villagers should be friendly to and support each other. Do not fight, drink too much alcohol, libel or slander others, or spread rumors about others. (i) If a villager gets into scuffle with a neighbor or a family member, he/she will be fined 500 yuan; (ii) if a villager causes any trouble during a village meeting under the influence of alcohol, he/she will be fined 200 yuan; (iii) if a villager libels, slanders, or takes revenge on village officials or other villagers, in addition to compensating for the loss of the other party, he/she will be fined 500–1000 yuan; (iv) a villager having inappropriate marital conduct or an inappropriate relationship outside marriage will be fined 1000 yuan; and (v) a couple will be fined 500 yuan upon divorce.

Article 3: Villagers should behave oneself in public places. Do not cause disturbance in public spaces. Do not obstruct executive officers in the performance of their duties.

Article 4: Do not steal money or property from a person or a place; do not rob any person or any place; do not extort state or collective property; do not gamble or hide property of any criminal. In the case of theft, in addition to giving back property or compensating for property loss, the offender will be subject to an additional penalty amounting to ten times the value of the property stolen. In the case of extortion, libel or slander, the offender will be fined 500 yuan. If a villager damages others' property, in addition to compensatory damages, he/she will be fined 1000 yuan.

Article 5: Villagers should not damage public property, including publicly owned water works, transportation infrastructure, power supply infrastructure, and production assets. Otherwise, in addition to compensatory damages, the offender will be fined 500 yuan.

Article 6: Do not dry grains, pile up soil or other things, or set up stalls on a road or otherwise. Do not play around on the road or block the road at night. In the case of a traffic problem arising from a villager's violation of this rule, in addition to compensatory damages, the offender will be fined 2000 yuan.

Article 7: Do not cut trees that are the property of the state, the collective, or others. Do not dig holes on the side of a road near a field. Do not damage or allow livestock to damage crops. Otherwise, in addition to compensatory damages, the offender will be fined 200 yuan.

Article 8: Villagers should follow *hukou* (household registration) management regulations. Report births and deaths of family members in a timely manner. If an outsider needs to stay in the village for a short period of time, he/she should pay a temporary residence fee to the villager committee (100 yuan per year if the outsider is the husband/wife of a villager and 360 yuan per year if the outsider is not the husband/wife of a villager.)

Article 9: Villages should attach importance to education and the standardization of schooling. Parents should send their school-age children to schools. Otherwise, they will be fined 3000 yuan. If a student drops out of school before finishing the nine years of compulsory education, the student's parents will be fined 3000 yuan.

Article 10: Villagers should believe in science rather than superstitions.

Article 11: Villagers should follow the housing construction plan of the village. Do not expand the coverage area of the house or allow the height of the house to be higher than the stipulated height limit. In the case of land requisitions, unreasonable requirements are not met. Villagers must obtain the approval of the villagers committee for house renovations. If a villager starts a renovation project without approval from the committee, he/she will be fined 50 yuan per square meter.

Article 12: If a villager fails to show at a village meeting on time, he/she will be fined 20 yuan.

Article 13: If a villager does not participate in a village-organized volunteer event, he/she will be punished 30 yuan.

Article 14: If a villager does not pay stipulated fees such as the agricultural tax to the villager committee, he/she will be fined 20 yuan for every 100 yuan not paid.

Article 15: If a villager transfers a quarry or land plot without first obtaining the approval of the villagers committee, the villagers committee has the right to order the villager to terminate the contract, revoke the villager's land use right, and impose a fine of 1000 yuan.

Article 16: If a villager intends to rent out a land plot or quarry, he/she must obtain approval from the village-level branch of the Communist Party and the villagers' team. In addition to the percentage drawn by the villagers' team, the villagers committee will also draw 10 percent from the rent.

Article 17: Villagers should follow the family planning rules of the country. In addition to punishments specified by the relevant policies of the country and the township, villagers who are in a de facto marriage without being legally married would be fined 1000 yuan and ordered to complete the marriage registration procedure.

Article 19: If an outsider temporarily staying in the village violates any of the abovementioned regulations, in addition to the punishment according to the above regulations, the villagers committee will ask him/her to leave the village permanently.

Article 20: The staff of the villagers committee and the villagers' teams must obtain the approval of the villagers committee and the villagers' teams before acting on their behalf. Otherwise, they will be punished according to disciplinary rules and procedures.

Article 21: To protect the public from dangers, villagers are encouraged to report violations of village rules and regulations. The villager committee is committed to protecting whistleblowers' identities. Furthermore, the whistleblowers will be rewarded with 15–20% of the fines collected from the reported offenders.

The Villagers Committee of the Dai People
DD/MM/2000.[2]
Signatures of the leaders of major clans:

The drafters of *Ordinances of the Villagers Committee* consulted the relevant policies and regulations of the government. Therefore, it contains many standard narrative elements. This has reduced the endogeneity of these rules and regulations to a certain extent. Nevertheless, public consultation was an important part of the regulatory process and increased public support for these regulations. The draft was sent to the villagers' teams for review. After review and modification, the villagers'

[2] The Chinese version of the *Rules and Regulations of the Residents Committee of the Dai People* only contains the year (2000) when the rules and regulations were issued. However, there is a specific date (January 26, 2001) on the Dai language version.

teams were convened to cast their vote. The rules and regulations were "enacted" in both the Chinese and Dai languages. More than 800 families in the jurisdiction were asked to sign the officially printed version of the regulations. Some regulations, such as Article 2, reflect the moral position of the majority of the villagers. Therefore, one can say that these rules and regulations are consensus-based. Public consultation and the consensus basis laid the foundation for the smooth adoption of these regulations. After being elected in December 2003, the second villagers committee of the Dai people convened villagers' teams and village-level communist party branches to discuss whether it was necessary to amend the regulations promulgated in 2000. After discussion, they concluded that there was no need to revise the original regulations. Therefore, when I visited Mancun Village in 2004, the original regulations were still in force.

Before the village-level organization reform, the nine villages under the jurisdiction of the village affairs office of the Dai people, including Mancun Village, all had their own village rules and regulations. The village affairs office also had established rules and regulations. The village regulations of Mancun Village were adopted in 1994, but before that, Mancun Village had similar village regulations. The printed version of the regulations cannot be found anymore. The following is a summarized version based on the memory of the village head Yan Han:

7.3.2 Ordinances of Mancun Village

Article 1: If a villager gets into scuffle with others, he will be punished by the villagers committee or handed over to the village affairs office or the township police department, depending on the severity of the offense. The severity of the offense is determined based on whether the medical expenses incurred are below 1000 yuan.

Article 2: In the case of a theft offense, the offender will be reprimanded and fined by the villager committee if the value of stolen property is less than 1000 yuan or handed over to the village affairs office or the township police department if the value of stolen property is above 1000 yuan.

Article 3: Rules about gambling: Except for within the seven days following the death of a villager, no gambling is allowed. Otherwise, the offender will be handed over to the police.

Article 4: A major dispute between villagers should be settled by the villager committee. If the villager committee cannot settle the dispute, it should be handed over to the village affairs office. If the village affairs office cannot solve the dispute either, the dispute should then be handled by the township police department.

Article 5: If a husband beats up his wife, the husband will be reprimanded by the villager committee. If domestic violence continues, he will be fined by the villager committee.

Article 6: Villagers who display hooliganism will be fined 100 yuan.

Article 7: Rape cases should be handled by the police.

Article 8: In the case of adultery, both the adulterer and the adulteress will be reprimanded and fined 50 yuan.

Article 9: If an outsider wants to marry a villager in Mancun Village, he/she must pay a certain amount of money to the villager committee. If the outsider is from Duancun Village or Encun Village, he/she should pay 100 yuan; if the outsider is from other places, the amount of money to be paid by the outsider will depend on his/her specific circumstances.

Article 10: If the marriage ceremony is held in the village, the couple should pay 50 yuan to the villagers committee and sacrifice 10 chickens as an offering to the Hearts of Village.

Article 11: Rules about divorce: If a couple agrees to divorce, they should pay 50 yuan to the villager committee; if only one member of a couple file for divorce, the one who proposes the divorce should pay 100 yuan to the villager committee.

Article 12: Rules about house warming. Whoever wants to hold a house warming ceremony should send a bottle of wine and two packs of cigarettes to the head of the militia squad (*huo zi tou*) who will distribute the gifts to the elders in the village.

These regulations were closely related to village life. Many provisions reflected the majority's moral values in the village. These values arose spontaneously from community life within the village. Although the villagers might not clearly remember the specifics of the regulations, they had internalized many of them in the process of socialization. Therefore, these consensus-based regulations were well observed. After the village-level organization reform in 2000, the village regulations of Mancun Village were abolished, but in fact, some of the regulations remained "alive" in the village.

Although important, these village regulations are not the most important contributors to the creation and maintenance of social order in Mancun Village. The most important contributors are the harmonious relationships between the different social control agents and wide acceptance of consensus-based norms.

Before the village-level organization reform, village affairs in Mancun Village were handled by the villager committee. The village head convened a meeting at a time that was convenient for village officials to discuss village matters. The place of meeting could be any village official's home. In case of a dispute with another village, villager officials, members of the communist party branch, and eminent elders would meet to discuss how to handle the dispute; other matters were usually handled by the village head, the deputy village head, and the village accountant together. The villager committee made decisions based on the majority's opinion. If the communist party branch participated in the meeting, the opinion of the party branch would also be taken seriously by the villagers committee. For matters concerning all villagers, a village meeting would be held to discuss the matters. Most villagers held a positive attitude toward village meetings. Every family would send at least one member to a village meeting. Within the villagers committee, there was also a division of labor between village officials. When villagers need help, they usually go to the village head, the deputy village head, or the village accountant. Mancun Village's broadcast system was installed in the 1950s and has been in use since then. The villager committee would use the system to notify villagers of things such as anti-gambling rules, caution against fire disasters, and farming tasks. Sometimes, the villager committee also used the broadcast system to communicate meeting information. Because of the broadcast system and the high concentration of villagers' dwellings, the villagers committee had a relatively high transparent work environment.

Transparency in the village governance system and the consensus-based regulatory process are crucial for the formation and maintenance of social order in Mancun Village. Their importance lies in the fact that they allow the development of new consensus-based norms to prevent new types of disputes and conflicts. For example, Mancun Village built a triangular-shaped barbecue marketplace in 1996. Only one side of the market faced the road. The profitability of the stalls largely depended on their locations. Therefore, how to allocate barbecue stalls was a tricky issue. In the face of this problem, the village officials of Mancun Village did not abuse their power. Neither did villagers fight over more profitable stalls. They held a village meeting to discuss the matter. After discussion, they decided to rotate the booths in such a way that every family had an equal chance of using the more profitable stalls and the less profitable ones. Because the barbecue stands of the villagers were small and thus very easy to move, this solution was feasible. It guaranteed fairness and prevented unnecessary conflicts.

From 2002 to 2004, Mancun Village broke ground on many public infrastructure projects in accordance with decisions made at village meetings. In 2003, Mancun Village and three neighboring villages decided to build an irrigation canal. Officials of these villages tried their best to obtain funding from higher-level government. Therefore, the four villages only needed to prepare construction materials. The villager committee held village meetings to announce the budget, the construction plan and the cost allocation plan. Most villagers agreed with the decisions made by the villager committee. The project was successfully completed in the same year. From 2002 to 2004, the construction of the village's garbage pit, public toilet, and cement paved roads, as well as renovation of the village entryway, were all decisions made by the villagers at village meetings. Village officials successfully secured funding for these projects from the prefecture or county governments by leveraging their social networks, especially relations with the members of their family clans. When the village decided to pave the roads within the village, funding from higher-level government was not enough to cover all the roads within the village. The villagers' team decided to slice the project into phases and raise funds from the villagers to cover the costs. The villagers' team held a village meeting to inform the villagers of the construction plan and the budget. After many rounds of discussion, the construction plan was finalized based on the majority opinion. Another problem was that some of the roads were too narrow. The villagers' team invited a professional who worked for the urban planning department of the township government to develop a road transportation plan for the village. According to the final plan, some villagers needed to retract the walls of their houses. This issue was also discussed at the village meeting. According to the final decision made based on the majority's opinion, the walls were removed, and the losses were borne by the relevant villagers themselves. Although some families would suffer losses and some villagers needed to wait longer than other villagers before they could enjoy the benefits of the project because the project was divided into phases, the plan was approved and signed by the villagers without fuss. During the three-year construction period, the village raised funds for the project three times (78 yuan per family each time). By the end of 2004, 60 percent of the roads in Mancun Village were cement paved. In 2002, Mancun Village built a public toilet. In 2003, the village entryway was renovated, and two garbage pits were built. Improvement of infrastructure has given rise to new norms in Mancun Village:

1. Mancun Village had no public toilet before 2002, and the villagers went to the nearby bamboo forest or the tea forest to answer nature's call. After the public toilet in the village was built in 2002, the villagers' team held a village meeting to discuss who should be assigned the task of cleaning the public toilet. After discussion, the task was assigned to a family, and the village would pay an amount of money raised from the villagers at the end of year to the family every year.
2. Before the construction of the garbage pits in 2003, residents of Mancun Village dumped garbage in the two bamboo forests flanking the village, which seriously affected public hygiene in the village. In 2003, two garbage pits were built in the village. Every day, the villagers dumped the garbage into the garbage pits. However, a new problem emerged: how to dispose of garbage? The villagers' team held a village meeting to discuss the matter. The villagers believed the cost of hiring workers to clean garbage would be too high. In the end, they decided that each family should take turns to clean up the garbage pits and transport the garbage to the shore of the Liusha River, one kilometer away from the village. The villagers were good at reducing the cost of standard operation. They produced a wood sign. Once a family finished their duty for the day, they would hang the sign to the next house to notify that it would be their turn to clean the garbage pits on the next day. This process saved a lot of trouble.
3. In 2002, the construction of some sections of cement paved roads in the village was completed. A regulation was established at a village meeting: each family is responsible for cleaning the section in front of their houses and taking care of the roadside flowers and trees of that section. During my stay in Mancun Village, I would saw villagers cleaning the road or watering the flowers every morning.

Due to the construction of cement paved roads, Mancun Village abolished an old custom. In the past, when a villager demolished an old house and built a new house on the original site, the walls of the garden would be moved outward a bit, meaning that life would be getting better and better. However, if villagers continue to follow this custom after the construction of cement paved roads, the roads would be damaged. Therefore, after discussion, the villagers agreed to abolish this custom.

No punishment was stipulated for violation of these new norms. It seemed that it never occurred to the village officials and villagers that someone might violate the new rules. In fact, based on my observation during my one-month stay in Mancun Village in 2004, ensuring that villagers abide by the rules had never been a problem.

In Mancun Village, the consensus-based decision-making process is the key to the formation of rules and decisions with strong support for follow-through. Furthermore, it could significantly reduce the cost of rule enforcement. In addition to the above new rules, the decision of the village to finance the Theravada Buddhist temple was also consensus based.

After the Theravada Buddhist temple in Mancun Village was built in 1990, there was no institutional guarantee for food supply, which became a major challenge faced by the temple. The young monks often went to villagers' homes to ask for food. After discussion, the villagers decided to take turns to donate food to the temple. Every day, four families in the village would prepare food and send it to the temple. When I visited Mancun Village in 2004, there were some changes in the temple support system. Two wood signs, similar to the wood sign used for notification of garbage cleaning duty, were made and hung at the houses of two families who were responsible for sending food (meals per day) to the temple on that day. The villagers told me with certainty that they rotated once in 24 days. This wood sign eliminated the cost of information transmission. Villagers would know it was their turn if they see the wood sign hung in front of their house.

A change in consensus would lead to the invalidation or change of the norm, as illustrated by the following case.

7.3.3 Case 1: A Dispute over the Roof Design

Before 1993, all houses in Mancun Village were made of bamboo and wood or brick and wood with a hip roof. In 1993, Yan Guang, a resident who had recently made some money from his business, decided to build a two-story brick house with a flat roof, which was both cheaper and more practical than a hip roof. This had never happened before. After discussion, the elderly, including *bu zhang*, decided to set a new rule: no resident was permitted to build a house with a flat roof until the number of households in the village reached 100; otherwise, the flat-roofed house would wreak havoc on the village. When Yan Guang learned about this rule, he had already bought all the construction materials. Therefore, he ignored the new rule and went ahead with the construction. In July 1993, the first house with a flat roof in the village was completed. However, overtaken by the celebratory mood over the completion, Yan Guang did not heed the builders' advice to install a lightning rod. On the third day after the house warming ceremony, the roof of the new house was struck by lightning, fulfilling the prophecy that a house with a flat roof would bring disaster to the village. Yan Guang was roundly rebuked by other village residents. He and his family had to move out of the new house and into a makeshift tarpaulin tent set up at the edge of the field At the same time, at the request of the elders in the village, the monks at the temple moved into the new house. A month later, it was said that the ghosts in the new house had been banished by the monks. Yan Guang spent 700 yuan symbolically buying the new house back from the monks and held another house warming ceremony. The first thing Yan Guang did was to install a lightning rod. After this lightning strike incident, with the "help" of natural forces, this new rule for building a house with a flat roof was accepted by the villagers. In the second year (1994), villagers built three new houses, all of which had a hip roof. However, nothing ominous happened to Yan Guang's new house in the year, casting doubt on this rule. In 1995, another village resident built a house with a flat roof. At present, Mancun Village still has fewer than 100 households, but there are nearly 30 houses with flat roofs, effectively making a mockery of the prohibition.

This case is a good illustration of the importance of consensus-based decision-making for formal and informal social control in Mancun Village. In this example, the elderly individuals headed by *bu zhang* acted as a social control agent. Public opinion led toward the elderly only after the lightening strike verified the prophecy. Before that, most villagers did not know this rule. Therefore, Villager A's behavior became a deviant behavior in the eyes of most villagers. The elders gained support. It became the consensus of the villagers that villagers should not build houses with flat roofs. However, in the third year after the establishment of this rule, a second person violated this rule. However, nothing ominous happened to both Villager A and this second offender. Therefore, the majority's opinion in the village changed again, and the bizarre rule became a joke.

Many norms and decisions in Mancun Village are consensus-based. If the villagers could not reach a consensus on an issue, this issue often could not be resolved. The following is an example of the villagers' failure to reach a consensus:

In 2004, Macun Village proposed the idea of building a drinking water treatment plant. According to the advice of the villagers committee, Mancun Village held a village meeting in early December. Before the village meeting, some residents of Mancun Village leveraged their social networks to secure a pledge from county- and prefecture-level governments to provide financial support. The three villages would only need to invest 100,000 yuan, and the remaining fund (approximately 200,000 yuan) would come from the prefecture and county governments. Village officials and some residents thought that this was a perfect opportunity because they heard that the government would not care about rural areas after the abolition of agricultural taxes and that rural areas would receive no government support in the future. This rumor made the village official more determined to build the water treatment plant. At the village meeting, the village officials reported on the fundraising plan and the budget of the project. Some villagers agreed, but some villagers raised doubts. Some worried that the water plant might affect water supply to farmland; some worried about water quality; some villagers said there was no need to build a water treatment plant because almost every family had a well and besides there was a public well in the village. Moreover, although all villagers contributed money to the cement paved road project, the roads in front of 40 percent families were still mud roads. It was more urgent to complete the road project than to start the tap water project. This time, the village officials lost patience and said that the project would be launched regardless of whether they agreed or not, and villagers not contributing to the project would not be able to enjoy the benefits in the future. These words caused indignation among villagers.

When I left Mancun Village in December 2004, the villagers still had not reached an agreement. When I returned at the end of March 2005, I learned that because a considerable number of villagers were unwilling to fund the project, the plan was put on the shelf. After talking with these irked villagers, I found that they were not so adamantly opposed to the project. If the village officials had shown more patience and made more efforts, they might be persuaded. The reason why they were angry was that the village officials did not follow the consensus-based decision-making process, and their voices were not heard by the village officials.

The following case is another example where the villagers failed to reach a consensus. In 1994, villagers from Mancun Village and Duancun Village began to set up barbecue stalls together in a place in Duancun Village near a local tourist attraction rated as A. However, later, villagers of Duancun Village thought that people from Mancun Village took market share away from them and asked the villagers from Mancun Village to leave. After several rounds of negotiation, Duancun Village refused to give in; thus, Mancun Village withdrew from the marketplace. This was the reason why Mancun Village built its own barbecue marketplace in 1996. The conflict between the two villages over the barbecue market did not end amicably, and the two villages have never been as close as before. In fact, the tension between the two villages had escalated due to some minor incidents. The unresolved economic conflict was the reason behind the dispute between the two villages over the incident where a villager from Mancun Village entered Duancun Village when a recently deceased person in Mancun Village had not been buried.

Whether dealing with internal affairs or relationships with other villages, consensus-based decision-making is very important in the social control system of Mancun Village. Failure to reach a consensus is often ensued by the escalation of conflicts or the occurrence of unnecessary disputes and adversaries.

The consensus-based decision-making process has given rise to high-quality decisions in the public domain with strong support to follow through. Social norms arising from the consensus-based decision-making process are the key to the maintenance of social order in Mancun Village. Therefore, I believe consensus building is the most important feature of the governance system of Mancun Village. The disappearance and change of consensus means that old norms are abandoned, and violation of a consensus may result in punishment by the social control system.

7.4 Formal Social Controls in Mancun Village

Regarding the handling of disputes in Meng County where Mancun Village was located, I interviewed a judicial assistant who has been engaged in administrative and judicial mediation for a long time. The following is his account of dispute handling situation in Meng County:

Disputes in villages in the township were mostly related to marriage and land. The villages have done very well in maintaining public safety since the launch of the safe community campaign in 1999. Most disputes occurred in the busy season from March to May, mostly related to the use of water and land. In 1999, the county government provided a mediator training program for officials of villagers' committees (natural villages) to help them learn to distinguish laws and policies as well as laws and customs and conduct mediation according to law. There are more than 500 mediators in the township. Every staff member of the villagers' teams is a mediator. Villagers committees, party members, village officials, and elders participate in the settlement of village-level disputes as mediators. Village rules have some influence over mediation, but some village rules may impose penalties that exceed the limit prescribed by law.

The people of Mancun Village rarely take disputes to court on their own initiative. By December 2004, no villagers from Mancun Village had ever submitted a dispute to the judicial office in the township. It is not because they know nothing about state laws. Legal cases that have taken place around them as well as law and public safety programs broadcast on TV have made them aware of laws that affect everyday life, especially criminal law. They know that gambling is illegal, unlicensed driving is punishable by a fine, and drug trafficking is a felony. They also know that they can go to the police in case of "big troubles" and that they can file a lawsuit in court. However, in general, state law is far from everyday life in Mancun Village. First, legal texts are written in Chinese. For residents of Mancun Village who are generally less educated, it is difficult for them to read, let alone Chinese-version legal texts. In practice, law enforcement officials and judicial personnel also use the Chinese language in most cases. Although most of the villagers speak Chinese fluently, they are far less familiar with the Chinese language than the Dai language, which after all is their mother tongue. Second, legality is difficult to understand even for well-educated laypeople, let alone less-educated villagers. For the villagers, the information costs of using the law are too high. When I visited the police department of Meng Township, a young police officer who had just been transferred from another prefecture told me that his current task was to master the Chinese dialects as soon as possible or he would be worthless in investigation. Apparently, language is a major obstacle for both villagers and law enforcement officials. It is not that the people of Mancun Village do not need the law at all. It is that information barriers and costs smother their desire to use the law. During my stays in Mancun Village, some villagers consulted me about legal issues. One of them even asked about the details of the law relating to the organization of the villagers committee. Third, Mancun Village has a well-functioning social control system that can meet the needs of villagers to maintain social order in the village. The villagers are familiar with these folkways and dispute resolution methods in the village. Furthermore, the village is a harmonious community. Most disputes, which rarely occur in villages, can be resolved outside the court system. The residents of Mancun Village and surrounding villages are all Dai people. They have similar social norms and speak the same language. Therefore, most disputes between villages can also be settled amicably through negotiation and mediation. Therefore, for the residents of Mancun Village, the need to use the law to settle disputes is low.

As mentioned before, the residents of Mancun Village rarely invoke state laws as a first resort, except in the event of the three criminal cases. The primary formal social control that can be observed in Mancun Village is government controls. State law in Mancun Village is mainly enforced by the government. The key role of the government in law enforcement is not to raise villagers' legal awareness but to deter the crime rate and stop violations. There are both clashes and collaboration between formal and informal social control agents in the village life of Mancun Village, and we can also observe different effects of government social controls on the social order in the village. In general, in addition to the necessary punishments, the effectiveness of government social controls in the village depends largely on the support from the villagers and whether the villagers reach a consensus with the government. The following is an example of government social control supported by villagers.

7.4.1 Case 2: Enforcement of the Marriage Law by the Township Government

The government of Meng Township passed the *Marriage Registration Regulations (Provisional)* on March 19, 1999, stipulating that (i) the age of marriage should not be earlier than 22 years for men and 20 years for women; (ii) the applicants should have hukou in the township and personally bring hukou certificates, proof of marital status (issued by the employers, the villagers committee, or the village affairs office), ID cards, and pre-nuptial training certificates (issued by the township marriage training school) to the Civil Affairs Office of the Township Government to register their marriage; (iii) if the applicants do not meet the criteria for marriage registration, the Civil Affairs Office would refuse to register their marriage; (iv) if the employer or the villagers committee knows the applicant does not reach the statutory minimum marriage age but still provide proof of marital status, the employer or the head of the villagers committee will be fined 3000; (v) if the village affairs office knows the applicant does not reach the statutory minimum marriage age but still provide proof of marital status, the officials at the village affairs office (director, village head, secretary, and director of women's affairs) will be fined 3000 and other staff members of the office will be reprimanded (and fined depending on circumstances); (vi) if a staff member at the Civil Affairs Office registers marriage for applicants who do not meet the criteria, the staff member will be fined 3000 yuan; if a staff member violates the rule more than twice within one year, he or she will be subject to administrative punishments; (vii) if a couple who do not meet legal requirements for marriage enter a de facto marriage without completing the marriage registration procedure, the couple will be reprimanded and fined 3000–5000 yuan and their marriage will be annulled; (viii) if the applicants submit false information, they will be fined 5000 yuan; and (ix) if a civilian reports illegal marriage, the government will protect the identity of the whistleblower and award 10 percent of the fine collected from the couple who violated the marriage registration regulations.

The township government has also issued a regulation regarding divorce registration: If a person remarries, the Civil Affairs Office will require a copy of his/her divorce certificate.

In the 1990s, most people in Mancun Village and nearby Dai villages married at a young age. Many village residents became parents when they were approximately 20 years old. After the township government strengthened the enforcement of marriage law, early marriages in Mancun Village and nearby villages were effectively controlled. There were two key reasons behind the success of this government control. First, according to the regulations, village officials will be fined if they issue proof of martial status for villagers who do not reach the statutory minimum marriage age. This rule strengthened the village officials' involvement in the enforcement of the regulations. Second, public opinion about early marriage has changed. In the past, early marriage could bring certain benefits to villagers. Early marriage sped up reproduction. If a couple gives birth to a child at the age of approximately 20, their children also have children at the age of 20. Then, in the eyes of the local people, this couple would be considered elderly at the age of 40 and could transfer the responsibility of putting bread on the table to the next generation. However, if people get married too early when they are still emotionally immature, the marriage could end disastrously. In Mancun Village, the divorce rate for young people is astonishingly high. There is a young man who has divorced twice and got married three times in a year. In rural areas, both marriage and divorce cost a lot in financial terms. Furthermore, divorce could put a strain on interpersonal relationships, thus leading to social capital loss. Life experience tells people there are both advantages and disadvantages to get married at an early age, but how do we explain the large number of early marriages in Mancun Village in the 1990s? According to my investigation in Mancun Village, young people in Mancun Village did not choose to get married early by intention. They felt peer pressure to get married. In this way, getting married early became a social norm in Mancun Village. Society expected them to get married at an early age. If they did not do so, they would be considered deviant. Many young people in Mancun Village in fact considered early marriage a trap. Therefore, the marriage regulations issued by the township government came as a relief for young people and thus were readily accepted by them. As we can clearly see from this case, the key to the success of government social control lies in whether the social control agent receives strong support.

In addition to social control exercised by functional departments of government, the public security department, as a law enforcement agency tasked to provide protection to citizens, is also a social control agent and plays an important role in maintaining social order. When I visited the police department of Meng Township in December 2004, it had 15 police officers, including five patrol officers, one front desk officer, and one hukou management officer. The police department is responsible for handling both public safety crimes and felony crimes in the township, which consists of five police districts. There are more than 52,000 permanent residents in Meng Township. The police department was overloaded with work most of the time. Under such circumstances, it would be impossible for society to rely solely on the police and the government to maintain order. This is the reason why informal social controls come into play. There are many villages similar to Mancun Village in the jurisdiction of the township government. They have a well-functioning social control system to ensure well-ordered village life, which has greatly reduced the pressure on law enforcement officers. The police department has also recognized the importance of the spontaneous social order in these villages to their work.

Due to limited police resources, the police department can only focus on fighting against more serious crimes. The biggest issue in Meng Township is drug dealing. Meng Township is located near China's southern border with Myanmar. It is on a primary route for drug smuggling into China. Therefore, the police department of the township invests a considerable part of their energy into the fight against drug-related crimes. Drug abuse has also posed serious threats to the social order in Mancun Village.

7.4.2 Case 3: Drug Abuse in Mancun Village

The drug menace cast a shadow over the peaceful village life in Mancun Village in the first half of 2003. There was a small ephedrine distribution center near the village. Some young people in the village began to use ephedrine for pleasure. Ephedrine is a stimulant, and the abuse of ephedrine is problematic. However, young people in the village did not know the problematic consequences of ephedrine abuse. They would give ephedrine to friends after drinking at a social gathering, saying that it is good for hangover. In the first six months of 2003, these young people were addicted to ephedrine. They often partied until midnight or dawn and were reluctant to work during the day. This caught the attention of other villagers. However, they did not know what happened to these young people. This time, the informal social controls in the village failed. In June 2003, the police department became aware of the drug abuse situation in Mancun Village. It ordered villagers who had abused ephedrine to participate in the rehabilitation program at the drug rehabilitation center of the police department. The drug rehabilitation program costs 500 yuan per person. Some young people were reluctant to participate in the program. However, after persuasion by village officials, 22 people participated in the one-week drug rehabilitation program. The village also specially arranged vehicles to send these young people to the drug rehabilitation center. When the program ended, some village officials also went to pick them up. During my stay in Mancun Village in 2004, some of the young people told me that they were tricked by people who told them ephedrine was for hangover. They also told me the effects of various drugs that they learned about when they were at the drug rehabilitation center. In 2003, a person in a neighboring village died from ephedrine overdose, ringing alarm bells for young people in Mancun Village. During my stay in Mancun Village in 2004, I did not encounter drug use.

The key to the police's successful control of the drug abuse situation was the strong support from the village officials and villagers. This social support actually came from two negotiation processes. First, the police department negotiated with village self-governing organizations to obtain their support. Second, village self-governing organizations negotiated with young people to gain their support. The talks between the village officials and the young people led the young people to recognize the problematic consequences of drug abuse and made village officials and other villagers understand what caused the behaviors of the young people. In the end, the deviant and the social control agent reached a consensus.

The following is an example of the township government's failure to gain support from villagers.

7.4.3 Case 4: Failure of Government Fundraising

In 1999, the government of Meng Township decided to build a square on the street where the office of the township government was located. The township government believed that it would accelerate the urbanization of the township and serve as the venue for celebration of the New Year's Day on the Dai people's calendar. To compensate for funding shortfalls, the township government asked the village affairs office to collect a fee (50 yuan per household) from villagers in the township. In addition, each household must pull two carts of sand or soil to the project site. The residents of Mancun Village completed the task of pulling two carts of sand or soil, but they thought the fee was unreasonable. They said that they hardly went to the street. What benefits could they gain from building the square? Why should they pay the money? Therefore, the people of Mancun Village refused to pay this fee.

Regarding this matter, an official of the township government told us that this project was very important to the town and that support from farmers was crucial for the development of an agriculture-based town such as Meng Township. He believed that there was only a slight minority of villagers opposing the plan and that the money would eventually be collected as long as the government stood firm on this issue.

In this case, there was a confrontation between government and citizens. The villagers believed the government's order was irrational. For the villagers, the government's behavior constituted misconduct. This confrontation could be seen as a conflict between two social controls. The villagers were trying to control the "deviant" behavior of the government. The government was the loser in this confrontation. The key to the government's failure in this case did not lie in whether the decision to build the square was right or wrong. The problem was that the government attempted to impose a fee on the villagers without first consulting public opinion. This government directive violated villagers' property rights and completely ignored villagers' wishes. Such a decision would of course encounter resistance from the public.

7.5 Conclusion

There are multiple social control agents in Mancun Village, representing different voices in the village. They form a system of checks and balances and contribute to the maintenance of social order in the village. Consensus-based decision-making is the key feature of village governance in Mancun Village. The consensus-based decision-making process brings together villagers with different viewpoints and positions so they can elucidate their opinions and try to reconcile differences and then reach a consensus. Failure to follow this process is often ensued by escalation of conflicts. The consensus-based decision-making process has given rise to social norms that are not only widely accepted by members of society but also constantly evolving to adapt to new situations and needs. It also brings together the different social control agents, including the village self-governing organization, religious figures, eminent elders, and young leaders, to form a well-functioning pluralistic social control system and prevent the occurrence of conflicts between the different social agents. It drives social norms and endogenous order in the village to constantly evolve and adapt to changes in village life. Like all other places, Mancun Village is no paradise. There are also deviant behaviors (including illegal and criminal behaviors), disputes, and conflicts in the village. However, most of the time over the past two decades, the multiple social control agents in Mancun Village have turned to the consensus-based decision-making process and kept village life in perfect order.

Mancun Village is a village with a high level of autonomy. Its social order depends largely on endogenous informal social controls. However, Mancun Village has not cut itself from the rest of the world. External factors, such as economic reform, government decisions, and regional social issues (such as drug trafficking), also affect the social order in Mancun Village. Therefore, when studying the social order in Mancun Village, formal social control produced and enforced by the state is a dimension that cannot be ignored. Although there are few formal social control agents operating in Mancun Village, formal social control remains an important component of the local social order. The introduction of marriage regulations and the handling of the drug abuse case in 2003 are two examples of the government exercising formal social control in Mancun Village. The marriage regulations banned early marriage and profoundly changed the married life of the villagers. In this case, formal social control gained strong support and was readily accepted by the villagers. In the case of the police handling the young people who were addicted to ephedrine, without support from the villagers, the police's effort to send the drug addicts to the rehabilitation center would run into difficulties. Without police intervention, the drug abuse problem among the young people in Mancun Village would become more serious. In this case, the collaboration between formal and informal social control agents effectively put an end to social deviance and kept society in order. In the case of the square construction project, the township government imposed a fine on the villagers without first consulting the public opinion, triggering indignation among the villagers and undermining the social order.

The following are some takeaways from the case study of Mancun Village: (i) The maintenance of village-level social order does not depend entirely on external coercive power. Consensus-based norms and social controls are more likely to gain strong support and bring conformity to society. Moreover, the endogenous social order arising from consensus-based social controls can constantly adapt to emerging social needs. (ii) Formal social controls are important components of social order. They can effectively deter and punish violations. Collaboration between formal and informal social controls could bring conformity to local communities in a more effective manner. (iii) Consensus-based formal social controls are more likely to gain strong support from members of society and eventually succeed. (iv) Endogenous social order in village communities greatly reduces the operation cost of formal social control institutions of the state and is therefore essential for the social harmony of the countryside and border areas where formal social control resources are limited.

Reference

Zhang, X., & Wang, Q. (2005). Social control and the rule of law in rural settlement areas of ethnic minorities. *The ideological front, 2*.

Chapter 8
Breakdown of Traditional Social Controls and Absence of National Legislation: A Case Study of Pingcun Village

8.1 Breakdown of Village-Level Order Amid Social Changes

Pingcun Village, located in Jinping County, Honghe Hani and Yi Autonomous Prefecture, Yunnan Province, is home to more than 1400 Yao people (over 200 households). The Yao people here call themselves "*yu mian*" or "*ji men*". Outsiders call them "Red Yao". The village is nestled in mountains and across from it is a Vietnamese village on the other side of the China-Vietnam border. Pingcun Village is divided into four sections that are connected by narrow and rugged paths. Apart from transportation, this crisscross of paths also serves as a network of grapevine communication, bonding the villagers closely together.

Currently, social life in Pingcun Village is very different from that in the past. Most families in the village still adhere to interethnic marriages, but there are some girls who marry Han people and move to places such as Guangdong and Guangxi. Most families still follow the traditions associated with religious sacrifice and rituals, but some decide not to hold the ceremonies or hold them on a selective basis. Some women choose to cut their hair and wear a traditional headdress made of red cloth after marriage, while other married women still keep their hair long. When encountering "unusual" things such as landslides or illness of farm animals, some villagers would still ask *mao gong* to carry out divination rituals, while others believe divination is pure nonsense.[1] Funeral ceremonies are still lengthy but much simpler than in the past. The village has not offered sacrifice to dragons in the past decade. Neither have villagers held the traditional rites of passage to adulthood in the past three or four years.[2] There is frequent cross-border trade between villagers and Vietnamese. Some villagers have become semiprofessional traders, frequently traveling between Pingcun Village, Vietnam, and Jinping County. Some young villagers are seeking

[1] *Mao gong* is how the Yao people call clergymen of their folk religion.

[2] The Yao people's traditional rite of passage to adulthood is called "jie du" in the local dialect (Editorial Committee, 1989, p. 205).

Q. Wang, *Sociology of Law*,
https://doi.org/10.1007/978-981-16-5509-8_8

jobs outside the village. The village is undergoing profound social changes. Its culture is changing at an unprecedented speed. Some of its traditional customs have disappeared, and some of its traditional beliefs are being questioned. Lives of villagers are becoming increasingly diverse.

Since the 1990s, social order in Pingcun Village has gradually deteriorated. Robbery was rampant in the mid-1990s but dropped in recent years. Theft and gambling have definitely been on the rise and are posing serious threats to the peaceful lives of villagers. During the harvest season, melons, beans, and corn are major targets of thieves. Some corn growers have seen nearly the entire season's harvest stolen. Thieves are also stealing other items such as livestock. Burglary is also rampant, and even the village affairs office has been broken into by burglars. Currently, villagers are constantly worried about being burglarized. Gambling is also a major threat to the social order in the village. As far as I know, there are at least four illegal gambling sites in the village. Some villagers are compulsive gamblers. They hardly work. Some of them have gambled away houses and land. A gambling addict even sold his children to pay off his debtors. Villagers who are deep in gambling debts or have gambled away everything pose a threat to the social stability of Pingcun Village. How has Pingcun Village entered into such a state of disorder that has seriously derailed the economic development of the village? What drives the village to the brink of anomie? Is anomie unavoidable in modernization? Is it a necessary evil a modernizing society must face? These are the major questions we discuss in this chapter.

8.2 Breakdown of Traditional Social Controls in Pingcun Village

8.2.1 Traditional Social Controls in Pingcun Village

Before the dissolution of the chieftain (*tu si*) system in 1922, the most important political authority figures in Pingcun Village were *tu si*, *guan zhai*, *zhao ba* and *zhai lao*. After 1922 (the Republic of China), the *tu si* system was changed to the *bao jia* system, but the two systems were similar in substance.[3] Since the existence of *zhai lao* did not pose a threat to the rule of *tu si* or the Government of the Republic of China, the *zhai lao* system survived.

Zhai lao, *zhai zhang*, and *long tou* (collectively called *zhai lao*) were eminent male elders elected by the male adults in the village when the village offered sacrifice to the dragon. Their term depended on whether the village was safe and prosperous under their rule. A person could only be *zhai lao* once in a lifetime. It was considered a great honor for a villager to become *zhai lao*. *Zhai* Lao was the highest-ranking leader and

[3] *Guan zhai* and *zhao ba* were two positions under the chieftain (*tu si*) of the Dai people. Each *zhao ba* had control over two or three large villages or four or five small villages. After the dissolution of the chieftain (*tu si*) system, the areas originally under control of a *zhao ba* ware handed over to *a bao zhang*. (Editorial Committee, 1982, p. 146).

decision-maker in the village. They were in charge of policy-making and political, military, religious, and diplomatic affairs of the village. *Zhai lao* were held in high esteem by the villagers. However, they were also subject to the supervision of the villagers and had no privilege. They were also responsible for enforcing customary laws and presiding over civil mediation.[4]

The following are some of the customary laws of Pingcun Village before the founding of the People's Republic of China:

Below are rules relating to theft, adultery, man slaughtering, mortgage sale, and marriage: If a villager steals melons or vegetables of another villager and is a first-time offender, he will be ordered to return the stolen property to the owner and invite the owner to lunch or dinner as a gesture of apology. If the offense is serious, the offender will be required to repair roads. Those who steal cattle and horses will be fined 5–60 *ban kai* (local currency) or sometimes even up to 100–200 *ban kai*, depending on the financial standing of the offender as well as the relationship between the offender and the owner of the stolen property. In case of unmarried pregnancy, if the man who got a woman pregnant is unmarried, the man must marry the woman and invite friends, relatives and the head of village to the marriage ceremony. If a married man gets a girl pregnant, the man may acquire the girl as a secondary wife. If he refuses to marry the girl, the man must pay twelve *liangs* (local currency) to the girl. If a man commits adultery with a married woman and is caught by her husband, he will be fined three to six *liang* and a red cloth. If the woman gets pregnant, the custody of the child she gives birth to should belong to her husband. *Zhai lao* are responsible for presiding over divorce mediation and writing divorce certificates. If they have one child, the custody of the child will belong to the husband. If they have two or more children, they may split the children evenly. If the woman remarries, the man the woman remarries must pay 50–60 *ban kai* to her ex-husband. The surname of the child/children the woman has custody over should be changed to the surname of her new husband. The head of household should be a man. The head of household has the highest authority in the family. Important family matters are generally decided by the head of household. A man could have his own family after he gets married. Family property may be divided evenly among male heirs. If the parents are still alive, the parents should receive one share. The village does not practice primogeniture or ultimogeniture. Aging parents can choose one of their sons to take care of them. The property of the parents will be inherited by the son who takes care of them. Before the parents die, the house owned by the parents should still belong to the parents rather than the son the parents choose to take care of them. Sons should split the burial expenses of the parents. The division of family property is a solemn matter. *Zhai Lao* and other eminent people in the village were invited to serve as witnesses. A property division document would be written, and the family would pay the one who writes the document five *jiao* or one *ban kai*.[5]

In addition to government social control and a relatively complete system of customary laws, the Yao people's folk religion was also an important social control

[4] Editorial Committee (1989, pp. 193–194; 1982, p. 146).

[5] Editorial Committee (1976, p. 128).

agent in Pingcun Village at the time.[6] Offering sacrifices to dragons (*ji long*) and the rite of passage to adulthood (*jie du*) were two of the most important rituals of the Yao people's folk religion. The villagers believed making offerings to dragons would help them avoid diseases, misfortune, and natural disasters. They made sacrificial offerings to dragons four times a year (the third day of the first month, the third day of the third month, the sixth day of the sixth month, and the eighth day of the eighth month of the lunar calendar). Before the sacrificial ceremony, the village would hold a three-day cleansing ritual presided over by *long tou*. A convention regarding work in the village and punishments for violations of the convention would be decided at the ceremony. The Yao people's traditional rite of passage to adulthood is called "*jie du*". After entering adulthood, villagers would be subject to more constraints. For example, they must not eat dog meat, steal, or say dirty words and must conduct themselves properly. Every adult villager had a master, referred to as *mao gong* in the local dialect. The master has the right and responsibility to educate and discipline disciples.

In the old days, *mao gong* played an important role in the social life of Pingcun Village. They were well versed in Yao literature and the Chinese language. They were considered clergymen of the Yao people's folk religion and living embodiment of the Yao people's culture. They were candidates for *long tou*. *Mao gong* were both religious and political authority figures in the village and held in high esteem by the villagers.

Clan leaders were also an important social control agent in the village in the past. A clan leader was usually a well-respected elder in the clan, mainly responsible for mediating disputes between families within the clan and negotiation over clan rules. Both clan leaders and *zhai lao* were responsible for presiding dispute settlement (family disputes such as divorce) in the village. Clan leaders often show respect for the authority of *zhai lao*.

Before the 1950s, the various informal social controls of Pingcun Village were mostly less integrated into the *zhai lao* system. The *zhai lao* system brought social stability, a sense of security, spiritual fulfillment, and a convenient way to settle disputes to the villagers. Thus, *Zhai Lao* had strong support and high social status in the village community. They were the "glue" that brought the community together. At the core of the informal social control system of Pingcun Village was not the specific content of the customary laws but the villagers' acceptance of *zhai lao*'s authority in law enforcement and public life of the village as well as the constraints imposed by religion on the behaviors of villagers.

When the villagers had difficulty settling a dispute, they also sought help from the nationalist government. However, in most cases, the government was beyond the reach of the villagers. Government officers at the grassroots level (*bao zhang* and *jia zhang*) were mainly responsible for managing political, economic, and military affairs rather than community affairs. Therefore, Pingcun Village enjoyed a high

[6] The people of Pingcun Village are multifaith. They believe in Taoism and the Yao people's folk religion and ancestor worship.

degree of autonomy. The social order of Pingcun Village at the time was primarily maintained through endogenous informal social controls.

8.2.2 Social Controls in Pingcun Village After 1949

After the democratic reforms in the 1950s, the social form of Pingcun Village underwent fundamental changes. The *bao zhang* and *jia zhang* system established by the government of nationalists was abolished. From 1949 to 1958, the Communist Party gained support from *zhai lao* and other informal social control agents in Pingcun Village. Therefore, despite political transitions, traditional social controls in Pingcun Village continued to function smoothly, keeping village life in perfect order. However, the twenty years from 1958 to 1976 were tumultuous. The Communist Party launched a series of political, economic and social campaigns, including rural reform, anti-rightist campaigns, the Great Leap Forward, the Four Clean-ups campaign, and the Cultural Revolution. Ethnic culture, beliefs, and knowledge were criticized as outdated leftover from the age of feudalism, and work and life in Pingcun Village became monotonous. The traditional social structure of Pingcun Village completely collapsed, and many folk cultural phenomena, beliefs, and customs disappeared (but this does not mean the folk culture of the village died out). *Mao gong* and *zhai lao*, who were once held in high esteem, were stripped of authority and persecuted. This period saw rapid expansion of state power. State power penetrated every crevice of Pingcun Village's social life. The production team replaced all traditional social organizations and performed political, economic, education, cultural, and propaganda functions. In such a social context, as a part of the village's traditional culture, the traditional social control system of Pingcun Village was on the brink of collapse. Without the support of traditional culture, the village's customary laws lost grip on the behavior of villagers and gradually faded away. The Cultural Revolution drew to an end in the late 1970s. After the Third Plenary Session of the Eleventh Central Committee, the Communist Party veered from the extreme left stance. It began to protect the right to freedom of religion and promote the household contract responsibility system. Alongside the restoration of economic order, the villagers began to restore their traditional beliefs, customs, and way of life. *Mao gong* and *long tou* once again became active in the public life of the village. The villagers were keen on holding various folk rituals and ceremonies. *Mao gong* were invited to chant scriptures. *Long tous* were invited to preside over the sacrificial ceremonies. The nearby mountains were once again resounded with folk songs of the Yao people. The villagers of Pingcun Village completely restored their traditional way of life in just one year or two after the end of the Cultural Revolution. The social life of Pingcun Village returned to the traditional order and once again demonstrated the basic characteristics of a rural community. Some customary laws, as part of traditional culture and order of the village, were also restored but to only a limited extent.

Village life in Pingcun Village was perfectly in order prior to the end of the 1980s. However, this does not mean that there was no problem with the village's social control system. There were primarily two reasons behind the relatively stable social order in the village at the time. First, in the early 1980s, the villagers were busy reviving traditional culture and economic order. The focus of the village and families was on production. The shared goal bound the villagers closely together. Second, wrenching social changes did not conceal the problems of the village's social control system. When problems such as excess labor and low productivity were exposed, many problems in the social control system also came to the fore.

In the mid-1980s, Pingcun Village, like other rural areas, replaced its production team with a village affairs office. Pingcun Village established a villager committee, which was also the residence of the local village affairs office. Since then, the village has entered an era of self-government. However, its initial experiment with self-government was not very successful. The villager committee was responsible for enforcing the village's own rules and regulations. However, because the villager committee failed to establish authority among the villagers, the village rules and regulations were but an empty shell. Since the village's primitive form of democracy embodied in the election of *zhai lao* was abolished in the 1950s, there had never been a similar democratic experience in the public life of Pingcun Village.[7] Villagers over 40 years old knew, either from their own experience or their father's experience, that *zhai lao* were elected by villagers themselves, although many of them might not recall the details of the *zhai lao* system. In contrast, the legitimacy of the officials serving on the villagers committee was often questioned by villagers, making it difficult for them to establish authority and perform duties, which in turn led villagers to believe these officials were incompetent. In addition to village officials, clan leaders and *mao gong* also failed to exercise social control in the village. Due to rapid population growth, the implementation of the household contract responsibility system and the influence of the Cultural Revolution, the villagers' views about family changed. They began to focus more on the nuclear family than the extended family. The social status and the influence of clan leaders were declining. Clan leaders existed in name only. They rarely made clan-related decisions anymore. They were still invited to participate in the settlement of family disputes but as witnesses rather than mediators. Clan leaders themselves began to lose interest in clan affairs. The villager committee also no longer relied on the influence of clan leaders to manage community affairs. Clan leaders were no longer considered authority figures in the village community. After the Cultural Revolution, *mao gong*,[8] on the one hand, began to distance themselves from politics and rarely intervened with village affairs. On the other hand, the village affairs office and the villagers committee did not need the help of *mao gong* to establish their own authority in the community. Village officials believed that folk religious authority should not intervene with law enforcement or state affairs. Under such circumstances, it is difficult for *mao* to establish political

[7] Before the village-level organization reform, although the members of the villagers committee were elected, the candidates were selected by the higher-level administrative organs, therefore seriously undercutting the residents' trust and public participation, which is one of the cornerstones of democracy.

[8] There are currently six *mao gong* in the village.

authority or participate extensively in the public life of the village community. They became pure religious figures.[9] Moreover, because *mao gong* no longer assumed a leadership role in the political life of the community, the *ji long* ceremony, which was more a political event than a religious event, organized by *mao gong* began to lose its appeal. The fact that *mao gong* could not bring any real benefits to residents beyond the spiritual world further weakened their authority and influence in the community.

Currently, the residents in Pingcun Village are still more or less religious. However, they no longer hold collective religious rituals. They believe religion is a private matter and the community has no place in the private lives of individuals. Moreover, due to the extremely high cost of the traditional rite of passage to adulthood (approximately 6000 yuan) and the sheer number of taboos associated with it, very few residents are willing to hold the rite, which means that Pingcun has lost another form of social control. Religion is no longer a source of cohesion in the community.

In the nearly 40 years since the early 1960s, no social control agent emerged in the village to fill the blank left by *Zhai Lao*. In this case, the formal social control agent of the state should be held responsible. The new formal social control agent failed to establish authority within the community and adapt to the new political system and social context. It did not become a new source of cohesion for the community. Therefore, Pingcun Village's traditional social control system lost its soul and became dysfunctional, which further deprived the possibility of achieving endogenous growth. Even though there are still informal society controls in Pingcun Village, the absence of a mechanism that supports their effective operation since the 1950s has weakened the authority of informal social control agents and undermined social cohesion in the community.

In the last 20 years, the entire country has undergone enormous changes. Cities have been modernizing rapidly, while rural areas have been developing at a slower pace. Pingcun Village is located in a mountainous area near the China-Vietnam border. Its cultivated land per capita stands at 0.8 mu per person. The surplus labor force and poverty pose serious challenges to the village. The widening urban–rural gap is not making things better. This is the background for social and cultural changes in Pingcun Village. The culture of the village fails to adapt to violent changes in society, putting the spiritual world of the residents at risk. Therefore, the village has seen a dramatic increase in incidents of deviance, and its existing spontaneous social controls (customs, clans, religion, and political organizations) have become too weak to maintain order.

---

[9] The residents would invite them to chant scriptures and exorcise ghosts at weddings and funerals. Sometimes, *mao gong* are also invited to perform divination or expel misfortune.

8.3 Present Informal Social Controls and Enforcement of State Law in Pingcun Village

8.3.1 Present Informal Social Controls in Pingcun Village

Most marriage-related customary laws of Pingcun Village are still effective. They are the most effective part of its traditional social control system largely because of the social structure of Pingcun Village, where family is still the basic unit of social life (including marriage, economic activities, political activities, and education). However, penalties for violating informal society controls have changed considerably. For example, the following is how the residents handle thieves: (i) if a resident is caught in the act of stealing property of another person (except when stealing cattle), in addition to requiring the thief to return the property or compensate for the value of the stolen property, the owner of the stolen property may impose a fine on the thief or take his property as punishment; and (ii) if a resident is caught in the act of stealing cattle, in addition to the above punishments, the owner may beat up the thief. This is an epitome of the current informal social control system in Pingcun Village. The way a dispute is handled varies depending on the severity and nature of the dispute and the relationship of the involved parties. The procedure for settlement is basically as follows: (i) family/clan disputes → family/clan meetings → residents committee → village affairs office → township justice department → court; or (ii) self-resolution → residents committee → village affairs office → township justice department → court.[10]

The following are examples that could offer insight into the present informal society controls in Pingcun Village:

Case 1

One morning in 1999, Villager A discovered that an ox of his was stolen. Villager A immediately asked more than 10 residents, including his niece's husband Villager B, to help him find the ox. They decided to follow the "old rules"; that is, after finding the cow and the thief, they would beat up the thief and then ask the thief to pay 2000 yuan to Villager A as compensation. Villager A would use this amount of money to invite the helpers to eat something good and split the remaining money among the helpers as compensation for time spent on helping him find the ox. The group of residents found the thief in Vietnam. After finding the thief, they, except Villager A, returned to Pingcun Village, and Villager A stayed overnight in Vietnam because he had to drive the ox back. When the group of helpers left, Vietnamese thief revealed to Villager A that Villager B had also participated in the stealing of the ox. After returning to Pingcun Village, Villager A found that Villager B had fled for fear of

[10] This procedure is not set in stone. The way to settle a dispute is often chosen based on the needs of the involved parties. Due to the vicinity of the village affairs office, when the residents are involved in disputes, they are more willing to go to the village affairs office rather than the villagers committee because they believe the villagers committee is incompetent. This has unavoidably increased the workload of the village affairs office.

being beaten. So Villager A and his helpers went to Villager B's home and demanded Villager B's family to give them 2000 yuan. Villager A used a part of the money to host a banquet for the helpers. According to agreement, the remaining money should be split among the helpers. However, Villager A and his wife got greedy. They only paid 20 yuan to each helper and kept the remaining money for themselves. Other residents were put out by Villager A's behavior, saying that they would no longer help Villager A in the future. A month later, Villager B returned to Pingcun Village and brought a gift to Villager A in a gesture of apology. Villager A did not beat up Villager B.

Case 2

In 1995, a pig of Villager C's was stolen. After finding out that it was stolen by Villager D, Villager C went to Villager D's home to confront him. According to the "old rules", Village C had the right to take part in Villager C's property as compensation. Villager C knew that Villager D was poor. However, after Villager C arrived at Villager D's house, he found the poverty of Villager D far beyond his exp ectation. In the end, Villager C only took a pig of Villager D as compensation.

As seen from the above two cases, *vigilance* is an important part of the social control system of the village. The formal social control agents (the village affairs office and the villagers committee) were not involved in the handling of the disputes in either case. In Case 2, Villager C himself was a member of the villagers committee, but he did not act in his capacity as village official in dealing with this dispute with Villager D. Instead, he followed the old rules like other residents. Villager C did not seek justice for himself through the villager committee because the villager committee existed in name only and failed to establish authority among the residents. However, informal social control entails customary laws that are not necessarily compulsory. They are easy to break.[11] For example, Villager A violated the local custom relating to the handling of the money.[12]

The current social control system in Pingcun Village is very different from its social control system in the past. Before the founding of the People's Republic of China, at the core of the village's social control system was *zhai lao*, who was responsible for the management of public affairs and had the power to enforce customary laws in the village. Currently, there is no such authority in the village to enforce customary laws. Instead, residents often take the law into their own hands. The lack of authority to fill in the blank left by *zhai lao* is what leads the residents to resort to *vigilante* and it also directly leads to the following two consequences: (i) clash between formal and informal social controls, as illustrated in Case 3 below; and (ii) disorder because over-reliance on *vigilante* could not lead to the establishment of a normative social system widely accepted by the residents.

---

[11] This is mainly attributable to the lack of authority in public life of Pingcun Village. It rarely happened under the *zhai lao* system.

[12] Of course, this does not mean that Resident A's behavior was not punished. Shaming and refusal to help in the future are also forms of punishment.

8.3.2 *Enforcement of State Law in Pingcun Village*

In addition to the ineffectiveness of the present informal social controls, the chaos in Pingcun Village today can also be attributed to the weak enforcement of state law in the local area.

The following are some examples used to illustrate this point:

Case 3

In April 2000, Villager E escaped after being caught in the act of stealing. Villager E had been caught red-handed several times. This time, the residents were really angry over his lack of repentance. On the night Villager E was caught again, dozens of residents dragged Villager E with his hand tied behind him to a local school and beat Villager E to death. For the handling of the accomplices of Villager E's, the villagers committee held a village meeting and invited the local police and the staff of the village affairs office to sit in on the meeting. At the village meeting, the residents unanimously agreed that the accomplices should pay a fine of 1000 yuan per person. This money would be used to hold a feast to which the whole village would be invited. Later, at the request of the accomplices, the fine was changed to 800 yuan per person. The police and the village affairs office agreed to this decision.

Local police investigated the death of Villager E but failed to pin down the mastermind behind this incident of collective violence. But one thing is for sure: village officials were not present, and they were not part of this collective violence.[13]

There are so many questions relating to this case.

Such a tragedy gives pause for reflection. Should the occurrence of tragedies be attributed to the cruelty of residents? Why had the residents not killed Villager E's accomplices? Why not kill all the thieves regardless of the value of the stolen items or whether it was the first offense of the thieves? Was vigilante killing a tradition in the village? The answer is no. Theft is punishable by a fine according to local regulations. Physical punishment was never a popular form of punishment for theft before the 1990s. As theft grew increasingly rampant, this cruel form of social control emerged. This seemed to have nothing to do with state law, but reality told another story. In Case 3, the residents knew what would happen if they had handed the unrepentant thief Villager E over to the local police. "The police would simply keep him in custody for several days and impose a small fine and then let him go. "[14] They believed such a punishment was too light for an unrepentant thief like Villager E. Therefore, they took the law into their own hand.

---

[13] The case occurred in a neighboring village of Pingcun Village. Violent incidents also occurred frequently in Pingcun Village but not as serious as this one. The incidents in Pingcun Village did not result in death. Neither did they involve so many residents. The people in Pingcun Village were not as united as those in the neighboring village. The occurrence of this case was attributable to the ineffectiveness of the law enforcement system of the state on crackdown on theft. Rampant theft was also posing a serious challenge to social order in Pingcun Village.

[14] Based on comments from the people in Pingcun Village and neighboring villages.

The residents in Case 3 were good at circumventing the law. The village officials "just happened" to be absent from the scene, therefore protecting themselves from any liabilities that might arise from the incident. One of the village officials told me that he knew what would happen. They had their own way of dealing with such matters. "It is not appropriate to kill people. But if the involved parties do not ask for my help, I will not intervene." Obviously, the village officials knew their duties. If they got involved, they would not let the residents beat Villager E to death. However, deep down, they were also disgusted with the behavior of Villager E. Therefore, they turned a blind eye on the violence of the residents. Between state law and customary law, they chose customary law in a seemingly passive manner.

The reason for residents' choosing to punish Villager E on a dark night was obvious that they could say it was such a dark night that they couldn't see clearly who were involved. The purpose of the villagers committee to invite the staff of the village affairs office and local police to attend the village meeting was to show that they were innocent. It was also a gesture of defiance against the authority of state law. In China, we often say *fa bu ze zhong*-the law cannot be enforced when everyone is an offender. Could we really say these residents were ignorant of the law?

It is hard to tell that local police's approval of the resolution of the villagers committee was because local police, as representative of the state, backed down in face of the defiance of the residents (vigilante violence) or forget their law enforcement responsibilities. It is more like that there was an unspoken agreement between local police and the residents. The village affairs office also approved the residents' behavior.[15]

Case 4

Villager F stole an ox of Villager G. Villager G demanded Villager F to pay 5000 yuan to him as compensation. However, Villager F did not have so much money and reported it to the local police. The police station reprimanded Villager G and imposed a fine of 200 yuan on Villager F.

Why did Villager F report his own offense to the local police? The reason was very simple. Because the penalty imposed by the police was far lower than the penalty required by Villager G. This is also why some residents believe that the law protects bad people.

Case 5

Villager H once went to a border patrol checkpoint to go through the formalities necessary to leave the country for a while. When he was at the checkpoint, he had to answer the call of nature. He emptied his bladder in an alley behind the checkpoint. A soldier standing guard at the checkpoint saw his behavior. He reprimanded that Villager H. Villager H responded, "No one told me I couldn't pee here." The soldier

---

[15] An official of the village affairs office told me that they usually would not intervene in disputes between residents unless the residents asked them to get involved. He said that an offense that was punishable by a fine of 1000 yuan according to village rules might be punishable by a fine of 200 yuan according to state law. He could not violate the policy.

got annoyed. He dragged Villager H into a room and locked him up. He told Villager H that he would stay here to work for the checkpoint for three days before he would be released. Villager H said, "I have not broken the law." The solider released Villager H in an hour. Villager H later told me that this incident led him to realize that law was not fair and it was just a tool of law enforcement officials.

Villager H's experience seemed insignificant. The soldier neither beat Villager H nor really detained him for three days. However, he threatened Villager H, which was a very inappropriate behavior for a law enforcement official. This small incident had a huge impact on Villager H's views about law.

In summary, the enforcement of state law in Pingcun Village was not in an ideal state. On the one hand, residents have been vacillating between formal and informal social controls. On the other hand, formal social controls often fail to respond effectively to the needs of residents, making it different for residents to associate formal social controls with justice, fairness, and their expectations.

Of course, there are many reasons why state law is not ideally enforced at the local level. On the one hand, there is a lack of law enforcement resources in the township where Pingcun Village is located. First, there is only a police station in the township responsible for maintaining social order. There are 12 people on the payroll of the police station, but in reality, there are only six staff members working there. However, the right to appoint and dismiss its personnel vests in the border security force. The police station is also accountable to the police department of Jinping County. Such a system itself spells trouble. Furthermore, the staff of the police station hardly receive any training in law enforcement. Their law enforcement capability is questionable. Second, there are 16 village offices and 42 natural villages in the township. The residences are scattered, making it impossible for law enforcement officials to respond to every call in a timely manner. They do not have enough resources to investigate every criminal case in a timely manner, let alone minor offenses. There is no wonder that stealing and gambling have gone rampant in Pingcun Village. Third, the local court is far away from Pingcun Villige. The residents needed to walk more than three kilometers and then take the bus to the county seat. Litigation is lengthy, costly, complex, and unfamiliar to residents. Furthermore, the rules of court may be completely different from what they expect. As far as costs are concerned, it is reasonable that courts are not the residents' first choice for civil dispute resolution. Fourth, the judicial office of the township government has only one full-time employee and four part-time staff members. It also has a tight budget. The judicial office has neither manpower nor financial resources to investigate cases in a thorough and timely manner.

On the other hand, the traditional social control system in Pingcun Village has broken down. There is no social control agent within the village that is powerful enough to fill the blank left by traditional social control agents, leading to a decline in social cohesion and a surge in conflicts. The village is tittering on the brink of anomie. Furthermore, clashes between state law and informal social controls also hinder the enforcement of state law in the village.

8.3.3 Interaction Between State Law and Informal Social Controls

In Pingcun Village, state law and informal social controls are not isolated existence. They interact with each other. Such interactions are achieved through the actions of the police, village officials, ordinary residents, and other people involved in legal actions (not just the parties involved in a case). State law has never lost its influence on informal social controls (regardless of whether the influence is good or bad), and informal social controls have never stopped responding to state law. In Case 1, Villager A knew that the local police was not helpful, so he chose to settle the dispute in the old way. It is precisely because the residents knew how the police would handle thieves that residents in Case 3 took the law into their own hands, which led to the tragic death of Villager E and that Villager F in Case 4 confessed his own crime and leveraged state law to invalidate the customary law. In Case 5, an accidental encounter with formal social control led Villager H to lose trust in state law.

In Pingcun Village, informal social controls have not been aligned with state law, and formal social controls have failed to address conflicts with customary laws. In summary, the interaction between formal and informal social controls is not good for social order in Pingcun Village. One major cause of this situation is the failure of state law to address local needs. Take Case 3 and Case 4 for example. In Case 3, the residents knew the provisions of the state law, but they did not internalize these provisions. This is why they knowingly violated state law. Villager F in Case 4 knew how formal and informal social controls would handle theft. To Villager F, state law was just a leverage against informal social control. If the punishment under state law was harsher than that under customary law, he would have readily chosen customary law. Villager F chose state law because he knew state law would protect him from harsher punishments under the "old rules".

8.4 Why Did the Social Order in Pingcun Village Break Down?

After the 1950s, amid abrupt social changes, the state destroyed some informal social controls that were important components of social order in Pingcun Village. Clans or folk religion are important parts of local culture and social life. It is not appropriate to excessively suppress them. In some locales, informal social controls can indeed play a major role in delivering justice and maintaining social order and power balance (Wang, 1997, p. 326). Informal social control agents were driven out of political life in Pingcun Village by formal social control agents under the guidance of extreme political ideologies. This "governance" approach is inappropriate and extremely destructive. The weakening of informal social controls was inconsistent with the basic social conditions of Pingcun Village. As far as Pingcun Village is concerned, social order in the village still needs informal social controls, as it seems that a well-established rule of law system will not happen in the near future in China. Furthermore, in the past 50 years, some factors that may be conducive to the establishment of a modern rule of law system have not been effectively leveraged but undermined. Pingcun Village used to have a primitive democratic system that, if reasonably preserved, would contribute to the establishment of modern democracy and rule of law. Unfortunately, this primitive democratic system was destroyed. This has led many residents to distrust formal social control institutions, such as the villager committee.

However, although the breakdown of the traditional social control system of the village is an important factor contributing to disorder in Pingcun Village, this does not mean that the breakdown of the traditional social control system in a village would definitely lead to social disorder in the village. As long as state law meets the needs of the village when the internal social control system is weak, the social order in the village can still be effectively maintained. Unfortunately, this is not the case in Pingcun Village. People's trust or distrust of state law manifests in their actions. This is why law (including the means through which people know law) is closely related to other social factors, such as government behavior and social relations. The attitudes of the residents towards customary laws and informal social controls are not formed overnight. Only when residents feel the superiority of state law will they truly trust and comply with state law. The residents' limited knowledge of law is gained through their encounters with law, as illustrated in Case 5. Their understanding of law ("law only protects the wicked") is one-sided. The people of Pingcun Village primarily base their understanding of law on their encounters with law enforcement. Because of the limited knowledge of the residents, it is difficult for them to distinguish law enforcement from law. They may distrust state law simply because of the bad behavior of certain law enforcement officials. Poor law enforcement is a key contributor to the negative interactions between state law and informal society controls. Another contributor is problems in legislation. The cases in the previous section reveal that the residents' attitude towards state law depends on whether state law can effectively respond to the needs of the residents.[16] However, state laws are not specifically designed to address the needs of residents. Therefore, no matter how law enforcement officials enforce the law, they cannot enable benign interactions between state law and informal social controls in Pingcun Village. The disorder in Pingcun Village was caused by the failure of state law and the lack of new informal social controls powerful enough to fill the blank left by traditional informal social controls.

In summary, there are two direct reasons for disorder in Pingcun Village: (i) imbalance of the village's internal social control system caused by the breakdown of its traditional social controls amid social changes and (ii) failure of state law to bring conformity to the village community. No wonder Pingcun Village is tittering on the brink of anomie.

[16] This principle also applies to customary laws. When a customary law fails to address the needs of the residents, it will also be abandoned. For example, Resident F in Case 4 leveraged state law to circumvent customary law.

8.5 Conclusion

The situation of Pingcun Village reminds me of Mr. Fei Xiaotong's depiction of the encounter between the rule of *li* and the modern justice system amid social changes in the rural part of China sixty years ago: "The current justice system has an enormous side effect on the country. It destroys the original order shaped by Confucian values but fails to establish the rule of law in the country." (Fei, 1998, p. 58). The new justice system failed to solve the problems of that era. Instead, it made the situation more complicated. Although the breakdown of the traditional social order system of Pingcun Village has nothing to do with the current justice system, the situation in Pingcun Village is eerily similar to the Chinese countryside in the 1940s depicted by Mr. Fei.[17] Moreover, whether it is the rule of *li* in villages of the Han people or the *zhai lao* system of Pingcun Village, both informal social control institutions dissolved amid abrupt social changes. This gives me pause. Does it mean disorder caused by the breakdown of informal social controls is the price a modernizing society must pay?

Although the Pingcun Village case cannot represent the social order problems across all types of villages and localities, it shows that if a village's internal or traditional social control system is broken or weakened to an extent that it is unable to maintain the existing social order or give rise to a new social order and, at the same time, state law fails to come into full effect or respond to the normative needs of the village, which will result in a lack of normative underpinning in social transition, the village is very likely to form an informal social control institution in conflict with state law. A lack of beneficial interactions between state law and informal social control will in turn exacerbate the negative effects of the absence of normative order, resulting in a vicious circle that can lead to social chaos. A takeaway from the Pingcun Village case is that when the traditional system of a village has been changed/destroyed, the lack of a new system in its stead will cause the collapse of the cultural system that supports the way of life, values, and worldviews of the residents, leading to social chaos in the process of modernization. This is a dilemma faced by many villages in the process of modernization. It is also the root cause of the sustained absence of social order in these villages. To overcome this dilemma, the state needs to pay attention to every detail of law enforcement, establish authority of state law, increase the trust of the public in state law, and improve the ability of the legislator to respond to the needs of society. More importantly, to solve the dilemma, we need to recognize that "modernization" and "traditions" are not mutually exclusive. It is important to transform local social control institutions in a prudent and gentle manner rather than forcefully. The law imposed must be able to promote the formation of an endogenous social control system in the village.

---

[17] Perhaps the orderly life of Pingcun Village in the 1940s was not broken down as Fei depicted because the justice system did not forcefully penetrate into the social life of Pingcun Village.

References

Editorial Committee. (1989). *An ethnographic study of the Honghe Hani and Yi Autonomous Prefecture*. Yunnan University Publishing House.

Editorial Committee. (1982). *A sociological study of the Yao People in Yunnan*. Yunnan Ethnology Publishing House.

Editorial Committee. (1976). *A sociological study of the Miao and Yao Communities in Jinping and Pingbian of Yunnan Province*. Yunnan University (for internal use).

Fei, X. (1998). *From the soil and institutions for reproduction*. Peking University Press.

Wang, M. (1997). *Culture and power in village settings*. SDX Joint Publishing Company.

Epilogue

Constructing Legal Theories with Chinese Issues at the Core

"A person who does not expect the unexpected will not discover unexpected things; such things will never be discovered or found by him. " (Popper, 1996, p. 209) The purpose of our research is to discover such unexpected things. For me, to expect the unexpected is the way to better understand China and to seek solutions to Chinese issues.

A few years ago, after reading Mr. Deng Zhenglai's *What is the Future of Jurisprudence in China?*,[1] I was overwhelmed by a strong feeling of frustration. This lengthy article made me think of Boaventura de Sousa Santos' analogy between law and a map (Santos, 2002). A bitter irony is over the past 30 years (or ever since the end of the Qing Dynasty), and we have been attempting to establish a rule of law in China by using the "map" of the Western world.

However, after calming down, I began to realize that this "paradigm crisis" in China's jurisprudence is not as serious as what is suggested by Mr. Deng. In fact, we can look at this paradigm crisis from another angle.[2] In my opinion, the "ideal legal landscape" in China is not a priori. It must be discovered through theoretical and empirical research. At least so far, no one would be arrogant enough to say that he knows what jurisprudence in China truly needs. I prefer to regard the previous works of scholars, such as Su Li and Liang Zhiping, as brave attempts that we could use as stepping stones to reach the "ideal legal landscape". The views of any scholar would be affected by existing knowledge and the social context he is in. When the existing knowledge system or the social context changes, his views also change. Therefore, it is not uncommon for a scholar to change his or her views during a research project or his academic life. For the jurisprudence field in China, what is important is whether

[1] This article of Mr. Deng's, nearly 180,000 words in length, was published in the first to fourth issues of *Tribune of Political Science and Law* in 2005.

[2] Mr. Deng has never denied the desirability of the "ideal legal landscape" in China, which is one of the commendable position of this article.

Q. Wang, *Sociology of Law*,
https://doi.org/10.1007/978-981-16-5509-8

such changes have improved our understanding of Chinese society and the rule of law in China.

What gives a theory the possibility to become "truth" is that a theory is testable, refined, and modified. As long as the majority of scholars in the field of jurisprudence are still theoretically sensitive, theories of law will continue to be refined and corrected. In this process, theories of law that apply to the social context of China will continue to mature, and Chinese scholars will ultimately create their own theories. Of course, whether this vision will become reality will depend on our attitude towards knowledge production.

In *What is the Future of Jurisprudence in China?*, Mr. Deng Zhenglai articulates two criticisms about scholars of jurisprudence in China: (i) failure to give due attention to real problems in China and (ii) employment of the paradigm of modern jurisprudence in the Western world to explain situations in China without a second thought, which contributed to cultural hegemony of the Western world (Deng, 2005). These bad research habits would ruin our career as legal theorists. They prevent us from constructing theories of law that apply to the social context of China.

With regard to the criticisms of Mr. Deng, I want to point out two dilemmas faced by contemporary Chinese legal theorists. First, failure to give sufficient attention to problems in China leads to the lack of an in-depth understanding of China's social reality. If we borrow Santos's metaphor, it would be like building a city on a vast expanse of land. The rule of law is the blueprint of the city, which provides information on building styles, roads, and regional planning. However, if we do not know the total area, topography, geological conditions, and other basic information of this piece of land, how could we develop a reasonable and feasible blueprint? Second, we do not truly understand Western societies and theories, especially the reasons behind the emergence of these theories and the problems they address, which, in combination with the first dilemma, has trapped many scholars in the maze of theories. We, surrounded by a cloud confusion, don't know what kinds of Western institutions and theories are worth borrowing. It's like building a new city by using the blueprint of another city without knowing the reasons behind the design and the different conditions of land. Due to a lack of endogeneity, existing theories of law and rule-of-law institutions in China cannot evolve and address real problems in China. With so many Chinese scholars, as Mr. Deng puts it, succumbing to the lure of the paradigm of modern jurisprudence in the Western word, it is hardly surprising that we have difficulty constructing theories of law that apply to the social context in China.

To overcome these two dilemmas, scholars of jurisprudence in China will need more effective methodologies. First, we should pay more attention to fieldwork research. The famous journalist Robert Capa said, "If your pictures aren't good enough, you're not close enough."[3] Mao Zedong also criticized those who like to talk about things they don't know (Mao, 1991, p. 109). It is always ignorance that leads to vague explanation or overgeneralization. We are too far away from the core of the problem. We cannot draw out an ideal blueprint for the establishment of the

[3] Opening line of the famous documentary *War Photographer*.

rule of law in China because we still do not fully understand the Chinese society in which we live. Only when we know the social context of law can we develop an ideal blueprint for the establishment of the rule of law in society. In other words, we need to take a sociological approach and examine the various "fields" related to law—families, villages, ethnic groups, courts, markets, and so on.[4]

Only when we place law back to its social context can we truly solve the problems in China's jurisprudence. The purpose of fieldwork is to observe and gain first-hand information. Fieldwork research will allow us to discover the real problems in China. It is a useful tool for Chinese jurists who attempt to put law back to the social context of China. However, it must be pointed out that to construct theories of law that apply to China, we need to observe the social groups and daily life of Chinese people to identify what kind of order Chinese society needs. Fieldwork research shortens the distance between jurists and society and brings different ideas and claims to the forefront of jurists' attention, thus preventing the emergence of predominant theories.

Of course, just walking into the "fields" of law is not enough.

There are many ways and frameworks that can assist human beings in understanding the world. For example, religion and science can help us come to grips with social and natural phenomena. Theories also offer frameworks and ways to understand the world, especially for scholars. If we, as scholars, want to answer all the questions about Chinese society and its order, it is imperative for us to construct necessary theories. In regard to the construction of theories of law, Mr. Deng's question—on what we should base our imagination of law and order—will need to come to the fore (Deng, 2005). It is entirely possible for scholars to arbitrarily create a label based on a certain theory or theoretical framework and then stick it to the social reality of China. Therefore, it is dangerous to just walk into the "fields" of law without the guidance of theories and values. If we do not have theoretical sensitivity, we would not be able to discover the mistakes of existing theories and space of improvement in the so-called "legal landscape" through fieldwork research. We may be lost in the labyrinth-like real world without the guidance of theoretical frameworks, disregard or misinterpret observations of issues in China under the guidance of Western theories, or attempt to circumvent Western theories at all costs and put the "Chinese" label on every observed problem. Such observations have no value at all.

In conclusion, the premise of constructive fieldwork findings is that researchers must be theoretically sensitive. Only theoretically sensitive jurists could make constructive observations that can help to advance the system of legal theories and

[4] The famous legal sociologist Roger Cotterrell, as a critic of the paradigm of jurisprudence in the western world, argues that perhaps the most obvious characteristic of law is its apparent intellectual isolation. The idea of law as a discipline and profession can only be understood in terms of "its own internal categories" and "without reference to the social environment within which it develops". This idea is especially popular in the modern western societies as mentioned in this book. For this reason, "the typical legal view that the jurists have formed in their professional environment has made them overconfident, and they think they understand so deeply that they endeavor to resist different views of the nature and the role of the law." (Cotterrell, 1992, p. 16–17) Therefore, entering the "field" of law requires to abandon its intellectual isolation as Cottwell said so as to obtain help from different disciplines such as anthropology, sociology, etc.

establish the rule of law in China. Observations themselves cannot provide a blueprint for the construction of theories and the establishment of the rule of law, but observations under guidance of theories can substantiate or modify theories or provide evidence to prove a theory to be wrong. Observation is an important way to verify an existing theory of law or a practice of the rule of law.

As long as we remain theoretically sensitive, it is entirely possible for us to construct theories of law that apply to Chinese society and propose a feasible plan to make substantial progress in the establishment of the rule of law. Western theories or models should not be predominant in international academic dialogue in jurisprudence. Instead, they should be appraised more critically, filtered, and modified to suit the local social context. Comparative study of Western societies and theories and the local social context is an effective way to combine emic and etic perspectives, which will allow us to find China's position in the world. In a similar vein, theoretically conscious observations can force local theories to constantly readjust and evolve.

We need to observe how law works in the real world. As Mr. Su Li puts it, "We are deeply embedded in this world." (Su, 1997) We are in a web of norms and institutions produced by our predecessors. What we could do is to observe, recognize, understand, and change this web. The generation of theories should be a cyclic process consisting of the following steps: continuous observation—modification of existing theories and institutions—proposing new theories and institutions. It will help us gain a more comprehensive and in-depth understanding of the social reality in China, and then we will be able to put forward and refine our own theories to truly explain our life and provide solutions to real-life problems. Only theories generated through such a process are likely to be recognized in the academic world. This book is just my first step towards developing such theories.

References

Popper, K. R. (1996). *Emancipation through knowledge* (F. Jingzhong, & L. Benzheng, Trans.). China Arts Publishing House.
Zhenglai, D. (2005). The future of legal studies in China. *Tribune of Political Science and Law*, (1–4).
Zedong, M. (1991). *Selected works of Mao Zedong* (Vol. 1). People's Publishing House.
Li, S. (1997). You and me are embedded in this world. *Frontiers*, (6).
Santos, B. de S. (2002). Law: A map of misreading. Toward a postmodern conception of law (Z. Jingwen, & N. Xi, Trans.). In Z. Jingwen (Ed.). *Studies for postmodern jurisprudence*. Law Press.
Cotterrell, R. (1992). *The Sociology of law: An introduction*. Butterworths.

Uncited References

I. Books
Becker, E. (2000). *The Denial of death* (L. Hesheng, Trans.). Huaxia Publishing House.
Benton, L. (2005). *Law and colonial cultures: Legal regimes in world history, 1400–1900 (Studies in Comparative World History)* (L. Yaping, & Z. Wei, Trans.). Tsinghua University Press.
Berman, H. J. (2003). *The interaction of law and religion* (L. Zhiping, Trans.). China University of Political Science and Law Press.
Black, D. J. (2004). *The behavior of law* (T. Yue, & S. Li, Trans.). China University of Political Science and Law Press.
Bojun, Y. (1960). *The interpretation of the Mencius*. Zhonghua Book Company.
Bonsignore, J. B. et al. (2002). *Before the law* (D. Zibin, Trans.). Huaxia Publishing House.
Chanda, N. (2008). *Bound together: How traders, preachers, adventurers, and warriors shaped globalization* (L. Bo, Trans.). CITIC Publishing Group.
Dahua, W. (1997). *Lectures on legal ethnography*. Ethnic Publishing House.
Douglas, J. D., & Waksler, F. C. (1987). *The sociology of deviance: An introduction* (Z. Ning, & Z. Xinmin, Trans.). Hebei People's Publishing House.
Duan, L. (2002). *Confucian ethics and legal culture: Sociological perspectives*. China University of Political Science and Law Press.
Editorial Department of Law Yearbook of China. *Law Yearbook of China (1999–2006)*. Law Press.
Fuller, L. L. (2005). *The morality of law* (Z. Ge, Trans.). The Commercial Press.
Giddens, A. (2000). *The consequences of modernity* (T. He, Trans.). Yilin Press.
Guanzi, Z. (2000). *The growth of law: Ethnographic interpretation of law in the southern mountainous regions of China*. Social Sciences Academic Press.

Q. Wang, *Sociology of Law*,
https://doi.org/10.1007/978-981-16-5509-8

Dalie, G., & Shiguang, Y. (Eds.). (1991). *Dongba culture*. Yunnan People's Publishing House.
Hart, H. L. A. (1996). *The concept of law* (Z. Wenxian et al., Trans.). Encyclopedia of China Publishing House.
Hayek, F. A. (2000). *The fatal conceit: The errors of socialism* (F. Keli, et al., Trans.). China Social Sciences Press.
Lemin, C., & Hong, Z. (2003). *The process of European civilization*. SDX Joint Publishing Company.
Huaizhi, C. (Ed.). (1996). *Theories behind the fight against prostitution, production and distribution of indecent materials, human trafficking, drug-related crimes, illegal gambling, and superstition*. China Procuratorial Press.
Jingwen, Z. (1994). *Modern western legal sociology*. Law Press.
Kasper, W., & Streit, M. E. (2002). *Institutional economics* (H. Zhaohua, Trans.). The Commercial Press.
Kechang, M. (Ed.). (1996). *A brief history of modern western criminology*. China Procuratorial Press.
Kleinheyer, G., & Schroder, J. (2005). *Deutsche und Europäische Juristen aus neun Jahrhunderten: eine biographische Einführung in die Geschichte der Rechtswissenschaft* (X. Lan, Trans.). Law Press.
Largo, M. (2008). *Final exits: The illustrated encyclopedia of how we die* (Z. Juanjuan et al., Trans.). New Star Press.
Larsen, S. U. (Ed.) (2002). *Theory and methods in the social sciences* (R. Xiao, et al., Trans.). Shanghai People's Publishing House.
Yong, Z., & Lundberg, M. (Eds.). (2008). *Minorities autonomy and development: Studies on regional national autonomy of China*. Law Press.
Mingliang, W. (2004). *Rational evaluation of crackdown on crimes*. Peking University Press.
Montesquieu. (1982). *The spirit of the laws* (Z. Yanshen, Trans.). The Commercial Press.
Peihua, H., et al. (2003). *China: National development and subnational finance*. CITIC Publishing Group.
Postman, N. (2004). *Amusing ourselves to death* (Z. Yan, Trans.). Guangxi Normal University Press
Pound, R. (1984). *Social control through law* (S. Zongling et al., Trans.). The Commercial Press.
Qicai, G. (2003). *Customary laws of ethnic minority groups in China*. Tsinghua University Press.
Rong, J. (2004). *Wolf totem*. Changjiang Literature and Art Press.
Ronggen, Y. (2000). *The customary laws of the Qiang People*. Chongqing Publishing Group.
Ross, E. A. (1989). *Social control* (Q. Zhiyong, & M. Yongzheng, Trans.). Huaxia Publishing House.
Russell, B. (2001). *History of western philosophy* (Vol. 2) (M. Yuande, Trans.). The Commercial Press.
Schotter, A. (2003). *The economic theory of social institutions*. Shanghai University of Finance and Economics Press.
Seymour-Smith, C. (1986). *Macmillan dictionary of anthropology*. Macmillan Press Ltd.
The Intermediate People's Court of Liangshan Yi Autonomous Prefecture. (1957). *Customary laws of the Yi community in Liangshan (For Internal Use)*.
Wanzhen, S. (1998). *Law yearbook of China* (Collector's Ed.). Law Yearbook of China Publishing House.
Watson, A. (1977). *Society and legal change*. Scottish Academic Press.
Weber, M. (2004). *Max Weber's complete writings on academic and political vocations* (Vol. 1) (Q. Yongxiang et al., Trans.). Guangxi Normal University Press.
Xiaoping, D. (1993). *Selected works of Deng Xiaoping* (Vol. 3). People's Publishing House.
Xiaotong, F. (1984). *Introduction to sociology*. Tianjin People's Publishing House.
Xinjiu, Q. (2002). *Analysis of the power of criminal law*. China University of Political Science and Law Press.
Xueyi, L. (2002). *Theoretical study of agriculture, rural areas and farmers in contemporary China*. Social Sciences Academic Press.
Yiqun, X. (2008). *30 years of Chinese mass culture*. Guangxi Normal University Press.

Zedong, M. (1996a). *Selected works of Mao Zedong* (Vol. 1). People's Publishing House.
Zedong, M. (1996b). *Selected works of Mao Zedong* (Vol. 2). People's Publishing House.
Hangsheng, Z. (Ed.). (2003). *Introduction to sociology* (3rd Ed.). China Renmin University Press.
Zhongqi, X., et al. (1998). *Study of customary laws of ethnic minorities in China*. Yunnan University Press.

II. Scholarly Papers

Berman, H. J. (1999). The western legal tradition in a millennial perspective: Past and future (L. Liwei, Trans.). *Twenty-First Century*, (4).
Bohannon, P. (2002). Law and legal system. In B. Malinowski (Ed.), *Crime and custom in savage society* (Y. Jiang, Trans.). Yunnan People's Publishing House.
Canpulaaolibu. (1997). A preliminary study on the customary laws of inheritance in nomadic communities of China. *Journal of Minzu University of China (Social Sciences)*, (5).
Chang, L., & Xi, R. (1997). A tentative study on the customary laws in Chinese Villages. *Studies in Law and Business*, (1).
Chunsong, L. (2002). Reshaping customary laws of ethnic minorities to serve economic growth in settlement areas of ethnic minorities. *Guangxi Ethnics Studies*, (2).
Chunying, X. (2007). Theory and practice of legal transplantation. *Northern Legal Science*, (3).
Cuiyu, J. (2000). Crackdown on trafficking in women and children. *Theoretical Studies*, (6).
Dahua, W., & Xiaoguang, X. (2000). Preservance and social functions of the Miao People's customary laws. *Journal of Guizhou Minzu University (Humanities and Social Sciences)*, (1).
Di, S. (1998). Analysis of the social structure and customary laws of the Jino People in Longpa Village. *Modern Law Science*, (5).
Hao,D., & Qiang, Y. (2003). An empirical study on the outflow of women in rural settlement areas of ethnic minorities. *Guizhou Ethnic Studies*, (1).
Fengming, S. (1998). Non-local wifes and structural violence in rural areas. In Y. Fang (Ed.). *Sociologists' views: Changes in marriage and family in China*. China Social Sciences Press.
Fitzpatrick, P. (1989). Custom as imperialism. In J. M. Abun-Nasar, & U. Spllenbert (Eds). *Law and identity in Africa*.
Jianyuan, Z. (2007). Social order arising from good interaction between social groups. *Chongqing Social Sciences*, (12).
Jiaqing, X. (1999). The customary law of the Miao People and its evolution in modern Era. *Journal of Chongqing Preschool Education College*, (3).
Jide, M., & Yuanhai, Z. (1997). A preliminary study of family-related customary laws of the Yao Community in Gongcheng. *Guangxi Ethnics Studies*, (2).
Kaizhong, S. (2000). Linguistic analysis of the customary laws of the Dong People. *Journal of Guizhou Minzu University (Humanities and Social Sciences)*, (1).
Kanda, H., & Milhaupt, C. J. (2004). Re-examining legal transplants: The director's fiduciary duty in Japanese corporate law. In W. Jinglian (Ed.). *Comparative studies* (Vol. 11). CITIC Publishing Group.
Lin, T., et al. (2003). The life of women migrating for marriage. *Sociological Study*, (2).
Longyingqiang, N. (2009). The implications of customary law of Tibetan Buddhism for criminal justice in China. In X. Hui, & C. Jinzhao (Eds.). *Customary law* (Vol. 8). Shandong People's Publishing House.
Man, X. (1997). Implications of the customary laws of the Yi Community in Liangshan for modern society. *Journal of Southwest Minzu University (Humanities and Social Sciences)*, (5).
Merry, S. E. (1991). Law and colonialism. *Law and Society Review*, 25(4).
Mingdong, W., & Shaomei, Y. (1998). Waterworks- and forestry-related customary laws of the Yi People in Yunnan. *The Ideological Front*, (3).
Mingliang, W. (2005). Anthropological interpretation of legal transplant. *Journal of Guangxi University for Nationalities (Humanities and Social Sciences)*, (6).
Moore, S. F. (1971). Law and anthropology: A reader (H. Weixing, Trans.). In L. Yiyuan (Ed.). *Selected readings in cultural anthropology*. Shihuo Publishing House.
Na, L. *Social context of human trafficking*. Unpublished manuscript.

Nader, L., & Todd, H. F. (2007). The disputing process: Law in ten societies. In W. Jinglian, J. Ping, & L. Zhiping (Eds.). *Journal of Legal and Economic Studies* (Vol. 8). China Legal Publishing House.

Qiang, Z. (1997). Legal transplant and legal change—Analysis of Alan Watson's legal theories. *Global Law Review*, (3).

Qiang, L. (2003). Analysis of the factors affecting rural-urban migration in China. *Social Sciences in China*, (1).

Qiliang, W. (2007a). Ideal roadmap for the establishment of the rule of law system in China—Development of legal theories. *Modern Law Science*, (4).

Rong, C. (2002). Effects of the open up the west campaign on the customary laws of the Mongolian People. *Forward Position*, (2).

Sen, W. (2000). Nature and emergence of customs. *Social Sciences in China*, No. 5.

Sen, W. (2003). Preface: The first milestone in the history of game theory analysis. In A. Schotter (Ed.), *The economic theory of social institutions* (L. Ming, & C. Kang, Trans.). Southwestern University of Finance and Economics Press.

Shigong, Q. (2005). Legal philosophy of the legislator—Reflections on contemporary jurisprudence from the perspective of legal transplantation. *Social Sciences in China*, (1).

Shijie, Y. (1998). Study on the Yao People's customary law. *Journal of Minzu University of China (Social Sciences)*, (2).

Shumei, B., & Yu, C. (2002). On customary law. *Forward Position*, (5).

Strathen, M. (1985). Discovering 'Social Control'. *Journal of Law and Society*, 12(2)

Temuerbaolidao. (2002). On several issues of Mongolian customary laws. *Journal of Inner Mongolia University (Humanities and Social Sciences)*, (1).

Tingju, B. (2002). Customary laws of the gentry. *Journal of Qinghai Nationalities University (Social Sciences)*, (3).

Weber, M. (2004). The sociology of Max Weber. In M. Weber (Ed.). *Max Weber's complete writings on academic and political vocations* (Vol. 1) (Q. Yongxiang et al., Trans.). Guangxi Normal University Press.

Wei, M., & Furong, M. (1997). Customary laws of the Salar People. *Journal of Qinghai Nationalities University (Social Science Edition)*, (2).

Weimin, Y., & Xiaoyong, W. (2002). Preservation and social functions of the Achang People's customary law. *Journal of South-Central University for Nationalities (Humanities and Social Sciences)*, (5).

Xiaoming, W. (1997). A tentative study on the customary laws of the Zhuang People in relation to Women's Property Rights in Guangxi. *Guangxi Ethnics Studies*, (1).

Xiaoyang, Z. (2007) Confusion in legal discourse and the holistic approach to legal anthropology. *Social Sciences in China*, (2).

Xiaohui, Z., & Qiliang, W. (2001). Evolution and functions of customary laws—Study of customary laws of 25 ethnic minority villages in Yunnan. *Modern Law Science*, (5).

Xin, X. (2007). Suicide as a way of Chinese migrant workers to fight for their own rights. In W. Yi (Ed.). *Studies of the Chinese countryside* (Vol. 2). Shandong People's Publishing House.

Xin, X. (2008). Launching pilot programs on judicial reform. *Journal of Yunnan University (Law Edition)*, (2).

Xing, Z. (2000). Customary law and ethnic minorities. *Journal of Yunnan Minzu University (Humanities and Social Sciences)*, (1).

Xisheng, Z. (1989). The conflict between customary law and the marriage law of the PRC. *Ethnography*, (1&2).

Xisheng, Z. (1990). A tentative study on the customary law of the Wa People in Ximeng. *Ethnic Studies*, (1).

Xisheng, Z. (1991). Traditional culture and criminal legal system of ethinic minorities. *Journal of Comparative Law*, (3).

Yi, G. (2002). Tracing the customary laws of the Miao People. *Journal of Jiangxi Provincial Police Academy*, (2).

Yu, F. (2005). *Economic globalization and China's legal system—Sociological approach to law.* Science of Law, (1).

Yumiao, Z. (2002). Effects of the customary laws of ethnic minorities. *Journal of Southwest Minzu University (Humanities and Social Sciences)*, (7).

Zhengjin, G., & Qiang, Z. (2002). Customary law and establishment of the rule of law in Western China. *Journal of Southwest Minzu University (Humanities and Social Sciences)*, (7).

Zhiping, L. (2007). The death of the one in custody—The dilemma of identity politics in contemporary China and the way out. In W. Yi (Ed.). *Studies of the Chinese countryside* (Vol. 2). Shandong People's Publishing House.

III. Journals, Magazines, and Websites

ABC Radio: *Cambodia Gets Six Patrol Boats from China.* Retrieved from http://abc.net.au/ra/news/stories/s1451382.htm

Bing, H. *The ultimate goal of the reform of the justice system should be to deliver justice to the people.* Retrieve from http://www.law-thinker.com/news.php?id=1868

Cross-border Human Trafficking Continues to Pose a Serious Challenge to Chinese Police. *Global Times.* Retrieved from http://www.cctv.com/news/society/20060515/100090.shtm

Fengzhimoduan. *Report of the investigation task force of the "Hide-and-Seek" Case.* Retrieved from http://www.tianya.cn/publicforum/content/free/1/1507781.shtml

From an infamous village known for involvement in trafficking in persons to a law-Abiding Village. (2004, October 20). *Yunnan Daily.*

Guangxi Police Rescued 37 Vietnamese Human Trafficking Victims. *Legal Daily.* Retrieved from http://www.legaldaily.com.cn/bm/2005-07/13/content_166691.htm2

Government Officials Respond to Questions regarding the Hide-and-Seek Incident in Yunnan (February 22). People.cn. Retrieved from http://news.china.com/zh_cn/domestic/945/20090222/15337554.html

Gu Xiulian Speaks Highly of Yunnan Government's Achievement in Combating Trafficking in Children and Women (2005, August 4). *China Women's News.* Retrieved from http://www.women.org.cn/allnews/1301/689.html

Haiqing, L. (2009). Restarting the reform of the justice system. *South Reviews*, (4).

Huiying, L., & Jianmin, L. *Police of thirteen countries hope to strengthen collaboration on non-traditional security issues.* Retrieved from http://www.gx.xinhuanet.com/newscenter/2005-08/18/content_4911166.htm

Internet Users Join the Investigation of the Hide-and-Seek Incident. (2009, February 13). *Yunnan Information.*

Investigation Task Force of the "Hide-and-Seek" Case. *Report of Investigation Task Force of the "Hide-and-Seek" Case.* Retrieved from http://www.Yunnan.com.cn/feature/content/2009-02/21/content_248238_12.htm

Jie, C. *Wu Wei, Deputy Director of the Propaganda Department of Yunnan Provincial CPC Committee, Disapproved the Investigation Results of the Hide-and-Seek Case.* Retrieved from http://news.kunming.cn/subject/content/2009-02/22/content_1763894.htm

Jun, L. The truth behind the hide-and-seek incident. Retrieved from http://news.ifeng.com/opinion/200902/0223_23_1027916_1.shtml

Kun, W. *Evidence found by private civilians are not admissible in court and police should be involved in the investigation.* Retrieved from http://news.sohu.com/20090221/n262382128.shtml

Lei, W. (2009, February 13). Internet users release an investigation report of the hide-and-seek incident. *Yunnan Information.*

Min, B. *Reflection on the Hide-and-Seek Case.* Retrieved from http://bbs.ynxxb.com/show-topic-1187.aspx

Ministry of Public Security. *China and Myanmar Held Ministerial Conference on Cooperation in Combating Cross-border Crimes.* Retrieved from http://www.china.org.cn/chinese/news/929778.htm

Ministry of Public Security. *Report: Combating trafficking in women and children*. Retrieved from http://www.mps.gov.cn/cenweb/briCenweb/jsp/common/atricle.jsp?infoid=ABC1365&category=700710005

Peng, W. *Successful crisis management by the government: The investigation of the hide-and-seek incident by internet users draws to an end*. Retrieved from http://media.people.com.cn/GB/8846689.html

Peng, W. *The investigation results of the Hide-and-Seek Incident presented by the investigation team made up by Internet users were questioned*. Retrieved from http://www.yunnan.com.cn/2008page/society/html/2009-02/22/content_249327_2.htm

Propaganda Department of the Provincial CPC Committee of Yunnan. *Announcement regarding the investigation of the death of Li Qiaoming*. Retrieved from http://www.yunnan.com.cn/2008page/www/html/2009-02/19/content_246031.htm

Shengjun, W. (2008). The justice system should keep up with the times. *Journal of Law Application*, (10).

Shengjun, W. *Practice the scientific outlook on development and deliver justice for the people*. Retrieved from http://www.court.gov.cn/news/bulletin/release/200902170002.htm

Shichuan, W. *Hide-and-seek incident: Where are the NPC delegates when their voice is needed?* Retrieved from http://news.ifeng.com/opinion/200902/0223_23_1027825.shtml

Shihua, T. *Vice president of the Yunnan high court Tian Chengyou asked, "What if they are your brothers and sisters?"* Retrieved from http://www.chinacourt.org/html/article/200808/14/317046.shtml

UNIAP. *Anti-trafficking Liaison Officers Border from China and Myanmar Meet for the First Time to Carry out Joint Inspection*. Retrieved from http://uniap.law.pku.edu.cn/UserImages/00000285.pdf

Wei, W. *The justice department should be involved in the investigation of the death of the suspect who died while in police custody*. Retrieved from http://society.yunnan.cn/html/2009-02/18/content_243937.htm

Wu, W. *Practice of Freedom of Religion in China over the Past 60 Years*. Retrieved from http://news.sohu.com/2009-09/04/content_1409389.htm

Weiwei, L. *NPC deputies and CPPCC members attach great importance to eight types of work of police*. Retrieved from http://news.cctv.com/china/20070301/105631.shtml

Wen, Z. *Police says Li Qiaoming accidentally hit his head while playing hide-and-seek*. Retrieved from http://news.kunming.cn/yn-news/content/2009-02/14/content_1758528.htm

Xiaojuan, S.. Vice chairman of all-china women's federation empathizes with Vietnamese human trafficking victims. *China News Guangxi*. Retrieved from http://www.gx.chinanews.com.cn/xw/show.asp?id=12554

Xin, H. (2009, February 22). Internet users launched a cyber manhunt on members of the hide-and-seek case investigation task force. *Yunnan Information*.

Xuan, F. *Internet users interested in the investigation of the hide-and-seek incident*. Retrieved from http://news.kunming.cn/yn-news/content/2009-02/20/content_1759979.htm

Xuan, F. *The provincial procuratorate released investigation results: Li Qiaoming was beaten to death by another prisoner*. Retrieved from http://news.kunming.cn/subject/content/2009-02/27/content_1777404.htm

Xiaoqiu, Z., & Xuefeng, Z. (2005). From combating human trafficking to preventing human trafficking. *Law and Life*, (11).

Xuelin, J. UNICEF pledges to support Guangxi Police's effort to crack down on cross-border crimes. *China News*. Retrieved from http://www.chinanews.com.cn/news/2005/2005-11-26/8/657007.shtml

Yaling, G, Peng, L., & Mingzhi, Y. *Cross-border women trafficking Gang busted by police of China and Myanmar*. Retrieved from http://www.yn.xinhuanet.com/news-center/2006-08/14/content_7769358.htm

Yan, W. *The justice department of Yunnan says false testimonies provided by witnesses affected the prosecutor's judgment.* Retrieved from http://news.xinhuanet.com/newscenter/2009-02/27/content_10913242.htm

Yang, Y. *Legal expert says the investigation results of Internet users could be presented to the court as evidence.* Retrieved from http://news.sohu.com/20090220/n262369606.shtml

Yihua, M., & Jie, C. *Wu Hao says there was no foul play in the investigation of the hide-and-seek incident.* Retrieved from http://www.yunnan.cn/2008page/society/html/2009-02/23/content_249617_2.htm

Yong, C. (2005, January 20). How to tackle the challenges faced by China in fighting trafficking in persons. *Nanfang Weekend.*

Yuda, D. *The root cause of the Huashuihe pollution incident in Zhejiang Province: Improper planning.* Retrieved from http://www.ce.cn/cysc/hb/gdxw/200505/10/t20050510_3788544.shtml

Zhihui, Y. *510 Internet users applied for joining the investigation team of the hide-and-seek incident.* Retrieved from http://news.xinhuanet.com/local/2009-02/20/content_10853102.htm

Zhijun, S. (2009, February 13). Deadly game inside the Detention Center. *Yunnan Information.*

Zhong, L. *China and Vietnam step up cooperation to fight cross-border crimes.* Retrieved from http://news.xinhuanet.com/newscenter/2006-05/11/content_4535942.htm

Zhuo, H. & Guitao, L. Chinese and Vietnamese police join hands to fight cross-border crimes. *Legal News (fa zhi kuai bao).* Retrieved from http://www.fzkb.cn/news/20060713/fz3b/013830.htm

The manufacturer's authorised representative in the EU is Springer Nature Customer Service Centre GmbH, Europaplatz 3, 69115 Heidelberg, Germany. If you have any concerns regarding our products, please contact ProductSafety@springernature.com

Printed and bound by CPI Group (UK) Ltd, Croydon, CR0 4YY
30/09/2026
02225264-0016